Modern Hebrew

ALSO BY
NORMAN BERDICHEVSKY
AND FROM MCFARLAND

An Introduction to Danish Culture (2011)
Nations, Language and Citizenship (2004)

MODERN HEBREW

The Past and Future of a Revitalized Language

Norman Berdichevsky

McFarland & Company, Inc., Publishers
Jefferson, North Carolina

LIBRARY OF CONGRESS CATALOGUING-IN-PUBLICATION DATA

Berdichevsky, Norman, 1943– author.
Modern Hebrew : the past and future of a revitalized language /
Norman Berdichevsky.
    p.   cm. / Includes bibliographical references and index.

ISBN 978-0-7864-9492-7 (softcover : acid free paper) ∞

1. Hebrew language.   2. Hebrew language—Revival.   I. Title.
PJ4551.B48 2014   492.4—dc23   2014019905

BRITISH LIBRARY CATALOGUING DATA ARE AVAILABLE

© 2014 Norman Berdichevsky. All rights reserved

*No part of this book may be reproduced or transmitted in any form
or by any means, electronic or mechanical, including photocopying
or recording, or by any information storage and retrieval system,
without permission in writing from the publisher.*

Front cover: information sign in three languages
(gkuna/iStock/Thinkstock)

Printed in the United States of America

*McFarland & Company, Inc., Publishers
Box 611, Jefferson, North Carolina 28640
www.mcfarlandpub.com*

The Danish philosopher Andreas Simonsen remarked on the great respect most Jews feel for the past, old friends and their parents, as well as the long historical memory of nationhood and the many religious obligations and commemorative holidays. This is what he termed "The Jewish ability to carry their past with themselves and be nourished by it. The better people remember their past and are able to integrate it with their appreciation of life, the better they are able to develop their intellect, humanity and vitality." It is the best definition of Zionism and explains the success of Modern Hebrew, a desk project initiated in 1880 by a few fanatics to turn what once had been an almost purely liturgical language like Latin, one that was nobody's mother tongue, into the vernacular of millions and the medium of a dynamic innovative society in the State of Israel, confounding all the forecasts of so-called experts. This book is dedicated to the many farsighted individuals who exercised an enormous intellectual effort to make Modern Hebrew live in the fields of journalism, literature, poetry, teaching, academic research and popular song, and who, in so doing, gave hope, pride and inspiration to Jews in their darkest hour of a bright future among the nations of the world.

Acknowledgments

My love of the Hebrew language is due in large part to the inspiration of my parents, teachers, mentors, colleagues and the people of Israel in the cities, academies, moshavim, kibbutzim and marketplaces of the country. I specifically owe a debt of gratitude to my wife Raquel, who again helped me with sound advice and counsel; to a former student of mine, John Janda, a proud son of the Czech nation, to academic colleagues in Israel, the United Kingdom and United States, Erich Isaac, Yehoshua Ben-Arieh, Amiram Gonen, Mrs. Orna Szpiro, Colin Shindler, Ken Hanson, Moshe Pelli; to the distinguished translators, Hillel Halkin, Risa Domb and Nicholas de Lange; to former comrades in the kibbutzim, Sasa and Barkai; to my relatives in Israel; and to the inspiration provided by three generations of masterful performers of Hebrew song.

Table of Contents

Acknowledgments vi
Note to the Reader viii
Preface 1

1—Hebrew in American Popular Culture 7
2—The Magnificent Heritage of Hebrew 15
3—Modern Hebrew's Inspirational Example 30
4—The Three-Thousand-Year-Old Treasury 43
5—How Hebrew Became a Modern Language 49
6—Do the Israelis Speak Hebrew or Israeli? 64
7—The Worldwide Rivalry with Yiddish 75
8—Negation of the Golah (Exile) and Hebraic Identity of a New Nation 87
9—Baltic Rebirth and the Zionist Staging Ground for a Jewish State 107
10—The First Modern Hebrew Textbooks Set in Palestine 117
11—The Soviet Persecution of Hebrew 124
12—Arab-Israeli Use of Hebrew 136
13—From Jewish State Toward a Hebrew Republic? 157
14—Slang and Profanity in Spoken Hebrew 172
15—The Current Assault on Hebrew at Home 178
16—Outlook for Hebrew Education in the United States and the United Kingdom 184

Epilogue 190
Chapter Notes 201
Bibliography 215
Index 223

Note to the Reader

Words reflecting concepts that are related in Hebrew often look alike, meaning that they have the same root consonant letters, and sound alike. Such words have been bolded throughout the text to emphasize their similarity. The first such instance appears on page 13: Re-Ĥe-M רחם = womb and Ra-Ĥ-Ma-nut רחמנות = mercy. Womb and mercy were obviously allied concepts in the minds of the ancient Hebrews—the womb protects the fetus in a merciful way from harm.

Also of note is that the symbol Ĥ represents the Hebrew letter ḥet ח and Ŝ represents the Hebrew letter shin ש.

Preface

Few subjects have commanded the attention and provoked, fascinated, excited, and enchanted so many readers like the saga of the Zionist rebirth of Israel. Yet in this monumental literature, relatively little space has been devoted to the epic transformation of the classical language of the Bible into modern "Ivrit," the national language of the dynamic State of Israel, its everyday vernacular spoken by seven million people. It was grafted successfully onto an older literature and longer historical continuity than Latin or Greek and is the official language of Israeli business, research, the law, and government.

For those with no previous knowledge of the language and those who may be superficially familiar with the Hebrew used in traditional prayer services at the synagogue or celebrations of festivals but little else, the momentous story of the trial and tribulations, growth and maturity, of Israel's national language remains an arcane subject. Words like *Sabbath*, *Amen*, *Satan*, *Hallelujah* and *Hosanna* have been incorporated into almost all the world's languages without any translation by any other term, a fact generally recognized by most Christians, but few of them are aware that the modern Hebrew language has for most of the past century been regarded as "dangerous" and the subject of active persecution. Three generations of Hebrew teachers and students risked imprisonment, social ostracism, financial ruin and the loss of their livelihoods in the Soviet Union for carrying on the "underground" movement to learn the language (see Chapter 11)—something that is either unknown or taken for granted by many Diaspora Jews who most commonly associate Hebrew with a tedious preparation for their bar mitzvah confirmation.

This book explores the historical background, past and current controversies, challenges, dilemmas and prospects facing the Israeli people that stem from the choice made four generations ago, dating from 1880, to create a renewed nation of Jews in the Land of Israel with Hebrew as their national language. It is a study in the politics, linguistics and sociology of language, exploring the relationship of the Israelis with the Jewish Diaspora as well as with their fellow non–Jewish citizens, the largely bilingual Arabic- and Hebrew-speaking Arab population.

I lived in Israel for many years and taught Hebrew at all levels in both the United States and the United Kingdom. It has long been my wish to write an accompanying book to be used as an overall introduction to the importance of Modern Hebrew and acquaint beginning students with the social and political role the language has played in the history of Zionism and the State of Israel.

The book examines some of the basic "mechanics of the language," including the many changes that have occurred in the transition to Modern Hebrew. It also explores how this language overcame many obstacles to become a spoken vernacular, along with its growing prestige. It is a book dealing primarily with the social aspects of the language to acquaint new students, both Jewish and Gentile, with the role model Modern Hebrew played for other national revivals. It does not cover literature, nor is it another biography of the pioneer founder of the movement to make Hebrew into a modern spoken language, Eliezer Ben-Yehuda.[1] It is rather the story of his vision and how it animated a large part of the Jewish world, gave new confidence and pride to Jewish youth during the most difficult period of modern history (on the eve of the Holocaust), and infused Zionism with a dynamic cultural content.

Over the past two generations, there has been a steady decline among many American Jews in the cultural and emotional identification they feel with Modern Hebrew literature, song and dance, elements that once drew them close to the Zionist project and the emergence of a modern national Israeli culture.

The lack of a common language is an obvious but overlooked factor in explaining why so many American Jews are insensitive to or unappreciative of the creation of a modern nation, national literature and spoken idiom that makes Modern Hebrew quite distinct from the language of ritual prayers recited in the synagogue. Many tourists in Israel miss out on much that is not available in instant translations. All laws, debates in the Knesset, the legal cases in court, and applications for patents are, of course, in Hebrew, but in both a literal and figurative sense, Israelis and Jews abroad "don't speak the same language." Israeli affairs portrayed by the media in the Diaspora are often based on highly fragmentary and specially selected

Eliezer Ben-Yehuda postage stamp honoring the father of Modern Hebrew.

extracts of published material translated (and occasionally mistranslated) from Hebrew.

Although many people with an interest in Israel are aware of the importance of the revival of Hebrew as a spoken language and may recognize the name of pioneer linguist Eliezer Ben-Yehuda, they do not appreciate the difficulties involved or the exciting story of what challenges were posed before the eventual accomplishment of what almost all linguists had declared impossible. Only a few books and periodicals in English, mainly for a specialized scholarly readership with considerable background knowledge of Hebrew, have dealt with these topics, and these are now more than fifty years old. The two most comprehensive books in English that are easy to understand are *How the Hebrew Language Grew* by Edward Horowitz (1960) and *Hebrew the Eternal Language* by William Chomsky (1957); much valuable material on the revival of the Hebrew language can also be found in the Israeli cultural periodical *Ariel*, number 25 (1969).

This is a remarkable story that deserves to be told to a mass audience. It is also an introduction to the special attributes of the Hebrew language, its borrowing from the rich historic flourishing of past civilizations and the ingenious mechanism of neologisms inherent in the "skeleton" of the language. Moreover, it is the story of the three-generations-long, worldwide rivalry with Yiddish and the techniques used to make Hebrew into a language capable of handling all the demands of a modern society.

The focus of contemporary Hebrew instruction in the Diaspora has shifted from what was the native earthy vitality of the vernacular to a loss of faith among the parents of many Jewish students who have only studied enough Hebrew to prepare for their bar mitzvah ceremony, and who regard Ivrit as an obscure provincial Levantine language of a Banana or "Falafel Republic" and no longer an inspirational tool. Not knowing Modern Hebrew, neither they nor their children are familiar with Israeli authors, playwrights, movie directors, actors, singers, athletes, or the standings of Israel's football (soccer) clubs.

Speakers of Hebrew outside Israel, the so-called *yordim* (ex–Israelis who have settled permanently abroad), constitute a widespread new Diaspora, but they retain knowledge of their primary or habitual language at home and, like other ethnic groups, follow events in their former homeland through the Internet, press, frequent visits and books so that they keep abreast of the country's development. Their language is not shared by the inhabitants of any other state, nor is it understood by their "fellow Jews" in the Diaspora. This gap in Hebrew and Israel knowledge is often embarrassingly detrimental to a sense of solidarity in many Jewish communities.

The State of Israel suffers from damaging attacks by considerable media bias, disgruntled academics with an axe to grind and many other hostile critics due to preexisting prejudices and a complete ignorance of Modern Hebrew. These same critics

1. are unable to directly check original Hebrew sources to accurately weigh the Israeli side of many issues; and
2. never question the legitimacy of wholly artificial creations such as Syria, Iraq, Jordan, Libya, Indonesia, Pakistan and a dozen states in Africa that cross linguistic, religious and tribal lines, all of which lack any historical identity, territorial contiguity and sense of nationhood.

Why I Wrote This Book

My love and appreciation of the Hebrew language was fostered by my parents and teachers in my Bronx neighborhood and through attending the City College of New York (CCNY), where I was fortunate to learn from one of the most renowned and distinguished scholars, Professor Simon Halkin. In retrospect, I discovered that many of the non–Jewish pupils came from homes with ancient traditions and exotic languages similar to the Hebrew I had acquired in preparation for my bar mitzvah. These other non–Jewish pupils of Chinese, Armenian, and Greek origin, as well as a few others with whom I became friends, were in many respects typical American teenage boys who shared the same passions for baseball, popular music and science fiction films with others of our age. I came to understand with heart and soul that through a long and perilous history Jews were not alone in having created a rich and ancient culture, albeit one marked by melancholy. The ability to retain a sense of a historic past and a deep sense of solidarity with a "Zion" state was something I shared with others. My knowledge of Hebrew and the eleven years I spent in Israel opened up new horizons and enabled me to participate in the resilience of spirit that Israelis feel in the face of adversity. There was also an added dimension—one that bespoke a tie with an ancient civilization older than even Christianity! There was another cuisine, another literary and philosophical world of great classical books, another music, another interest in political developments halfway around the world that made me feel that "being Jewish" was of a much higher spiritual order than the inane, materialistic and ceaseless quest for wealth, professional prestige and social status that has been endlessly parodied by books, films and plays as the hallmark of "how Jews live." My goal in writing this book is to reach as wide an audience as possible to make readers more aware of the role Hebrew has played in the forging of contemporary Israeli society and culture and its function worldwide as the new Jewish international language, replacing Yiddish.

Buenos Aires police station with word for "police" in Spanish, Hebrew and Chinese (author's photograph).

A dynamic nation has been created with a determined belief in a common origin, destiny and struggle, with a unifying common language, adapted and modernized by the only people who identified with it and its ancient homeland. Anyone wishing to understand modern Israel, its history and its development toward a more inclusive society for all its people should be familiar with Modern Hebrew and how this language grew and changed over the past 130 years through challenges and dilemmas resulting in startling achievements and new prospects.

1. Hebrew in American Popular Culture

The popular film *The First Wives Club* includes a telling scene in which Bette Midler, playing an American Jewish housewife, intrudes on her teenage son Jason, who is listening to some rock group on his Walkman, and triumphantly tells him that she was able to hire his favorite band for his bar mitzvah ceremony. He is overjoyed, exclaiming "that's cool!" and he kisses his mother, at which point she rips out the cassette he has been listening to and inserts another one. He listens for a moment, with a look of pained surprise on his face, to the cassette's opening words of every traditional prayer (which one can clearly hear on the Walkman): "Baruch Ata Adonai" (sounds like gibberish to him). He asks, "What's this?" She responds, "It's Hebrew! Your bar mitzvah is in three weeks. Learn it! It's the one thing your father is willing to pay for. Don't shame me in the synagogue."

Somewhat later on in the film, after the bar mitzvah, the three jilted wives are arguing in the kitchen, berating each other for not having been in close touch during all their married years. Goldie Hawn accuses Bette Midler of not inviting her to the bar mitzvah. Bette retorts, excusing that oversight "You wouldn't have come!" and then Diane Keaton attempts to pacify the angry Goldie by adding, "And it was in Hebrew!" (as if to say, how could a non–Jew expect to make heads or tails of anything?).

It is worth noting the striking contrast between *First Wives Club* and another movie dealing with an ethnic theme, *My Big Fat Greek Wedding*, which humorously deals with a Greek American woman, Toula Poutakalos, in Chicago struggling with her traditional family and the prospect of "intermarriage" with her Anglo-American boyfriend. Toula (an authentic Greek name) has been raised bilingually and, presumably without having to be bribed, is totally familiar with Greek history, philosophy, language and literature, the arts and the rites of the Orthodox Church, thus making her father proud.

The passive attitude of the present generation of American students in general toward foreign languages is prevalent in much of higher education today, and for many of them Hebrew appears to be of little use beyond the synagogue. On visits to Israel, they usually feel intimidated by the much more linguistically proficient Israelis their age, who easily use English to communicate. Many Americans have the impression that Hebrew is an exotic Eastern language with no relation to European languages, a Semitic tongue with an unfamiliar vocabulary, grammar and alphabet. This impression is reinforced by old world memories of traditionally taught classes in the synagogue, conjuring up images of a shabby, ill-lit *ḥeder* (room) somewhere in an East European *shtetl,* presided over by a bearded rabbi with a ruler in his hand, ready to smack anyone not paying attention, and monotonously teaching by rote.

Popular perceptions and attitudes, as well as much literature and film, continue to assume the existence of close relations between the Jewish Diaspora and the State of Israel and universally regard the latter as "The Jewish State," thereby ignoring the growing divergence between the two. This growing gap between the Diaspora existence and the culture, lifestyle, and critical security needs of most of Israel's Jewish population was demonstrably apparent in the 2012 American presidential election and will most likely widen still further in the future. Jews used to be regarded as either an ethnic or a religious group in their Diaspora communities, enjoying a large and growing measure of solidarity with Zionism and the State of Israel in the face of a common challenge or threat, as was the case between approximately 1920 and 2000. This is by and large no longer the case, and by 2030, a majority of the world's Jews will probably be Hebrew speakers living in Israel due to the substantial differences in the rate of natural Jewish population growth in Israel (trending toward 3 births per woman and almost reaching equality with the Arab birthrate there, dramatically greater than the meager American Jewish birthrate of only 1.86, this figure is even lower than in most Western European countries).[1]

An example of how American Jews bring with them inherently American attitudes, assumptions and prejudices was the recent attempt to establish a professional Israeli baseball league in spite of numerous warnings in the Hebrew press and from Israeli sports journalists "in the know" that the game was too slow and too complicated and would never appeal to the Israeli people. Nevertheless, the American promoters of the idea went ahead, consistent with their preconception that "Jews" (i.e., Israelis) should love baseball because Jews in America do. The league barely survived one year (2007) and needed to import many non–Jewish players from Latin American semi-professional leagues in order to mount a full six teams that had to share three "home" stadiums, only one of which had originally been a real baseball diamond.[2]

American Jews are at least 95 percent Ashkenazi (Central and East European) in origin, and many of them have not been to Israel. They retain an emotional attachment to Yiddish and the associated cuisine, music, and folklore of Eastern Europe. This memory of nostalgic Yiddish fragments and food preferences—smoked salmon ("lox"), herring, bagels, borscht, and *klezmer* melodies—outweighs any similar set of attitudes toward Israel and its Levantine setting, language, music and cuisine,[3] perceived as "foreign."

American Jewish Loss of Ethnicity and the Decline of Hebrew

Many of the students I teach in introductory courses enter the class not even knowing that "Ivrit" (עברית) is the Hebrew word for Hebrew! This indicates a serious deficiency in education and ethnic identification with Israel that would simply be unimaginable in the case of Finnish Americans not knowing what Suomi is, or Hungarian Americans, Magyar, or Greek Americans, ελληνική γλώσσα.

During the pre-statehood period, Jews in the Diaspora sympathetic to Zionism regarded Hebrew as the most productive part of the dynamic, largely secular culture being created by generations of pioneers. Today, by and large, it lacks even the attraction and fascination for Diaspora Jews that it held for many Christian theologians and clergymen who felt the power of the language they believed God first used to speak to humanity. This feeling of reverence and majesty was beautifully expressed by the great German writer Hermann Hesse in his largely autobiographical novel *Beneath the Wheel:*

> Hebrew kept all of them on their toes. The peculiar ancient language of Jehovah, an uncouth, withered and yet secretly living tree took on an alien, gnarled and puzzling form before the boys' eyes, catching their attention through unusual linkages and astonishing them with remarkably colored and fragrant blossoms. In its branches, hollows and roots lived friendly or gruesome thousand-year old ghosts; fantastically fearsome dragons, lovely naïve girls and wrinkled sages next to handsome boys and calm-eyed girls or quarrelsome women. What had sounded remote and dreamlike in the Lutheran Bible was now lent blood in its true coarse character, as well as a voice of an old cumbersome but tenacious and ominous life.[4]

What the 2012 Presidential Election Revealed

American Jews living in Israel favored the Republican presidential candidate, Governor Mitt Romney, and his much more pro–Israel stance, but they were outnumbered by American Jewish supporters of President Obama at home by a huge margin. In the last week of October, 80 thousand ballots, weighing 500 pounds, were sent to the U.S. embassy in Tel Aviv. The respected Shaviv Strategy and Campaign Service conducted an exit poll among the expats. With a sample of 1,572 voters, and a margin of error of around 2.5 percent, the results were Republican Mitt Romney, 85.0 percent; incumbent Democrat Barack Obama, 14.3 percent; and other write-ins, 0.6 percent.[5]

A large majority of American Jews living in Israel expressed a markedly different evaluation of President Obama's policies regarding U.S.–Israeli relations than their counterparts back home. Of course, a majority of American Jews did not see it this way and believed the Democratic Party platform represented their "values," while their counterparts in Israel were upset with the president over what they believed was an abandonment or significant lack of support for Israel's security needs.

Many teachers consciously use the word "Ivrit" to specifically refer to the modern vernacular as spoken in Israel and "Hebrew" for the classical language of the Bible, prayer and synagogue. They have frequently been disappointed by the Israeli political establishment and career-minded academics who prefer to write and speak in English at international forums.

It is a frequently lamented fact that in American academia, Jewish studies and Hebrew courses offered at universities across the country have entered into what appears to be a period of long-term decline. These conclusions match my own teaching experience: "Jewish Studies rose with the humanities and has seen its fortunes fall along with theirs. These are difficult economic times. There are far more jobs in technology and the sciences; the number of students majoring in humanities fields like history or English is at an all-time low. Even at the most elite colleges, professors are forced by their deans, departments, or both to choose between offering rigorous courses that attract few students and teaching classes that are popular—and watered-down. Jewish Studies has not escaped these pressures."[6]

These are the prevailing views among many educators in both the United States and the United Kingdom, where multiculturalism ironically seems to have initially benefited both ethnic studies and demands for wider use of foreign languages so that immigrants no longer are required to become immersed immediately in English-language courses. This seems to be the case for all languages dear to ethnic and religious groups, except Hebrew. The first table, opposite, tells a clear story. Modern Hebrew suffered the steepest decline among all major foreign-language course enrollments at American colleges and universities (while Biblical Hebrew showed only a modest decline and Arabic was in first place among the languages that gained students!).

A true story (names withheld to protect the innocent) and anecdote for the seismic gulf between Biblical and Modern Hebrew relates how a distinguished Oxford professor was stopped and questioned at Heathrow Airport by an Israeli security team regarding the motive for his trip to Israel. "To do research," he replied. "And what do you teach, professor?" He replied, "*Hebrew*," and so the next question they asked was in Hebrew: "What is in your suitcase?"

Fall 2002, 2006, and 2009 Language Course Enrollments
(Languages in Alphabetical Order)

	2002	2006	% Change 2002–06	2009	% Change 2006–09
Arabic	10,584	23,974	126.5	35,083	46.3
ASL	60,781	78,829	29.7	91,763	16.4
Chinese	34,143	51,582	51.0	60,976	18.2
French	201,979	206,426	2.2	216,419	4.8
German	91,100	94,264	3.5	96,349	2.2
Greek, Ancient*	20,376	22,849	12.1	20,695	-9.4
Hebrew, Biblical	14,183	14,140	-0.3	13,807	-2.4
Hebrew, Modern	8,619	9,612	11.5	8,245	-14.2
Italian	63,899	78,368	22.6	80,752	3.0
Japanese	52,238	66,605	27.5	73,434	10.3
Korean	5,211	7,145	37.1	8,511	19.1
Latin	29,841	32,191	7.9	32,606	1.3
Portuguese	8,385	10,267	22.4	11,371	10.8
Russian	23,921	24,845	3.9	26,883	8.2
Spanish	746,267	822,985	10.3	864,986	5.1
Other languages	25,716	33,728	31.2	40,747	20.8
Total	1,397,253	1,577,810	12.9	1,682,627	6.6

*The apparent drop in Ancient Greek may be attributed to changes in reporting; in earlier surveys, languages such as Biblical Greek, Koine Greek, and other premodern Greek language categories may have been reported under the category "Ancient Greek."

Source: The Modern Language Association of America, "Enrollments in Languages Other Than English in United States Institutions of Higher Education," Fall 2009.

The professor of Biblical Hebrew could not understand the question because "suitcase" (*mizvada*) was an unknown term for him. He was immediately whisked away to the special room for interrogation by the agents.

The second table, on the following page, shows enrollments for all major foreign languages—Hebrew just barely exceeds Korean and has only about half the numbers of Biblical Hebrew.

THE UNITED STATES

At the university level, Judaic studies and Hebrew are in decline. Nationally and locally, Modern Hebrew is a standard offering at approximately 140 U.S. colleges and universities. This includes the Ivy League schools, and almost all of the "Big Ten," but the statistics are not encouraging.

The situation among the Jewish community with regard to knowledge of Modern Hebrew has become a perennial source of despair. Dozens of Jewish community leaders, academics, Hebrew teachers, rabbis and parents of stu-

Undergraduate Language Course Enrollments in Four-Year Colleges and Graduate Language Course Enrollments
(Languages in Descending Order of 2009 Totals)

	Undergraduate Enrollments (Four-Year Institutions)			Graduate Enrollments			Totals		
	2002	2006	2009	2002	2006	2009	2002	2006	2009
Spanish	515,688	587,376	602,325	9,950	10,865	12,205	525,638	598,241	614,530
French	162,705	169,949	174,966	4,605	4,763	4,241	167,310	174,712	179,207
German	75,987	79,071	81,107	2,803	3,072	2,600	78,790	82,143	83,707
Italian	51,750	64,344	66,109	1,047	1,018	775	52,797	65,362	66,884
Japanese	38,545	50,035	54,080	930	859	717	39,475	50,894	54,797
Chinese	26,914	41,782	50,385	934	1,127	1,009	27,848	42,909	51,394
ASL	21,613	33,500	36,515	121	746	826	21,734	34,246	37,341
Latin	27,695	30,250	30,150	1,045	1,021	1,024	28,740	31,271	31,174
Arabic	8,194	18,650	28,066	531	940	782	8,725	19,590	28,848
Russian	20,208	21,721	23,596	770	749	596	20,978	22,470	24,192
Greek, Ancient	14,044	16,365	15,765	6,033	6,423	4,837	20,077	22,788	20,602
Hebrew, Biblical	9,014	8,517	8,331	5,133	5,581	5,091	14,147	14,098	13,422
Portuguese	6,945	9,029	9,877	487	458	438	7,432	9,487	10,315
Hebrew, Modern	7,693	8,437	7,399	418	697	355	8,111	9,134	7,754
Korean	4,045	5,687	7,085	111	237	348	4,156	5,924	7,433
Other languages	19,257	25,845	30,725	1,797	2,414	2,393	21,054	28,259	33,118
Total	1,010,297	1,170,558	1,226,481	36,715	40,970	38,237	1,047,012	1,211,528	1,264,718
% Change	NA	15.9	4.8	NA	11.6	-6.7	NA	15.7	4.4

Excluded from this table are enrollments in schools that did not specify their institutional type.

Source: The Modern Language Association of America, "Enrollments in Languages Other Than English in United States Institutions of Higher Education," Fall 2009

dents about to choose a foreign language requirement at college have sought to explain the decline. The majority have come to the conclusion that Modern Hebrew is not trendy, that it is no longer a source and sign of ethnic pride, that it is too remote and "foreign" from the usual texts students are accustomed to reading at synagogue services, and that it is too greatly linked with Israeli governments whose policies on a host of issues are not in line with the political stance of many American Jews. The currently popular revival of ethnicity has largely encouraged an emotional tie to the Yiddish language and folkways of the grandparents' generation rather than identification with Israel.

Sociologist Steven Cohen, co-author of the 2007 study "Beyond Distancing: Young Adult American Jews and Their Alienation from Israel" and an acknowledged expert in the field, concludes, The apparent linkage between ever increasing alienation among American Jews is a "reflection of deep-seated change in Jewish life, representing a shift away from an emphasis on the collective including the Jewish People, ethnicity and politics—and towards the private—prayer and spirituality. Jewish Intermarriage is a reflection of that shift and a cause."[7] Among the most amazing responses from the study is the high percentage (over half) of respondents under 35 who would not view the destruction of Israel as a personal tragedy!

Some critics of Modern Hebrew courses maintain that Jewish students are offered a curriculum that is no different from other foreign languages rather than a form of self-affirmation or insight into Jewish religious tradition and practice. It is indeed difficult to answer such disparate needs in introductory courses, but the criticism is valid up to a point. It might be fascinating for the students to learn how related words have a definite bearing on ethical issues—for example, the close connection between the words *ReĤeM* רחם (womb) and *RaĤManut* רחמנות (mercy)—or that the prophets preaching social justice nevertheless supported an independent priesthood maintained by a flat-tax "tithe."[8]

What do these students miss if they stop at a one- or two-years level of college Hebrew? Among other things, they miss out on much of the exciting developments in Israel ignored by the general media.

Symptomatic of the gap in Hebrew literacy between Israel and the United States is the relative paucity of translated literature from Modern Hebrew in terms of sales. Only about 3 percent of the new titles published each year in the United States are translated from all foreign languages combined. Compare this with as many as 40 percent in some European countries, such as Denmark, Switzerland, and The Netherlands, where foreign language proficiency is common. In 2009, only five new Israeli fiction titles were translated into English and published in the United States. In 2008, just 362 new novels appeared in translation in the United States, which represents less than 1 percent of the 47,541 fiction titles published that year.[9]

The truth has never been said better than by David Hazony[10] in his essay "Memo to American Jews: Learn Hebrew—The Gulf Between Israel and Diaspora Is Growing Fast":

> Israelis are suddenly appearing at the forefront of a whole range of previously unthinkable fields—not just medicine or military upgrades but also electronic music and fashion and television programming, avant-garde dance ... and world-leading architects and chefs and chemists. Every one of these successes sits atop a pyramid of incredible things, very little of which American Jews ever hear about, much less participate in.
>
> Herein lies our trouble. The more time goes by in which American Jews fail to get on the Israeli-civilization bus, the less qualified they become to say anything at all about who we are and what we should or shouldn't do.
>
> The harsh truth is that any discourse that says "I love Israel, but I can't stand Israelis," "I love Israel, but could never live there," "I love Israel, but can't stand that horrible rabbinate, that horrible Lieberman, that horrible heat," or, "I love Israel even though I don't know Hebrew"—all these are variations of a single bizarre theme, a theme very different from what Jews used to be, a theme in which ignorance and love are seen as somehow compatible, in which what you're loving isn't really Israel at all, but your own saucy dreams.
>
> But there is a simple solution to all this, perhaps incomplete and sure to cause many American Jews to bristle—but frankly it is the only way forward if this peoplehood thing is going to work. It's the 800-pound falafel ball sitting in the room
>
> American Jews have to learn Hebrew.

American Jews often regard such criticism as a stinging rebuke and resent any comparison with "ethnic Americans" who have continued to cultivate the language of their ancestors. Unlike all Jews in the United States, with the exception of "yordim" (ex–Israelis who have left the country for good), knowledge of an ancestral language derived from intimate contact with grandparents and was often regarded as a trait of their parents' generation, who had rejected Yiddish.

2. The Magnificent Heritage of Hebrew

No literate person can expect to read a daily newspaper or listen to a discussion of the arts and sciences, law, psychology, physics, mathematics, military affairs or any other professional field without encountering a wealth of phrases and expressions of foreign origin that have become part of the English language. Expressions such as *status quo, casus belli, laissez-faire, déjà vu, savoir-faire, haute cuisine, allegro, pogrom, de facto, de jure, sine qua non, prima facie, modus vivendi, leitmotif, blitzkrieg, lebensraum,* etc. (yes, even *et cetera* itself) and thousands more are part of our everyday speech. For those to whom "classical languages" are synonymous with "dead" ones, modern languages at least offer a practical tool to aid study in prestigious professional fields—French, so closely associated with high fashion, cuisine and art; Italian, with music and the opera; German, with science, philosophy, medicine and psychology; and Russian, with philosophy, physics, aeronautics and great literature.

The contribution of Hebrew is less obvious and often overlooked in our more secular age. Many students who have no major interest in religion often ask of what use is Hebrew, a minor language spoken by less than seven million people as their native, primary or habitual tongue. This question is never posed by those students considering studying Latin or Ancient Greek, well aware as they are of the immense respect accorded the classical civilizations of Greece and Rome.

During the Reformation and Renaissance, Christian scholars took a profound interest in the Old Testament and produced new translations directly from the original Hebrew, rather than using the Vulgate Latin texts. This interest can be seen, for example, in the poetry of William Blake (1757–1827) and John Milton (1608–1674), who both read and wrote Hebrew, and in Rembrandt's famous painting with its Hebrew "Writing on the Wall," illustrating the "Feast of Belshazzar."

Fidelity to the original Hebrew of the holy works had previously been demonstrated by the Christian scholar Johann Reuchlin (1455–1522), whose study of the Hebrew Scriptures resulted in strong support among enlightened clergymen to prevent the burning of the Talmud as a work of heresy. Because of a desire to read the Bible in its original tongue and a belief in Hebrew as "The Mother of Languages," it figured prominently in the Puritan movement in England, culminating in the Commonwealth under Oliver Cromwell.

The Puritans in New England were also instrumental in promoting Hebrew as part of the curriculum in such prominent universities as Harvard, Columbia, Yale, Brown, Princeton, Johns Hopkins, Dartmouth and the University of Pennsylvania (the first three still bear Hebrew inscriptions on their seals). In Harvard's early years, Hebrew enjoyed an exalted status and more time was devoted to its study than to Latin or Greek. This role of Hebrew in the curriculum endured until the 1820s. Graduates of Protestant Schools of Divinity had to be able to read the Old Testament in the original Hebrew—a practice still required in Scandinavia and Germany.

The English House of Commons in 1649 sought to substitute Saturday as the "True Sabbath" in place of Sunday as the Lord's Day. John Selden (1584–1654) was a noted legal scholar whose study of the biblical and Talmudic sources of ancient Jewish law (in Hebrew and Aramaic) helped reshape the British system of jurisprudence and establish the privilege of the individual against self-incrimination.

The designation in Modern Hebrew for the United States is "Artzot haBrit," which literally means "The Lands of the Covenant." For Hebrew speakers, this name struck an immediate responsive chord in stating that America was a country that placed the rule of law foremost above all persons and privileges. "Brit" means "covenant." It was also the term used for "circumcision," the act that made the covenant a visible sign in the flesh between God and the descendants of Abraham and Isaac. This covenant—the Torah—constituted the voluntary acceptance of a righteous moral code.

The Torah and the Constitution were elevated by Jews and Americans, respectively, as the final recourse and supreme arbiter of political disputes and moral conflicts. The "LAW," rather than any president or king, was acknowledged as the source of power in the state. A King Ahab and a President Nixon were removed not by armed insurrection or devious political maneuvering but by the sense of public outrage that they had abused the moral authority entrusted to them. The prophets had the Torah and the political opponents of the administration had the Constitution on their side. A King Solomon and a President Clinton, even if not deposed, suffered the scorn and humiliation of having betrayed their sacred trust. Nowhere else but in ancient Israel and modern America is there a document that is so respected and carries such weight.

Furthermore, there was esteem for the Old Testament reflected in the prevalence of biblical place names, such as Salem, Jericho, Shiloh and Bethlehem, as well as personal names. Colonial America, especially New England, was populated by countless Isaacs, Josephs, Jacobs, Joshuas, Solomons, and Abrahams (one American commander at Bunker Hill and in charge of the Continental Army in New York was Israel Putnam), as well as Sarahs, Ruths, Rebeccas, Rachels, Deborahs and Abigails. Reverence for the Old Testament even extended to requiring that the size of a barrel of beer in Massachusetts be constructed according to the dimensions specified in Deuteronomy.

All this evident regard for the biblical/Hebrew heritage made New England initially hospitable to early Jewish settlement. Nothing better illustrates this immense respect for the Old Testament than the words uttered in May 1775 by Ethan Allen, leader of the Green Mountain Boys in Vermont. When challenged by British soldiers at the gates of Fort Ticonderoga regarding on whose authority he was acting to demand its surrender, he replied, "By the authority of the Great Jehovah and the Continental Congress!"

Cecil Roth, one of the most prominent Jewish historians of modern times, had this to say: "Generation after generation of Englishmen heard the Bible read in church and studied it at home. In many cases, it was the only book; in all, the principal book. At last its cadences, its music, its phraseology, sank into his mind and became part of his being. Hence by slow degrees his daily speech was not merely enriched, but to some extent molded by its influence."[1]

Hebrew's Influence on English

Without knowledge of Hebrew and its majestic cadence and imagery, we are apt to assume that certain modes of expression are simply derived from old Anglo-Saxon speech, but the translation of the Bible into English directly from Hebrew exercised a major influence over the English language. When we use expressions such as a "heavy heart" or idioms like "the skin of his teeth" and "a drop in the bucket," or employ superlatives such as "Holy of Holies" (Kodesh ha-Kedushim), King of Kings (Melech ha-Melachim), or Song of Songs (Shir ha-Shirim), we are simply repeating a word-for-word translation of the Hebrew Bible.

Hebraic and Greek Roots of Western Civilization

The impact of Hebrew goes back much further than the Reformation and Renaissance! Our view of ancient history has been shaped by the enormous role Greece, Rome, and Christianity (and their bias toward its Jewish origins) played in the formation and development of what came to be known as Western civilization. This term is actually a misnomer, since many of its most important foundations—monotheism, the Judeo-Christian ethic (namely, the belief that each individual is created in the image of God and shares in an essential sanctity and dignity), as well as our alphabet—originated in the heartland of the ancient world, which stretched from the Aegean Sea and the Nile Delta across the Levant, Phoenicia, Israel and Mesopotamia (including the kingdoms and empires of Akkadia, Assyria, the Hittites and Babylonia).

It is now evident that many links existed between the Old Testament and Hebrew language and the early civilization of Greece and the classic works of *The Iliad* and *The Odyssey*. More than 30 years ago, Professor Cyrus Gordon pointed out in his epic work of scholarship, *The Common Background of Greek and Hebrew Civilizations,* that both drew on a common East Mediterranean heritage, with many cross-currents between them: "Only two of the ethnic groups that emerged historically in the eastern Mediterranean of the second millennium have enjoyed a historically conscious continuity down to the present: the Greeks and the Hebrews."[2] This fact had been long ignored because so few scholars were skilled in both Greek and Hebrew. A re-examination of the great works of Hellenic and Hebraic civilizations sheds light on similar customs and common aspects of kingship, military strategy and technology, sacrifice, music and the issues of humanity's fate as dramatically portrayed both in the Book of Job and in the greatest Greek dramas—the problems of evil and suffering. These central elements of "Western" civilization originated in the Near East—ancient Israel and Greece (which at that time included Crete, Cyprus and much of Asia Minor).

Carthage and Tyre

History is always written by the victors. Rome vanquished Greece, mostly peacefully, and absorbed much of the Greek legacy—mythology, philosophy, and laws. Two other rivals, however, were crushed in a series of violent wars—Israel and Carthage. These two shared much the same Semitic heritage in language and did not accept Rome's claims to a superior civilization.

The Phoenicians of Tyre and Sidon had been close allies of the ancient Israelite kingdom and helped King Solomon build the First Temple. Migrants from these two Phoenician cities founded Carthage and spread across the western Mediterranean to Sicily, Corsica, Sardinia and southern Spain. More than a thousand years before Islam, much of Mediterranean Europe and North Africa was characterized by a pre-Christian, pre-Muslim Semitic civilization.

In contrast to so many other subject peoples under Roman rule, these Semites put up stubborn resistance and even asserted the superiority of monotheism (first Judaism, and then Christianity). They were proud of their alphabet, which was borrowed first by the Greeks and later by the Romans. Our alphabet is a direct descendant and still bears the names of the first two letters of the early Phoenician-Hebrew alphabet (*aleph* and *bet*). The sequential order of the letters from A to Z closely follows much the same order in the Hebrew alphabet.

The last reigning emperor of Ethiopia inherited the title of "Lion of Judah" (claiming descent from King Solomon and the Queen of Sheba) and chose the name Haile Selassi (Hayl ha-Shlosha—in Hebrew, "The Power of the Trinity"). The Puritans held the Hebrew language in such high regard that their military banners were inscribed with the emblem of the Lion of Judah and their battle hymns were taken directly from the Psalms.

Biblical Hebrew Words of Major Importance in English Usage

Although regarded as a "minor language," the influence of the Jewish and Christian Holy Scriptures has magnified the importance of Hebrew so that it has continued to be of major significance in theological issues and questions and provoked thousands of volumes of commentary and debate. Four significant Hebrew words are marked with an asterisk below and have been the subject of endless debate and controversy over the past two thousand years: *Jehovah*, *Messiah*, *Satan*, and *Sheol*. These are among two dozen other Hebrew words that have been assimilated into English and many other world languages:

Alphabet, abbot, abbey, aliya, Amen, Armageddon, Ashkenazi
Babel, Cabal, Cherubim, ebony
Gauze, Gehenna (Gai-Hinnor, or Valley of Hinom), Gemara
Halacha, Hallah, Hallelujah, Hazzan, Hosanna
Jehovah YHVH* (Jehova), Jezebel, jeremiad, jot, iota, jubilee
Kabbalah, kaddish, Beit Knesset
Leviathan
Mammon, manna, matzah, menorah, Messiah,* mezuzah
Pharisees, Saducees, Sabbath, sabbatical, sapphire, Satan,* scallion, Seraphim, shekel, shibboleth, Sheol,* shofar
Tallit, Talmud, Tanakh (representing an abbreviation for Torah [The Law], Neviim [The Prophets] and Ketuvim [The Chronicles])
Torah
Yeshiva

Some of these Hebrew words of biblical origin were so distinctive that no attempt was made to find a word or phrase to render the exact meaning. The words were retained in the more than one thousand biblical translations into other languages in approximately the form they are pronounced in Hebrew, such as **Amen** אמן. The three letters, aleph-mem-nun, denote the concepts of faith, belief, affirmation, confirmation, confidence. When we say this word, we affirm our prayer. It was deemed improper to try and translate this word into a weaker euphemism in the local language, such as "may it be so."

On February 22, 1995, British Prime Minister John Major, speaking to the House of Commons in Parliament about the initiatives taken to reach a peaceful settlement in Northern Ireland acceptable to both Protestants and Catholics, appealed to both sides to "avoid the shibboleths of the past." He used the Hebrew term "shibboleth" with complete confidence that all members of the House would immediately grasp the significance of this solemn concept in the original language, drawn from the Old Testament (Judges 12:1–6).

Shibboleth שבולת (the Hebrew word for an "ear of corn") was pronounced with the "sh" sound by the Gideonites, while the hostile tribe of Ephraimites could not say the "sh" and pronounced it "sibboleth." The self-same strategy of dialect detection was used in a peasants' revolt in Flanders in the town of Brugge (Bruges) in the thirteenth century. The Flemish-speaking peasants distinguished their comrades from French-speaking nobility who were clad in peasant garb by asking them to repeat the Flemish slogan "Friend and Shield"; the French speakers inevitably could not pronounce the "sch" in the Flemish word for shield. A similar shibboleth technique was used in World War II by the Dutch resistance and British intelligence to uncover German SS officers pretending to be Dutch civilians, who were unable to properly pronounce the name of the town of Scheveningen.

The cherubim and seraphim כרובים וסרפים are two types of winged celestial beings who protected the Holy Ark (II Chronicles 3:10–13, I Kings 6:23–28) and God is said to dwell among them (Psalms 99:1). They are described in many verses in Exodus, Ezekiel, I Kings and II Chronicles, and they figure as benign protectors or muses in English art, sculpture, literature and poetry (see *Piers Plowman* by William Langland, *Paradise Lost* by John Milton, *A Song to David* by Christopher Smart, *Auguries of Innocence* by William Blake, *Cain* by Lord Byron and *The Rhyme of the Ancient Mariner* by Samuel Coleridge).

Sabbath (Shabbat and sabbatical) is derived from the root letters shin-bet-tav, denoting a cessation or stoppage of any kind. In the very first verses of the Old Testament, we read that God created the heaven and the earth, but on the seventh day, He "ŜaVaT" שבת. The modern word for a work strike, *shvitah* שביתה, was formed from the same root. The Jewish day of rest is Shabbat.

Hallelujah and Hosanna mean "Praise to God" and "Save us!" respectively. The root H-L-L הלל denotes praise and adulation, and השע means to save. Both terms became an important part of Christian worship to redeem mankind.

Cabal קבל indicates a secret group plotting conspiracies. The word is derived from the Kaballah, a mystical and esoteric book of Jewish wisdom that was held suspect by Christian clerics in the Middle Ages (from the root letters K-B-L, meaning "to receive").

Mammon ממון is a term used to refer to worldly wealth, riches and capital in the economic sense. It is derived from M-M-N. In Modern Hebrew it became a verb meaning "to finance."

Leviathan לויתן means "monstrous sea creature" (Isaiah 27:1, Psalms 104:26). Used later to indicate anything of huge abnormal size.

Behemoth בהמות is the plural form for a huge wild animal, probably the hippopotamus (see Genesis 1:25, Ecclesiastes 3:19, Leviticus 27:27, Jonah 3:7, Proverbs 30:30, Job 18:3, and Isaiah 46:1).

Golem גולם is a man-made creature that, according to the legend dating to the Middle Ages, was created by Rabbi Loew in Prague to help defend the Jewish community. The root G-L-M means "to create" or "embody." The term "Ĥomrei Gelem" is used in modern Hebrew for "raw materials."

Armageddon is a corruption of the words Har Megiddo (Mountain of Megiddo, near modern-day Afulah in Israel), the supposed site mentioned in the New Testament where the final battle between the forces of good and evil during the "End of Days" will occur.

Philistines and Philistinism: The root P-L-Ŝ פלש comes from the Hebrew meaning "to invade." The Philistines were one of the "Peoples of the Sea" who originated in the Aegean islands off the Greek and Turkish coasts before reaching the shores of the southwestern coast of what is today Israel and Gaza. In modern English, the term has come to denote the assumed characteristics of the biblical Philistines as they were regarded by the Israelites. Technologically superior to the peoples of ancient Palestine due to their knowledge of metallurgy (1 Samuel 13:19–21), the Philistines most likely crossed the Aegean Sea from Greece. They were accomplished blacksmiths who manufactured and sharpened iron tools for the Israelites, who nevertheless considered them indifferent, hostile or ignorant of spiritual and artistic values as personified by King David. He was not only a great warrior capable of defeating the Philistine giant warrior Goliath but also hailed as an accomplished singer, musician, poet and dancer (2 Samuel 6:5, 6:16 and 6:21).

For a number of creative Victorian-era authors such as Oscar Wilde, the term "Philistine" was used as an epithet applied to the British middle classes, deemed to only be interested in commerce and apathetic toward the arts.

CONTROVERSIAL HEBREW WORDS—WHY DO THEY MEAN SO MUCH TO SO MANY?

The five words marked with an asterisk are probably the most controversial in Hebrew or any other language due to theological disputes and rival interpretations of the translation of the Scriptures into other languages.

Messiah—from the Hebrew *mashiach* (M-Ŝ-Ĥ משיח)

The Messiah, or anointed one, was regarded as a prophet anointed by God to redeem mankind. It has since acquired a broader meaning to refer to political "messiahs" who promise "Heaven on earth." The Greek translation of messiah, "Christus," was attached to Jesus' name as part of Christian theology.

Satan שטן—the Hebrew designation for an evil or malicious spirit or messenger of God

The Book of Job, Psalm 109, and Genesis 27:33 all illustrate the original meaning of this word. Later, Christianity identified this word as the name of "the devil," whose seat of power came to be associated with the vision of Hell—a place of eternal damnation for the wicked. It is still used as an exclamation or profanity in the Scandinavian languages.

Sheol—שאול literally a pit grave, or "abode of the dead"

Sheol was where the "shades" (*rephaim*), entities without personality or strength, resided. It was the underworld in the Old Testament, a place of darkness to which all the dead went, both the righteous and the unrighteous, regardless of the moral choices made in life, a place of stillness and darkness cut off from God.

Sheol is identified as the place where the "Witch of Endor" contacted the "shade" (soul?) of Samuel for King Saul, although such practices were forbidden. The Old Testament writings describe Sheol as the permanent realm of the dead, but in the Second Temple period (roughly 500 BCE–70 CE), other, more sophisticated ideas evolved. In some texts, Sheol is the home of both the righteous and the wicked, separated into respective compartments; in others, it was a place of punishment, meant for the wicked dead alone. (See the two Books of Samuel).

When the Hebrew Scriptures were translated into Greek in ancient Alexandria around 200 BCE, the word "Hades" (the Greek underworld) was substituted for Sheol. This is seen in the New Testament, where "Hades" (eventually translated as "Hell" in English) is both the underworld of the dead and the personification of the evil it represents.

Alma עלמה and the Dispute Over the Hebrew Word for Virgin

"Therefore the Lord Himself will give you a sign: Behold, a virgin will be with child and bear a son, and she will call His name Immanuel" (Isaiah 7:14).

Of all the Hebrew words used in the Old Testament, the most controversial one in biblical translations was *almah* עלמה.

Isaiah 7:14 says that an *almah* will bear a son. Its use elsewhere makes it evident that what is most likely meant is simply a young single woman of marriageable age or one newly married. Therefore, the word *almah* does not necessarily mean virgin. The word occurs elsewhere in the Old Testament, especially Proverbs 30 ("maiden"): "There are three things which are too wonderful for me, for which I do not understand: the way of an eagle in the sky, the way of a serpent on a rock, the way of a ship in the middle of the sea, and the way of a man with a young woman [*b'almah*]. This is the way of an adulterous woman: she eats and wipes her mouth, and says, 'I have done no wrong'" (Proverbs 30:18–20). The first three examples cited here do not leave any trace after the act of flying through the sky, slithering along a rock or plowing through the sea. Similarly, a young woman who has committed adultery can wipe her mouth and leave no trace.

There is a specific word meaning "virgin"—*bethulah* בתולה. If Isaiah 7:14 was meant to indicate a virgin instead of simply a young maiden, then why wasn't the word used here? This translation was made around 200 BCE by 70 scholars of Hebrew. In Isaiah 7:14, they translated the word *almah* into the Greek word *parthenos*, meaning "virgin." This Greek word is used in the New Testament for the Virgin Mary (Matt. 1:23; Luke 1:27) and for the ten virgins in the parable (Matt. 25:1, 7, 11). Why would Isaiah choose to use the word *almah* עלמה and not *bethulah* בתולה?

The English word "virgin" comes from the Old French "virgine," meaning a sexually intact young woman. Both the word *almah* and the masculine form *elem* are in current usage in Modern Hebrew and retain the flavor they did in the Old Testament of particularly attractive unmarried youths. No Hebrew speaker in Israel today would countenance a translation of either word for "virgin" in the words of two popular hit songs—"*Tsarot tovot*" (Good Difficulties) and "*Elem ẖen*" עלם חן (Charming and Graceful Young Man)—which use both the male and female forms to clearly mean attractive young men and women who are most likely not married. They both use playful language, as shown below:

"Good Difficulties"
In my town there were two young women (*alamot*), two beautiful young women and twins, and I loved them both. They were so similar, so similar were the young ladies. And I loved the both of them and so experienced good difficulties. And the two of them didn't know about each other. One, I took away to the mountains in order to see the shining sun, and the other to the forests to see how the sun disappears.

The song goes on to relate how the angels hinted to the speaker that he had to make a choice, but the poor guy was unable to. In the song "*Elem ḥen*," we learn of the advice given to a charming and handsome young man and the "enticing" young ladies:

> Pride conquers your heart
> Young man of grace and charm
> but you don't dare to approach her,
> Young man, young man of grace and charm
> Come closer, sweetheart
> They are enticing and leaping
> Place your hand on the waist of one of these young ladies!

YHWH יהוה—the Tetragammaton and Jehovah

The term tetragrammaton (from Greek τετραγράμματον, meaning "the four letters") refers to the Hebrew name of God, the theonym transliterated to the Latin letters YHWH. It is derived from a verb that means "to be," and was originally regarded as a proper name of the God of Israel used in the Hebrew Bible. The most widely accepted pronunciation of the tetragrammaton (YHWH) is Yahweh יהוה, though the spelling "Jehovah" is used in many Bibles (and is the most widely known in the English-speaking world).

Copenhagen's famous "Round Tower" is engraved with the Latin word "Doctrinament," a sword, a heart and God's name in Hebrew (the Tetragammaton), indicating that the seventeenth century Protestant monarch King Christian IV let his heart be ruled by God's word.

Since ancient Hebrew had no written vowels, it is uncertain how the name was actually pronounced. Sometime before the first century CE/AD, it became common for Jews to avoid saying the divine name for fear of misusing it and breaking the second commandment ("You shall not take the name of the Lord, your God, in vain," Deut. 5:11). Whenever they read Scripture aloud and encountered the divine name, they substituted another Hebrew word, *Adonai* (which means "my Lord"), in its place.

Around the thirteenth century the term "Jehovah" appeared when Christian scholars took the consonants of "Yahweh" and pronounced it as "Yahowah," which has a Latinized spelling of "Jehovah." Jehovah's Witnesses today

The inscription on the Round Tower of King Christian IV in central Copenhagen is partly in Hebrew (God's name in the letters Y-H-W-H). The symbols show that the king has let his heart be ruled by the word of the Lord (Jehovah) (author's photograph).

criticize orthodox Christian denominations for "hiding the name of God" by replacing "Jehovah" with "the Lord" whenever "Jehovah" appears in Scripture.

A Hallmark of Great Literature, Oratory and Debate

The influence of the Hebrew language extends far beyond the fields of linguistics and religion. Its contribution is much more profound than the borrowing of individual words and concepts. Hebrew speech patterns have been so long encased in English words and phrases that we scarcely give a thought to their origins. Classics of English literature (both prose and poetry), political oratory, the popular stage, song and screen, and inscriptions on historical monuments are strewn with titles lifted directly from the pages of the Old Testament, where they appeared for the first time in Hebrew. These words and expressions serve as allegories, proverbs and parables for modern situations and events that recall the Bible. This has long been a hallmark of great literature and debate.

Below are just a few examples among many that were familiar to almost all Americans, including those without any formal education and whose only book at home was the Bible, a hundred and fifty years ago.[3] These sayings were used by professional people, convinced that their audience would immediately know the circumstances from the Bible where these words were first used. They evoked an immediate responsive chord. The following verses may be unfamiliar to many with a college degree or a high IQ in the English-speaking world today, but to be ignorant of them a hundred and fifty years ago meant being worse than "illiterate":

The Good Earth (*Deuteronomy* 6:18)
Man Shall Not Live by Bread Alone (*Deuteronomy* 8:23)
The Grapes of Wrath (*Deuteronomy* 32:32)
Proclaim Liberty throughout the Land and unto All the Inhabitants Thereof (on the Liberty Bell—*Leviticus* 25:10)
What Hath God Wrought! (*Numbers* 23:23–24)
Be Fruitful and Multiply (*Genesis* 9:1)
The Tower of Babel (*Genesis* 11)
Sell One's Birthright for a Bowl of Stew (*Genesis* 25:29–34)
Seven Years for Rachel (*Genesis* 29:18)
The Heart Goes Out (*Genesis* 42:28)
The Fat of the Land (*Genesis* 45:18)
Let Them Make Bricks with Straw (*Exodus* 5:7)
Let My People Go! (*Exodus* 7:14)
A Peculiar Treasure (*Exodus* 19:5)
An Eye for an Eye and a Tooth for a Tooth (*Exodus* 21:24)
Gone with the Wind (*Psalms* 103:16)
Nothing New Under the Sun (*Ecclesiastes* 1:9)
Vanity, Vanity, All Is Vanity (*Ecclesiastes* 1:14)

These and scores of others were chosen many times as the titles of books, plays, songs and films beloved by millions, and many readers could well extend the list by another hundred or more! Countless Christian churches and place names around the world bear testimony to the geography of Israel and the Hebrew language: *Beth-Lehem* (House of Bread), *Bedlem*, *Beth-El* (House of God), *Bethania*, Mt. Moriah, Galilee, Jordan, *Shiloh*, Mt. Hermon, Jericho, Goshen, *Kinneret* (the Hebrew word for the harp shape of the lake), Salem (Anglicized from *Shalom*), Canaan, Hebron, Nazarene, Lily of the Valley, Rose of Sharon, Mt. Sinai. In addition, Gethsemane is the Hebrew/Aramaic *gat-shemen* (oil press).

Hebrew as the Primal Language—The Tower of Babel Myth

A traditional Jewish view expressed in a Midrash (Genesis Rabbah 38) claims that Adam, who was created from the clay of the earth (*adamah*), spoke Hebrew because the names he gives Eve—"*Isha*" (Genesis 3:23) and "*Hava*"—only make sense in Hebrew. That is because *isha* (woman) was created from *ish* (man) and Eve, the name of Adam's wife, comes from the root HYW, meaning "life": "And Adam called his wife's name *Ḥawwāh* because she was the 'mother of all living.'"

The great Italian poet Dante Alighieri addresses the topic in his *De Vulgari Eloquentia* (1304) where he wrote, "Hebrew was the language which the lips of the first speaker formed," and argued that the Adamic language is of divine origin and therefore unchangeable; he also noted that the first act of speech is due to Eve, addressing the serpent, and not to Adam. In his *Divina Commedia*, however, Dante changed his view (Paradiso XXVI), concluding that Hebrew was a later derivative of the language spoken by Adam.

The prestige of Hebrew was thus so great in both ancient and medieval times that scholars and kings strove to prove that Hebrew was the "Mother of all Languages" by carrying out language deprivation experiments, isolating infants from the normal use of spoken or sign language in an attempt to verify that the first identifiable words such children would utter would be in Hebrew.[4] An alleged experiment by Holy Roman Emperor Frederick II in the thirteenth century used this technique to determine what language would have been imparted unto Adam and Eve by God. The tests were recorded by a monk, Salimbene di Adam, who wrote that Frederick encouraged "foster-mothers and nurses to suckle and bathe and wash the children, but in no ways to prattle or speak with them; for he would have learnt whether they would speak the Hebrew language (which had been the first), or Greek, or Latin, or Arabic, or perchance the tongue of their parents of whom they had been born. But he labored in vain, for the children could not live without clapping of the hands, and gestures, and gladness of countenance."[5]

James IV of Scotland engaged in a similar experiment and was said to have sent two children to be raised by a mute woman isolated on the island of Inchkeith, to determine if language was learned or an innate property. Unlike the earlier attempt by the emperor, James' experiment allegedly confirmed that the children "spoke good Hebrew."

The view that Hebrew is the original source of all the world's language families dating from the time of the Tower of Babel was subsequently repudiated as simplistic and biased by the religious view of the Bible as "The Word of God." However, some recent scholarship has indicated that Hebrew may indeed be much older than the other Semitic languages. Its geographic location at the crossroads of three continents may have been an important factor in it being the source of other language families. Hebrew's sister languages (first Akkadian, and then Aramaic) functioned for a time as the "lingua franca"—an international language of diplomacy and trade in the Near East. By contrast, Arabic was then a remote minor language without a significant literature and off the main trade routes connecting centers of civilization.

The origin of Indo-European languages such as English, Greek, Latin and Farsi (Persian) is thought to go back to Sanskrit and further in the remote past to the original prototype Indo-European language, which in turn may share similarities with other major families. Some innovative linguists who support this theory of a single original language, or "monogenesis," have indicated a few such shared similarities to support the position, claiming, for example, an ancestral source for the word for "wine" (*yayin* in Hebrew), as well as air and *avir*, earth and *eretz*, mother and *ima*, fruit and *perot* and others.

A major new thesis resurrecting the Tower of Babel view of Hebrew as the primal language was presented in Isaac Mozeson's *The Word: The Dictionary That Reveals the Hebrew Source of English* (first published in 1989), linking 22,000 English words back to Hebrew. The author and his supporters assert that legitimate linguistic methods were used to follow all the etymological steps leading back to Hebrew. However, *The Word* was the object of attacks by most philologists. The idea of a single origin of languages rests on the idea that, originally, the three-consonant roots of Hebrew words denoting a concept replaced an earlier single-syllable, two-consonant word. This view asserts that at least two of major super-language families recognized by linguists, Indo-European and Semitic, may have had a common ancestor and then diverged. Since human language may be 30,000 years old or even older, and the oldest written evidence is no more than 8,000 to 10,000 years old, it will be very difficult to trace these connections to find further support for monogenesis.[6] Nonetheless, Mozeson still has supporters who subscribe to the idea that this original Hebrew was subsequently diffused throughout the world by contact, trade, and migration at some stage of pre-history rather than many languages being independently invented many times and subsequently evolving further into the world's major language families and individual languages of today.

Even without such a grandiose view as the original tongue of mankind, no other language can rival Hebrew's magnificent achievements in influencing so many of the world's languages and literatures over so long a period of time—not even Chinese or Greek, or Hindi, Farsi, or any other modern language with a distinguished heritage and pedigree extending from ancient civilizations to the present. It is precisely this facet of a continuous three thousand year old historical tradition that was the most powerful argument for making a modern variant of Hebrew the national language of a reborn Jewish sovereign state.

No other aspect of what can be called Judaic Civilization or Judaism has remained so constant—not the disputed boundaries of the ancient Jewish kingdoms, the many religious disputes between different schools of thought and levels of observance (Pharisees, Sadducees, Essenes, the Rabbis versus the Karaites, the modern communities of Orthodox, Conservative, Reform, Reconstructionist or the diverse cultural heritages of Ashkenazim, Sephardim, Yemenites, Ethiopians, Georgians), and the great variety of Diaspora languages, such as Yiddish, Judeo-Spanish (Ladino), Judeo-Arabic of Baghdad, Judeo-Arabic of Morocco, Tat, Yevanic (Judeo-Greek), and a dozen others.

Estimates made by Israel's Ministry of Immigrant Absorption in 1999 stated that 75 percent of the 70,000 Ethiopian "Beta Israel" community members could not read or write Hebrew. They represent the only Jewish community that historically had not maintained at least some ceremonial level of Hebrew knowledge. They had also arrived from a largely subsistence economy without modern job skills. Since then, enormous progress has been made, primarily due to instruction of the younger adults and children in Hebrew and through military service.

3. Modern Hebrew's Inspirational Example

In contrast with the ancient language, Modern Hebrew may at first glance seem a poor cousin with only a few scattered terms such as *kibbutz* (figure 4), Knesset (Israel's parliament), *ulpan* (language studio) and *uzi*, (Israel's compact sub machine-gun) as universally recognized words, but it has played the major role in establishing a sense of unity for millions of Jewish immigrants from diverse cultural backgrounds and creating a truly national language. Many Jews in the Diaspora are not familiar with the great achievements of Modern Hebrew as an inspirational role model for the revival of Irish, Welsh, Scottish Gaelic, Catalan, New Norwegian, Basque and Maltese, as well as modernizing reforms of Turkish and Modern Greek (*demotike*) that deserve to be widely known. The patrons, poets and patriots of these "minor languages" never tired of pointing to Modern Hebrew as an example of what could be achieved with enough effort, willpower, diligence, and dedication to making their national historical language more accessible to the great majority of people. Proponents of a "national revival" embracing these languages have invited Israeli experts to demonstrate the ulpan method—intensive language courses taught to new immigrants in a "Hebrew" environment without reliance on any other language of instruction, a technique that has been subsequently imitated by the successful Rosetta Stone method.

The Irish Revival

"A Nation Once Again" was the most popular song of the Irish Republican movement—it expressed the deep longing for generations of Irish patriots that. "I might yet see, Her fetters rent in twain, And Ireland, long a province, Be a Nation once again!" This same sentiment of restoring lost pride and regaining its own distinct idiom was mirrored by the animating spirit of Zionism and the wish to return to a lost homeland and language.[1]

As early as 1927, Eamon de Valera lamented to the head of the World Zionist Organization, Nahum Sokolow, that the Irish, in spite of having all the tools available to a national government, had been incapable of imitating the successful revival of Hebrew that was already apparent in Palestine. The same view was repeated more than 30 years later by Arthur Webb, the longtime editor of *The Irish Times* in Dublin, in an interview with the *New York Herald Tribune* (March 17, 1960). Sean Cronin, writing in *The Irish Times*, repeated the accusation that the entire mass media of Ireland overwhelmed a high school graduate with English-language cinema, theater, radio, TV and press, in contrast to the Hebrew environment of Israel.

The same point has been made by Nuala Ni Dhomnaill, the best-known and most colorful woman poet writing in Irish today.[2] She is a major cultural personality who has won wide acclaim in her native Kerry and all of Ireland, and also throughout the Irish Diaspora. Nevertheless, much of her work is read in English translation in spite of her claim that it thereby loses its effectiveness. She has made direct reference in expressing regret that, unlike Hebrew, Irish was not imposed on a massive scale; yet she admits that it is too late to change the linguistic reality.

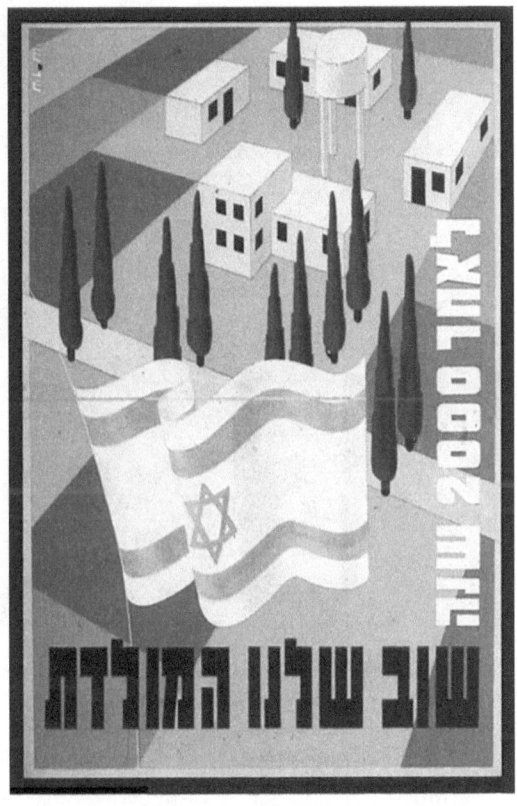

Poster celebrating the Kibbutz 1960, with the inscription "After 2,000 years, the Homeland is Ours Again" against a background of a kibbutz landscape (courtesy Palestine Poster Project Archives [PPPA]).

The Modernization of Maltese

In both Malta and the State of Israel, independence was re-created along with a cultural revival in the face of great odds and massive doubts as to the

Residents of Dimona study Hebrew after work at an ulpan, December 1, 1953 (Israeli National Photograph Collection).

viability of both states and languages. In both cases, a strongly based native, ethnic-linguistic nationalism evolved based on the Phoenician-Hebrew- and Canaanite-speaking city-states and colonies that extended from the Levant to southern Spain.

In the late 1870s, a handful of local scholars believed that Maltese, descended from the dialect spoken in Carthage and originally brought there by the Phoenicians, deserved to be respected. They argued that, as a language closely related to the Hebrew and Aramaic spoken by Jesus and the first disciples, Maltese had a noble pedigree. How could such a language be fit only for the market or the fisherman's wharf and boat? Why should it be denied as the language of instruction in the schools and the courts, and decreed incapable of producing a great literature?[3]

Only in the late nineteenth century did scholars finally adapt Maltese to a written standard using Latin letters and thereby greatly increase literacy. This success brought considerable prestige to the language that was the spoken vernacular of more than 95 percent of the island's population.

The publication in 1880 of a book in Italian titled *Saggio intorno alla lingua Maltese come effine all'Ebraico* enabled the cause of Maltese to finally make headway among many of the island's Italian-speaking intellectuals who had previously spurned the language. The author of the book, Annibale Preca, argued for the close association of Hebrew with Maltese. Although the original model for emulation was Biblical Hebrew, proponents of Maltese and educational authorities continued to follow the progress of Modern Hebrew in Palestine as proof that an ancient language could serve as the vehicle of a modern society. The modernization of Maltese even went a step further than Modern Hebrew by becoming "user-friendly" in order to increase literacy. Adoption of the Latin alphabet, a "reform" proposed many times for Modern Hebrew but ultimately rejected, won acceptance and greatly increased literacy in Malta.

Basque, Welsh and Catalan Language Revitalization

Three other examples in Europe of local government subsidies and initiatives designed to promote a regional language and grant it equality with the national language can be found in Wales, the Basque Country (El País Vasco in northwestern Spain) and Catalonia (northeast Spain).

Representatives from all three regions studied Israel's modernization of Hebrew and its progressive teaching programs to help implement the legislation and educational reforms that resulted in successfully increasing knowledge of Welsh through compulsory courses as a "foreign language requirement" in 1993 in all parts of Wales and instituting Catalan as the language of instruction in all subjects in public schools in Catalonia, where Castilian Spanish (perceived abroad as the sole national language of Spain) is the "compulsory *foreign* language requirement." One cannot today apply for many high-level positions in the regional government of Catalonia without fluency in Catalan. And in 1957, the Israeli cultural consul in Paris, S. Levine, received a confidential letter from a group of Basque intellectuals still in the anti–Franco underground asking for advice on how to implement the ulpan methods.

It is no accident that Welsh and Basque nationalists found a particularly sympathetic chord with the revitalization of Hebrew. Both groups claim that their respective languages are the "oldest in Europe" and that their national survival is intimately connected with the preservation and flourishing of their "national language."

*Modern Greek (*Demotike*) and Turkish*

The modern nationalist movements in Greece and Turkey both embarked upon a revitalization of their respective languages to make them more up to date and free from foreign influences in order to demonstrate that a "true national language" had to win favor with a majority of the common people who were unfamiliar with the established classical literary versions favored by scholars, the Greek Church or the Ottoman bureaucracy (the latter had in Turkey incorporated ornate Persian literary expressions and maintained the inappropriate and cumbersome Arabic script). Linguists and scholars in sympathy with modern nationalism in both countries found a solution that favored a modern and simplified form. Like Modern Hebrew, these linguistic projects were viewed as state-directed enterprises designed to increase a sense of solidarity and cohesion and integrate classes, diverse social strata, immigrants, and minorities, as well as reduce regional diversity.[4]

Hebrew and Esperanto—The Amazing Parallels

Esperanto, the only successful devised language, owes much of its origins and success to the original search for an answer to the Jewish language question. Its originator, Dr. Lazar Ludwig Zamenhof,[5] was a Jew whose knowledge of Hebrew undoubtedly played a major role in his search for a universal tongue. Although the Esperanto vocabulary is largely derived from the Romance, Germanic and Slavic families, it is certain that Zamenhof's profound knowledge of Hebrew contributed to the logical structure of Esperanto.[6] This was a two-edged sword. Initially, Yiddishists argued against Modern Hebrew, comparing it to what they called the "similar artificial character" of Esperanto. Later, proponents of Esperanto could demonstrate that Modern Hebrew had also suffered many of the same unjustified attacks as to its viability before achieving a modicum of success.

Both Zamenhof and Ben-Yehuda regarded the problem of Jewish identity as inseparable from the question of language. Ben-Yehuda's vision focused on the revival of Hebrew as a precondition for a Jewish national renaissance. At various times, Zamenhof had also toyed with the ideas of reviving Hebrew and using the Latin alphabet for Yiddish. He ultimately rejected both solutions in favor of a neutral international language. He hoped that this language would, at the same time, eventually be used as a common Jewish international language.

There exists considerable speculation on direct and indirect borrowings by Esperanto of elements from both Hebrew and Yiddish that can only be briefly touched upon here, but it reveals some of the workings of Zamenhof's "Litvak"-rationalist frame of mind. Hebrew and the other Semitic languages are built upon a root structure of tri-literal consonants that bear an essential concept. Words related to the same concept are immediately recognizable by the presence of the same three letters. Zamenhof utilized the structure of

3. Modern Hebrew's Inspirational Example

Hebrew to vastly increase the reader's familiarity with words that have related meanings; these are spelled and pronounced similarly. Compare how words in English are completely unalike, even though they may all relate to the concept of, say, monarchy. Compare with the words that share common root letters in Hebrew and Esperanto:

English	Hebrew (Hebrew letters)	Hebrew	Esperanto
1. King	1. מלך	1. MeLeCh	1. Reĝo
2. Queen	2. מלכה	2. MaLKah	2. Reĝino
3. Monarchy	3. מלכות	3. MaLCHut	3. Reĝeco
4. Royal	4. מלכותי	4. MaLChuti	4. Reĝa
5. Kingdom	5. ממלכה	5. maMLaCHa	5. Reĝlando
6. Royally	6. באופן מלכותי	6. bi-ofen MaLCHuti (literally in a royal manner)	6. Reĝe

Note that in Esperanto there is total recognition to distinguish parts of speech—all nouns end in o, all adjectives end in a, all adverbs end in e. He went much further to regularize the language so that there are no exceptions. Compare how many words can be derived that are all related to the basic concept of health (san):

malsana	sick, ill	saneco	healthiness
malsaneco	unhealthiness	sani	to be healthy
malsano	illness	saniĝi	to get well, recuperate
malsanulejo	hosptial	sanilo	health device, cure, medicine
malsanulino	sick person (female)		
malsanulo	sick person (male)	sano	health
resaniĝi	to convalesce	sanulino	a healthy female person
sana	healthy	sanulo	a healthy male person
sane	healthily		

Compare the above vocabulary utilizing the common root "san" with the many derivative words in Hebrew based on the three consonants *yod-daled-ayin* ע ד י (originally, probably the last two).

מדע, מודיעין, הודעה, מודעה, מודעי החברה, ידען, ידעון, ידעוני, ידיעות, ידע, דעת, דיעה.

> knowledge, science, opinion, information desk, poster, announcement, social sciences, pundit-expert, celebrity, sorcerer, bits of news or information

Gender of Nouns

A logical element in the vocabulary inventory of Hebrew that makes learning both fun and efficient is that often a student learns two words at a time because the feminine form of countless nouns is provided by adding a simple suffix (often one of only three types), creating such pairs as uncle-aunt, brother-sister, dog-bitch, stallion-mare (for those who are horse and dog lovers and need to immediately know the sex of the animal in question). The three most common such suffixes involve either a vowel change to "ah" (the kamatz vowel) or the addition of -et or -it. It also enables one to immediately know in Hebrew if the doctor, lawyer, axe murderer, police officer, teacher, or candlestick maker is male or female. The word pairs below indicate how easy the system in both Hebrew and Esperanto, as the same stem makes the word recognizable in its two variants, which look and sound alike except for one syllable.

    uncle, aunt dod, dodah דוד דודה onklo, onklino

    brother, sister ah, ahot אח אחות frato, fratino

    male dog, bitch kelev, kalbah כלב כלבה hundo, hundino

    policeman, policewoman policisto, policistino שוטר שוטרת shoter, shoteret

    waiter, waitress meltzar, meltzarit מלצר מלצרית kelnero, kelnerino

Just as Hebrew nouns for living beings, animals and those employed in the professions can be distinguished easily to denote gender, the same is true in Esperanto; the suffix -in performs the same function.

Many Esperanto verbs use the suffix -ig to correspond to the causative function of Hebrew verbs in the *pi'el* and *hif'il* formats and the passive nifal.[7] In Esperanto the causative is added by the suffix -ig and the passive iĝ: manĝas, manĝiĝas, manĝigas (1. eat; 2. is eaten; 3. feed).

    1. ochel   2. neechal   3. maa'achil   מאכיל 3 נאכל 2 אוכל 1

The use of the special grammatical marker "et" in Hebrew, placed just before a definite direct object, such as in "God created the heaven and the earth," is closely paralleled in Esperanto, with the final n attached to a noun that is the direct object of an action. In "Dio kreis la ĉielon kaj la teron," the same function is fulfilled by the grammatical marker "et" (את).

בראשית ברא אלוהים את השמיים ואת הארץ

This permits a much greater flexibility of the word order, allowing greater freedom for poetry, and it avoids cases of unintended confusion. For example, in the sentence "He loves the queen more than the king," does this mean....

1. Li amas la reĝinon pli ol la reĝon (He loves the queen more than he loves the king), or
2. Li amas la reĝinon pli ol la reĝo (He loves the queen more than the king does [more than the king loves the queen])

Compare the Hebrew:

1. ‏הוא אוהב את המלכה יותר מאת המלך.
2. ‏הוא אוהב את המלכה יותר מהמלך.

It is hard to ignore so many parallels. It is likely that Zamenhof copied these features from Hebrew and incorporated them into Esperanto. These features of Hebrew that Zamenhof used as a template for Esperanto evoked much favorable commentary among new learners of the language who had never studied foreign languages before and were in many cases "uneducated" and working class, but they provoked an avalanche of criticism from many "intellectuals"' and classic scholars resentful of an amateur.

Zamenhof was susceptible to the charges that he violated all the "holy traditions and canons of classical Western civilization" and that Esperanto was a barbaric innovation, a created "Frankenstein without a soul." These grotesque charges were thrown at him for using words like "patro-patrino" (father and mother) and "frato-fratino" (brother and sister). For many ultra-conservative Christians, such as patrician Swiss writer and intellectual Gonzague De Reynold, professor of history and literature at the Universities of Fribourg and Berne, who venerated Latin, Esperanto was "one more sign of the decadence" and corruption of European society since the French Revolution. De Reynold and others argued fervently against Esperanto and Zamenhof's Jewish influence. They rejected his "scheme" because accepting a word like "patrino" (mother) and all that word implied, with the initial PATR signifying father/fatherhood, was highly offensive to "civilized sensibilities." Such critics were naturally drawn to anti–Semitic movements and the Nazis during the 1930s.

For the record, this prejudicial criticism was, of course, nonsense, and thousands of children raised as native Esperanto speakers have used the word "patrino" in the same affectionate way that Europeans used their national languages, in which "mother" is represented by words deriving from the stem MTHR.

Zamenhof and Eliezer Ben-Yehuda were contemporaries, and the similarities of their lives and careers are nothing short of amazing. The monumental achievements of these two provide inspiring examples of devotion to learning, prophetic vision and identification with Jewish heritage and destiny. The parallels between them are uncanny, almost as if each one was the other's alter ego.

They were born within one year of each other (1858, 1859) and grew up in similar homes, infused with the "Litvak" (Lithuanian Jewish) atmosphere of the *Haskalah* (Enlightenment) movement, in which respect for secular learning was esteemed equally with Jewish tradition. Zamenhof's home town, Byalistock, lies 250 miles from Luzhki in the Vitebsk region in what is today's Belarus, where Ben-Yehuda (originally Pearlman) was born.

Both sought a career in medicine, one that Zamenhof achieved (he went on to become a respected eye specialist with an international reputation and, true to the noblest traditions of the profession, often treated the poor without charge). Both made enormous professional, material and physical sacrifices to advance the cause of their languages, despite their opponents' derisive claims that they were "eccentrics" or "fanatics," to the ultimate success of witnessing living communities of Hebrew and Esperanto.

The life and work of Ben-Yehuda are well known, and his memory is widely honored by the State of Israel and its institutions. But the life and work of Zamenhof deserve to reach a far wider audience than has heretofore been the case. The vision that motivated and sustained him throughout his life's work was that of a secure, productive, and culturally creative existence for the Jewish people living in a world of understanding and mutual respect among the nations.

A Polish ship bears Zamenhof's name, as do streets and memorial plazas in over two hundred cities (including Jerusalem, Tel Aviv, Haifa, Warsaw, Budapest, Vienna, Amsterdam, Hamburg, Zagreb, Marseilles, Antwerp, Barcelona and Rio de Janeiro). A silk factory in the People's Republic of China annually produces thousands of banners emblazoned with his picture, and a Japanese publishing house recently reissued his collected works. According to stamp collectors, after Einstein, Zamenhof is the Jew whose portrait has appeared on the postage stamps of more countries than anyone else. He also received belated recognition in this regard from the State of Israel in 2000. In spite of all these international honors, however, most Americans still fail to identify his name.

Why this is so is not difficult to understand. A very small proportion of the world's peoples have a reasonable command of a second language and only 8 percent of American colleges have any foreign language requirement. Most of the world's population are essentially monolingual speakers. Where the language in question is "prestigious," such as English, Russian, Spanish, German or French, speakers are liable to view the idea of an international neutral language as eccentric and superfluous. Esperanto's popularity has been greatest precisely among speakers of "minor" languages such as Hungarian, Bulgarian, Danish, Dutch, Finnish or Greek, who have already acquired one or more foreign languages in order to communicate beyond the boundaries of their own countries.

Why Zamenhof's Jewish Identity Played Such a Formative Role in Esperanto

The linguistic situation in the Diaspora today stands in sharp contrast to that of previous centuries, when Jews enjoyed a reputation for linguistic accomplishments. During the Middle Ages, translations by Jews of scientific, medical, and philosophical texts had helped bring about a revival of scholarly activity and secular interests. Jewish merchants in Europe and the Middle East were often, by necessity, fluent in two or more languages. A linguistic consequence of the Holocaust was a drastic reduction in the number of Jewish speakers of German and Yiddish, as well as Polish, Czech, Hungarian, Serbo-Croatian, Dutch, Greek, Lithuanian and Ladino. The centers of Yiddish cultural activity in Europe were obliterated, although a handful of refugee authors were able to keep the spark of Yiddish literature alive in the New World.

Jews constituted a large proportion of the pre World War II Esperantists in Central and Eastern Europe. One of the most pathetic and reprehensible chapters in the history of noble ideals is the lengths to which a considerable segment of the German Esperanto movement went in order to prevent the inevitable Nazi decision to eradicate the organization for obvious anti–Semitic motives. Who more than Zamenhof and Esperanto symbolized all that the Nazis detested—the Jewish, internationalist, pacifist and humanitarian character of its founder? Nevertheless, several high-ranking members of the German Esperanto movement tried to create a new "National German Esperanto organization," totally disregarding the "internal idea" of the movement to foster brotherhood. They vainly hoped to create a merger of the international language to serve the needs of the new Nazi Germany. This absurd idea was immediately rejected by the Nazis, who warned German Esperantists to simply cease and desist from all further propaganda and activity in the Third Reich.[8]

The Soviet Union initially adopted a favorable attitude toward the international language and supported an Esperanto theater during the 1930s. Many socialists referred to Esperanto as "the Latin of the Proletariat."[9] However, a reversal occurred when it became clear to Stalin that Esperantists outside the Soviet Union were unwilling to follow the party line as dictated from Moscow and, even worse, that Soviet Esperantists were able to inform correspondents abroad about the ugly realities of Soviet life. The result was that by 1938 the Soviet press and penal code had designated Esperanto as a "tool of Zionism and Cosmopolitanism," and almost all Soviet Esperantists either perished in the great purges or languished in Siberian labor camps until the Khrushchev thaw of 1956.[10]

To fully appreciate fully Zamenhof's life work, one should study his background, upbringing, character, and motivations. Several biographies have appeared, all written for an Esperanto-reading audience. In all but one of these biographies,[11] Zamenhof's Jewish motivation is omitted or considerably underplayed. Yet it was just that which was the very source of his success, whereas hundreds of professional linguists working full-time and with generous financial support and technical assistance managed to produce only paper projects (among others, Volapük, Ido, Latino sine Flexione, Basic English, Occidental, Novial, and Interlingua).

The goal of the Haskalah (Enlightenment) that figured so prominently in the life and work of both Ben-Yehuda and Zamenhof was the achievement of equal rights for Jews based on common loyalty and citizenship, without surrendering respect for heritage and traditions. The ideal of "a man abroad, a Jew at home" made significant inroads among an educated minority of Lithuanian Jews who had long been opponents of Hasidism. "Litvak," legalistic-Talmudic inclinations were transformed into a passion for secular learning that formed a common motif in the life and work of both Zamenhof and Ben-Yehuda.

Deep ethnic, religious, and linguistic divisions deeply impressed the young Zamenhof, who had already mastered half a dozen languages before entering the local gymnasium (including Hebrew, German and French through the influence of his father and grandfather). He had learned Polish from friends and at the state-run elementary school, and then Latin and Greek as a high school student. To these he added a good reading knowledge of English and Italian and perhaps several other European languages. Later he would make use of important elements from all of these languages in creating Esperanto.

Hitler later struck a raw nerve with German nationalists and extreme right-wing intellectuals in other nations who opposed Esperanto due to its relative success among the working class and the Jewish background and internationalist sentiments of its founder. For Hitler, Esperanto was more damning evidence of a Jewish plot, as expressed in his autobiography *Mein Kampf*, published in 1923, declaring Esperanto to be "the creation of Jews, Communists and Freemasons" and announcing his conviction that "as long as the Jew has not become the master of the other peoples, he must speak their languages whether he likes it or not, but as soon as they became his slaves, they would all have to learn a universal language (Esperanto, for instance!)."

Zamenhof's Jewish Identity Poses a Dilemma for the Esperanto Movement

Although careful to sublimate his Jewish identity following the initial successes of the Esperanto movement, due to fear of provoking anti–Semitic opposition in the wake of the Dreyfus trial, Zamenhof did not hesitate to express his deepest Jewish emotions and convictions in private correspondence or before select Jewish audiences. In a letter to French Esperantist A. Michaux in 1905, Zamenhof wrote:

> If I had not been a Jew out of the Ghetto, the idea of the unity of mankind would either never have come into my head or it never would have held me so obstinately during the course of my entire life. The unhappiness of the disunity of mankind can never be felt so strongly as by a Jew out of the Ghetto who is obligated to pray to God in a long-dead language, and who receives his education and instruction in the language of a people who oppress him, and who has co-sufferers throughout the world with whom he cannot inter-communicate.

The greatest irony in Zamenhof's life was his failure to appreciate the possibility of reviving Hebrew. Ben-Yehuda's efforts were yet in their infancy when Zamenhof first launched the Esperanto movement in 1887. Hebrew writers of his generation were still forced to use a stilted, unnatural style when using Hebrew for modern secular themes. Quite a few authors of the 1880s, such as Mendele Mokher Seforim (Shalom Jacob Abramovitsch), abandoned Hebrew for Yiddish, but later returned to Hebrew following the pioneering efforts of Ben-Yehuda.

Zamenhof's last great project, completed during World War I, was the translation of the Old Testament from Hebrew into Esperanto. Those who know both languages can appreciate the fidelity of Zamenhof's translation of the concepts, mood, and majestic rhythm of the original Biblical Hebrew. However, Zamenhof doubted that the Hebrew language could be made sufficiently flexible to accommodate the needs of modern society. It was another telling, if coincidental, parallel that Zamenhof published his first Esperanto textbooks in 1887 under the pseudonym "Doktoro Esperanto" ("Dr. Hopeful"), just a few years after the composition of the Zionist anthem *ha-Tikvah* ("The Hope"). Zamenhof finally abandoned his Zionist activities about the time of his marriage and graduation from medical school in 1884.

Although buffeted by the catastrophes of two world wars, persecution by both the Nazis and the Soviet regime, and the nasty, dismissive or condescending remarks that Esperantists lack a soul, Esperanto is, like Hebrew today, a living reality, supported by an "invisible" but active community of approximately a million speakers. It is a literary culture embracing more than 40,000 literary works (both original and in translation), hundreds of periodicals, scores of international gatherings, seminars, guided tours, theatrical groups, musical ensembles, and several university programs granting higher degrees. Moreover, it has been granted recognition as an official language of instruction at the International Academy of Sciences in San Marino, which utilizes Esperanto in diverse fields of study (subsidized by the European Union). There are a dozen or so hours of weekly radio transmissions (primarily from the Vatican and Communist China), and more than one hundred specialized dictionaries in the sciences, technology, arts and commerce, not to mention countless friendships made possible across linguistic barriers.

Prejudice and Persecution

It makes as much sense to denigrate Esperanto as to ridicule Welsh, Estonian or Catalan. Of course, "educated" people would never venture a censorious opinion about or mock a national language about which they know nothing for fear of offending a particular nationality and being "politically incorrect," but Esperanto is fair game for cynics and may provoke an off-the-cuff comparison with "Klingon" (imaginary language of aliens from outer space). The critics and the cynics are wholly ignorant of Esperanto's actual enemies with real power who took it seriously enough to retaliate against tens of thousands of its proponents. Esperanto was declared illegal and its practitioners suffered persecution and imprisonment under the totalitarian regimes of Hitler and Stalin; Fascist Italy during the latter period of Mussolini's rule; the Japanese government of the late 1930s and World War II, Nationalist Spain under Franco from 1939 to about 1950; all the "People's Democracies" in Eastern Europe from 1948 to 1955; and the regimes of miniature psychopaths like Enhver Hoxha in Albania, the Iranian mullahs and Romania's Ceausescu, who made learning a foreign language the equivalent of disloyalty. The only other language to suffer as much active persecution in the twentieth century was Hebrew in the Soviet Union (see Chapter 11).

What can one learn from the parallel lives and work of Zamenhof and Ben-Yehuda? The question of a language for the Jewish people has been resolved. Hebrew was and is the only authentic language of Jewish civilization and the vital link between Israel and the Diaspora. Ben-Yehuda's vision of a national-linguistic revival ultimately eclipsed Zamenhof's universalist ideal. Yet the promise of Esperanto for a future messianic time remains.

This was recognized by Itamar Ben-Avi, the son of Eliezer Ben-Yehuda. Ben-Avi argued on behalf of Esperanto as an international neutral language in his newspaper, the Hebrew daily *Doar ha-Yom* דאר היום. In a world of national, religious and language rivalries and frictions, Esperanto remains for hundreds of thousands a realistic hope for a neutral bridge that will allow all to meet equally without any feeling of inferiority. Zamenhof brilliantly borrowed much from his deep love of the Hebrew language to make Esperanto viable.

4. The Three-Thousand-Year-Old Treasury

One of the great joys and charms of the English language is the rich vocabulary and its one-thousand-year-old tradition of absorbing words from many cultures—Anglo-Saxon, Danish, Latin, Greek, Norman-French, Parisian French during the Age of Enlightenment, American Indian, Spanish, Italian, German, Russian and dozens of other ethnic groups. Why do our books begin with either a foreword or a preface? Quite simply, these are choices left to the individual and reflect the variety we have at our disposal from the thousand-year-old evolution, development and constant borrowings from other languages.

No one has expressed this idea better or more humorously than Bill Bryson in his best-seller *Mother Tongue*: "English retains probably the richest vocabulary, and the most diverse shading of meanings of any language. We can distinguish between house and home which the French cannot."[1] And again: "One of the glories of English—its willingness to take in words from almost anywhere—shampoo from India, chaparral from the Basques, caucus from the Algonquin Indians, ketchup from China, potato from Haiti, sofa from Arabia, boondocks from the Tagalog language of the Philippines, slogan from Gaelic."[2]

Now, imagine what glories await the polished Hebrew reader and speaker who has a language more than three times as old—three thousand years of a continuous literary history to draw from!

The history of the Near and Middle East and Jewish residence in the Diasporas of Europe is often revealed in a single Hebrew sentence that uses words borrowed from half a dozen civilizations. The following partial list is meant only as an appetizer for the real feast ahead. Each one of the foreign sources of interaction with Hebrew listed below represents just a smattering of the influence they exerted for centuries.

These foreign languages greatly influenced the addition of vocabulary and were drawn upon by scholars of the Enlightenment who sought to make

Hebrew a language fit for modern use in the latter half of the nineteenth century. It was due to the genius of Eliezer Ben-Yehuda and other scholars that authentic indigenous Hebrew roots could be utilized from the remote past of the Bible and the Mishnah to create the basis for the neologisms that came to play an essential role in creating the language of the twentieth century.

An educated Modern Hebrew reader will encounter dozens of words in an ordinary text that bear witness to the three-thousand-year pedigree and history of the Jewish experience, from its homeland in Ur of the Chaldees (from whence Abraham was commanded to find a new land in Canaan) to the thousand years of rival Hebrew kingdoms, to the confrontations with Assyria, Babylon, Greece, Rome and the exiles of Arabia, Persia, and Europe[3].

Akkadian

Akkad was the general name for the region of Babylon and Ashur starting from the fourth millennium BCE. It was an Eastern Semitic language similar in ancestral form to Arabic and written in cuneiform on clay tablets. The first great literary classics of the Near East—notably the Gilgamesh Epic, with its rival story of the Great Flood and the descent of Ishtar to Sheol—were written in Akkadian and exercised a major influence on Hebrew.

This is where we get *adrichal* (architect), *geser* (bridge), *ulam* (hall), *delet* (door), *haychal* (temple), *halon* (window), *yesod* (fundament-foundation), *tel* (hill), *kishuf* (magic), *mabul* (flood), *mazal* (not just luck but also the zodiac sign where the stars are located), *tahana* (station), *gan* (garden), *aron* (closet), and *igeret* (letter). Many of these and dozens of others are still in everyday use.

Greek

Many hundreds of words were absorbed from Greek during the period of close contact with the Sea Peoples and empires of Alexander and his successors.[4] Some of these terms underwent slight changes after being adopted first by the Romans in their own Latin language. Many were subsequently absorbed by the Romance languages and English and so are immediately recognizable to us. They are often easy to spot because they begin with consonants in combinations such as Psy-, Str-, Sf-, Sp-, and Ks-, which are not found in Hebrew and had to have a short initial vowel sound "a" (represented by the letter *aleph*) in order to facilitate their pronunciation for speakers.

Greek provides words like *aklim* (climate), *geografia* (geography), *avir* (air), *santer* (chin), *orlogin* (clock), *dugmah* (example), *zug* (couple), *mistorin* (mystery), *sfog* (sponge), *katedra* (faculty), *psicologia* (psychology), *architect* (architect), *askola* (school), *itztadion* (stadium), *itliz* (butcher shop), *namal* (harbor), *metropolyn* (metropolis), *sefel* (cup), *ogen* (anchor), *tik* (file), *michona* (machine), *filosophia* (philosophy), *hymnon* (hymn), *ochlosiya* (population), *archiyon* (archive), *polmus* (a polemic), *pumbi* (public), *senigor* (defense attorney), *pundok* (pub), *astrategia* (strategy), *sport* (sport), tarbut (culture), *tachsis* (tactics), and many more.

Persian

Persian (Farsi) exercised a major influence on the huge diaspora created after the destruction of the First Temple. It was the first Indo-European language to exert influence upon Hebrew, and it continued to do even after the Arab conquest in the seventh century CE. Original Farsi words entered Hebrew, Greek and Latin, going through several transformations, such as in *Ishpaz* (*Ishpooz* in Hebrew)—*aspinj* (hospital—hotel/hostel); *bazaar, gizbar* (treasurer), *duchan* (stall or high place), *balagan* (Hebrew slang originally meaning an attic but eventually with the connotation of a disorderly, untidy place, and then indicating a place of ill repute/prostitution), *bustan* (tree garden, grove), *dat* (religion), *handasa* (engineering), *khaki* (the color), *ethrog, shach-mat* (checkmate in chess, meaning the "king is dead").

Turkish

A few words and expressions remain from the 400 years of Ottoman rule in Palestine, where a majority of Jewish residents used Yiddish, Arabic and limited Hebrew among themselves. They rarely, if ever, needed to resort to Turkish in order to deal with the authorities. What remains is *dunam* (the unit of area for land, traditionally the amount a farmer could plow with an ox in a day and later standardized as one thousand square meters), *tabu* (the property deed to land ownership), and the popular board game "*Shish-Bish*" (Six-Five, or backgammon). A few other words still extant are *dugri* (talking straight to the point), *kiosk, burekas* (the popular baked item made with meat or vegetables), *tembel* (fool or a lazy person), *mangal* (a grill), *baklava, yoghurt* and *shislik*, all of which also entered the major European languages.

Arabic

This is a sister language of Hebrew but with a much younger alphabet and literature. Many words for parts of the body, numbers, and family relations are very close to Hebrew. Numerous Jewish rabbinical authorities and philosophers learned, spoke and wrote in Arabic during the Middle Ages due to its wide distribution. Ben-Yehuda and other linguists researched possible Arabic roots to evolve new Hebrew words in mathematics and geometry like *nadir, zenith, ofek* (horizon), and *merkaz* (center), as well as *machson* (warehouse), *sabon* (soap), *rishmi* (from *rasmy*, meaning official), nadiv (polite), and more modern terms such as *gerev* (sock), *boreg* (screw), *mishmish* (apricot), *finjan* (coffee pot), *buul* (postage stamp), *avzem* (buckle), and *digdug* (tickling).[5]

Much slang and coarse profanity were adopted by the early Jewish settlers in Palestine who were reluctant or unable to use equivalent Hebrew vernacular expressions because there weren't any. Many Arabic expressions are still in common use in everyday Modern Hebrew conversation as well as contemporary spoken Arabic (see Chapter 14).

German

The new Hebrew of the Zionist colonies was much influenced by the work and philanthropic contributions of wealthy German Jews, and it was used by a highly educated minority of Eastern European Jews in Poland, the Bohemian lands, the Baltic, Scandinavia and even the Balkans as the language of culture and technology. The German Protestant sect known as the Templars,[6] who established half a dozen agricultural colonies in Palestine at the end of the nineteenth century, cooperated with neighboring Jewish settlements and influenced their use of German in work processes, technology, construction and agriculture. The German Jewish school network HaEzra (The Help) and the technical schools in Haifa (Technikum) established German as the original language of instruction.

Many words in Hebrew were direct word-for-word translations of German words; such terms as *Gan-Yeladim* for kindergarten, the names for the months of the calendar, *installateur, gummi, beton, dubel, tapete, leiste, spachtel, spritzen, auto, gestalt, falsch, rezept, schnitzel, spitze* and dozens of others are in use in Hebrew with only a brief shift in pronunciation or stress. Some words were invented by Ben-Yehuda based on German words, such as *mivreshet* (brush) from the German word *bürste,* creating the root of a new word, B-R-Ŝ.

English

The commercial importance of Great Britain, the direct connection of the British Mandate over Palestine with Zionism and the service of Jewish volunteers in the British armed forces during World War II all contributed to the borrowing of many English words associated with automobiles, aviation, seamanship, agriculture and science. The growing influence of the United States and the American Jewish community, along with the worldwide appeal of Hollywood, greatly increased the number of loan words, such as *jack, exhaust, gas, gear, differential, distributor, tire, plus, tank, starter, switch, pedals, fuse, puncture, choke, camshaft, clutch, radiator, carburetor, chassis, underdog, fighter, free kick, knockout, foul, penalty, offside, timeout*, and so forth.

Although the Hebrew Academy has issued "native" Hebrew alternatives, many remain in dictionaries for legal use but are rarely consulted. The original English and American terms remain in popular usage due to the overwhelming importance of English in the current Israeli educational system, as a world language for diplomacy and business, and also as the most widely accepted language for publishing in international journals.[7]

Yiddish

The mutual influences of Yiddish and Hebrew on each other have been the subject of many lengthy volumes and commentaries, and this is a worthy subject for further study.[8] About 15 percent of Yiddish has a vocabulary that originally derives from Hebrew.[9] It was the language spoken by most European Jews outside the Mediterranean region and absorbed influences and words from German, Polish, Russian and Rumanian. Several aspects of Yiddish grammar, vocabulary, syntax, colloquialisms, and spelling remain in Modern Hebrew.

Many Yiddish words and expressions also entered English, including some that started out in Hebrew, like "mazal tov." According to Dr. Nissan Netzer of the Bar Ilan University Hebrew Department, Yiddish is the foreign language most prevalent in Hebrew slang (48 percent), followed by Arabic (26 percent) and English (14 percent), but of course these Yiddish-derived slang words and expressions are used less by Jews of Sephardi-Mizrahi origin than among Israelis of Ashkenazi origin. Many common colloquialisms are direct word-for-word translations from Yiddish.

The endings -lah (*beigelah* for beigel, *immahlah* for "little mother") and -er (*macher, shvitzer, shnorrer*) are universal, and Hebrew words corrupted in Yiddish pronunciation include Shabbos, *Balahbooste* (*ba'al ha bayit* in Modern Hebrew for a home owner), *dos* for *dati* in Hebrew (for a religious Jew) and expressions like *gournisht* and *bubkes* (nothing)—also used in English), as well as *drek* (shit) and *nudnik* (bothersome person). The suffix -nik denotes membership in any group, such as in *kibbutznik* and *Mapamnik*. Many expressions have been literally translated—the equivalents in English of "knock my head against the wall," "he is missing a screw," "don't take it to heart," "went lost," "it became black before my eyes," and hundreds more. The trend over the past few decades has been the replacement of Yiddish slang with English and neologisms based on authentic Hebrew words.

Clearly, English has taken the lead in most recent slang, with dozens of words simply given a Hebrew pronunciation, so there is little doubt of what words mean in their Israeli version, such as *hi, okay, job, good-bye, bitchit, fun, gay, boss, by!, cool, derling, deal, date, DJ, no vey,* and *fock* (see Chapter 14).

All languages have absorbed impulses from contact with other tongues through migration, conquest, expulsion, foreign rule, cultural interchange and increased familiarity with the literary heritage of other peoples. Each such contact inevitably presented challenges regarding whether new terms would be perceived as foreign intrusions or welcome for adoption. Once again, no other language has such a long pedigree of so many borrowed terms (with some adaptation in pronunciation) over such a long historical sojourn in different times and places as Hebrew. This is an achievement that has continued through the evolution of the modern language, albeit accompanied by the neologisms to retain a sense of authentic origins.

5. How Hebrew Became a Modern Language

*New Words (Neologisms)—
The Hebrew Press, Radio and the
Academy of the Hebrew Language*

The Status of Hebrew in 1880

At the time Ben-Yehuda arrived in Palestine in 1881,[1] there had been two Hebrew-language newspapers, *ha-Lbanon* and *ha-Havatzelet* (The Lily), founded in 1863 using a very limited vocabulary drawn largely from the Bible, with the additional use of a set of "international" (largely German, French or Russian) terms. Hebrew-language journals and periodicals of various types existed in Europe, but they invariably focused only on Jewish issues. In fact, Palestine had no newspapers in Arabic, Turkish, Ladino or Yiddish. Both newspapers competed with each other for a limited readership and were not above slandering and accusing each other before the Turkish authorities.

Ben-Yehuda was fortunate that a progressive and worldly editor, Dov Frumkin, was in charge of *ha-Havatzelet* and eventually supported his ideas on language and teaching Hebrew by modern methods. Nevertheless, Frumkin cautioned him against offending the ultra–Orthodox community. Ben-Yehuda used

Israeli postage stamp honoring the origins of Hebrew journalism—typesetting the early Hebrew newspaper *ha-Lbanon* in Jerusalem 1863.

the novel technique of introducing new terms for contemporary issues, devices, and everyday items not found anywhere in the Bible or in Talmudic and Mishnaic Hebrew. When his reputation had spread and more learned people were willing to read his newspaper, he would include newly coined words without footnotes or a long explanation, believing that readers would be able to pick them up from context.

Ben-Yehuda eventually established his own newspaper, *ha-Zvi*, in 1884, which propounded his ideas and demonstrated that Hebrew could serve as the language of journalism. New socialist-minded pioneers began to arrive at the turn of the century and founded their own newspapers, as did Ben-Yehuda's son in 1910 (*ha-Or;* The Light). Much increased immigration and the progress of Hebrew schools[2] made possible the establishment of additional newspapers, including the veteran *ha-Aretz*, founded in 1923.

The Inherent Logic of the Language and the Source of the Neologisms

The Hebrew vocabulary intrigues and challenges students who quickly learn to discern the relationship between words with similar roots—*zakan* and *zaken,* זקן, for instance, respectively denoting a beard and an elderly person. These two words appear identical without the vowel signs—dots and dashes for the vowel sounds that appear underneath, above or within the Hebrew letters and are called "nikud" (נקוד).

This also reveals the inherent patriarchal character of the ancient Hebrew society, but it becomes much more intriguing to discover that the word for knife, SaKiN סכין, is related to the words for danger, SaKaNa סכנה, and dangerous, miSooKaN מסוכן, as well as the word for risk, SeeKooN סיכון. The capitalized letters in English, **S-K-N**, and the letters in bold, **סכנ**, represent the "root letters," the three important consonants that immediately transmit a basic concept (the "n" letter known as *nun* has the form נ and a special shape as an end letter ן). A reflexive form as a noun or verb, מסתכן mistaken, is immediately understood as a risk taker (someone who puts himself in danger).

Students can thus appreciate how the social conditions of several thousand years ago made the concept of a knife—the most potent weapon that could be concealed—related to the ideas of danger and risk. This traditional word-building process in Hebrew was adapted and utilized in creating the many neologisms—new words to represent the many new concepts and devices of modern times.

Lack of Vocabulary—The Major Barrier to Making Hebrew Contemporary in the Latter Half of the Nineteenth Century

The transition to a modern vocabulary was extremely difficult among the first generation of Hebrew-speaking children, especially those who attempted to adopt a natural, unstilted vernacular to mirror their world. The American Yiddish poet "Yehoash" visited one of the early Zionist settlements in 1913,[3] and was impressed to hear teenage girls playing and making use only of Hebrew. However, when one was asked the name of a flower in her own garden, she replied, "Flowers don't have names." It would take another generation and the achievement of Israeli independence for Hebrew to catch up with the backlog of essential vocabulary. Consider, for example, all the diverse fields rich with terminology that one would need to have as part of his or her lexicon in order to become an educated speaker: flora, fauna, medicine, technology, art and science, just to name a few.

During the early "renaissance" from the 1880s to World War II, new words of Hebrew (or Arabic or Persian as indigenous to the Middle East) origin were coined and the public was encouraged to use them instead of the internationally recognized words that have German or Russian suffixes.

New Words—Relying on the Skeleton of the Roots

The inherent mechanisms for word formation have played a brilliant role in enabling linguists to draw upon indigenous sources for the necessary vocabulary to modernize the language.

The key to the vocabulary, and a source of wonder and surprise for many new students, is that words that sound alike and look alike share a similar concept. For example, in English the words *book*, *author*, *library* and *literature* are all quite different. They don't look alike, or sound alike but in Hebrew they share the common consonants S-F-R ס-פ-ר. Compare the English words book (*sefer*), author (*sofer*), library (*sifriyah*), and literature (*sifrut*).

ספר סופר ספרייה ספרות

They are all linked by the appearance of the same consonants, SFR ספר, and are related in having to do with the concept of books.

The ability of Eliezer Ben-Yehuda and other linguists to coin new words from the scant vocabulary stock of the Bible and the Talmud stems from this basis and the use of prefixes and suffixes that still retain the original consonantal root letters. For example, how did Modern Hebrew create the modern word for computer? Israel was one of the first countries to make use of computers in the 1960s, when the word had not yet acquired international acceptance. Why was this new word so readily adopted by the public on Israel as the "natural word" for a computer? It was named maĤŜeV מחשב, based on the root Ĥ-Ŝ-V חשב (pronounced ĥoŝev), "to think," which resulted in the words maĤŜaVa (thought) מחשבה and ĤaŜiVut (importance) חשיבות. The root letters Ĥ-Ŝ-V חשב indicate the basic action/process of thinking/thought. Note that in Hebrew the sounds of SH and CH are rendered by single letters (the letters *shin* and *chet*). The active verb is ĤoŜeV in the present tense (thinks חושב.).

The causative function carries with it an initial "m" letter and in the active or intensive form (*pi'el*), so that the form maĤŜiV מחשיב means to consider or esteem someone or something as important. The initial sound/letter "n" creates the passive form (*nif'al*), so that something that is neĤŜaV נחשב is considered/regarded as important. The reflexive form (*hitpa'el*)— thinking over and over to oneself about something—carries the prefix "mit," so we have mitĤaŜeV מתחשב, meaning to take something into account. The adjective "important" (thought of) is rendered as ĤaŜooV חשוב. Even the noun "a thought" makes use of the three basic consonants—maĥŝava מחשבה

The modern word for computer in Hebrew is thus maĤŜeV מחשב—a thinking device. In the text below, the words in bold all bear the consonants Ĥ-Ŝ-V חשב, illustrating the power of precisely rendering the related words.

> Nahumi is considered the most important expert in Israel on agriculture. The Minister of Finance accords great importance to his opinion and almost always takes his recommendation into account and the farmers always check what he thinks.
>
> Nahumi neĤŜaV lemumche heĤaŜooV biyoter biYisrael al haĥaklaut. Sar ha-Otzar maĤŜiV et da'ato umitĤaŜeV behamlatzotav vihaikarim tamid bodkim mah hu ĤoŜeV.
>
> נחומי נחשב למומחה החשוב ביותר בישראל על החקלאות. שר האוצר מחשיב את דעתו ומתחשב בהמלצותיו והאיכרים תמיד בודקים מה הוא חושב.

In the hands of a good teacher, this property of the language can help and intrigue students who are delighted to understand immediately the meaning of new words they never encountered before because they grasp the essential point—that words which sound alike also "look alike" and contain the consonants in the proper order to relate to diverse aspects of an essential concept. This logical element runs through the language in both its ancient and modern forms.

All verbs can be recognized in the variety of different constructs that denote passive, intensive, and reflexive aspects of the action that a verb indicates, called *binyanim* (literally "buildings" or constructs). All the different *binyanim* contain the three basic consonants. Variants of "think," such as an intensive aspect (calculated—thought of very intensely), reflexive (very strongly thought of—reconsidered), the adjective "important" (worthy of thought), and so on, all are formed by words that contain the three essential consonants. Not all verbs exist in all the different *binyanim*, but many have at least three or four such variants, making the recall of much of the Hebrew vocabulary a matter of repetitive patterns, starting with the original form of the three consonants called *pa'al*.

A major problem for new learners who have not grown up with the language is their unfamiliarity with the different forms in which a three-letter root may appear, and nor will many be aware that there may be additional letters that represent prepositions. In the sentence below the two underlined words without vowels appear identical as מדובר.

Medover Tzahal nimsar bitiguva: **Midubar** bimikrim hanogdim et orchei Tzhala.

מדובר צה"ל נמסר בתגובה: "מדובר במקרים הנוגדים את ערכי צה"ל

The first word combines an initial preposition מ, meaning "from," with the noun דובר (*dover*), meaning a spokesperson (noun), while the second word is "midubar" (a participle), meaning the subject that is spoken about. An English translation would thus read, "From a **spokesperso**n for the Israel Defense Forces: 'What is involved (**spoken about**) are cases that contradict the values of the Israel Defense Forces.'"

Students of Biblical Hebrew only have to contend with roughly 8,000 words, or approximately 2,000 recognizable "roots," some of which have disappeared, though a great many have survived through posterity to the modern era. During the period of the Mishnah, perhaps 8,000 new terms were added by Jewish scribes based on only 800 new "roots." Another few thousand words of Aramaic origin and new Hebrew terms were added in the period of the Talmud and later that enabled many of the *maskilim*, the writers and poets of the Enlightenment, to use the language for secular purposes. Since Ben-Yehuda's day, the estimate of new words, including technical and foreign terms, had produced something like 17,000 new items. Today's modern educated Israeli reader has a vocabulary of 60,000 words.[4]

Agreement on Two Major Controversies: Biblical vs. Mishnaic Grammar and Ashkenazi vs. Sephardi Pronunciation

It was Ben-Yehuda's editorial article "A Burning Question" in the journal *ha-Saḥar* (The Dawn) that launched the idea of a national restoration, making Palestine a spiritual center and reviving the Hebrew language as a written and spoken tongue, thus predating the political Zionism of Herzl by almost twenty years. The idea was debated and met with little approval due to the immediate practical problem of how to standardize a modern language when even the Hebrew in use by different communities was pronounced very differently, and objections were raised to Ben-Yehuda's initial plan to base the grammar of the new language on that of the Bible when, in fact, it was Mishnaic Hebrew that was closer to the morphology of modern European languages. It provided greater simplicity and exactness, especially with regard to the more precise expression of past and future tenses, and increased richness of vocabulary, although it surrendered some of the poetic imagery, vigor and austere solemnity of the Biblical language.

Mishnaic Hebrew refers to the language found in the Talmud, as preserved by the Jews after the Babylonian captivity and recorded by Jewish sages around the year 200 of the Common Era. About a century after the publication of the Mishnah, this language began to fall into disuse as a spoken vernacular and literary format, and later sections of the Talmud and the Babylonian Gemara (גמרה, circa 500) were written in Aramaic, which had become the "lingua franca" of the Middle East.

In the end, Ben-Yehuda won out on insisting that the Sephardi pronunciation in use by the Oriental communities be universally adopted. He had the advantage of support from the more prestigious Sephardi community in Jerusalem (which enjoyed a better and closer relationship with the Ottoman authorities) and the fact that it was deemed more logical to use Arabic as a model. To this day, many native Hebrew-speaking Israelis of Sephardi-Oriental origin correctly pronounce and spell the guttural letters *ayin* (ע) and *ḥet* (ח).

With regard to the grammar, Ben-Yehuda eventually came to acknowledge the view that it would be easier to manipulate the more flexible Mishnaic grammar than the archaic biblical constructions. It is, however, part of Hebrew's glorious heritage that many elements of vocabulary and grammar from both periods remain in use and provide speakers with a variety of modes of expression. Mishnaic Hebrew was a necessary rung on the ladder of transforming the language into a modern spoken vernacular.

After solving the matters of grammar and pronunciation, Ben-Yehuda devoted most of his time to adopting a new vocabulary to meet the needs of the end of the nineteenth century and incorporating a whole host of words for devices, concepts, issues and phenomena that were unknown in biblical or medieval times. Other modern languages, including French and German, were also used as models for new words. The modern Hebrew word for newspaper follows the German construction of *zeitung*—drawn from *zeit* (time). The new vocabulary constructed "iton" עתון from the root for time (et) and the common ending "on," used to indicate "a thing comprising the concept rendered in the noun." For example, from *milah* מילה (word), Ben-Yehuda derived *milon* מילון. This is the modern word for dictionary, instead of the previous *sefer-millim* ספר מילים (literally "a book of words"), an earlier attempt to create a compound word similar to the German *Wörtberbuch*. Similarly, *sa'on* שעון (watch) was coined from the root for the word meaning hour or time, *sa'ah* שעה, and the ending is used to indicate a material object.

Many new words were coined on the basis of roots (similar consonants) from past words in the biblical vocabulary. From *lahav* להב (flame), all the following words, indicating some form of enthusiasm, were created in modern times: *mishulhav* משלהב (enthused), *hitlahavut* התלהבות (enthusiasm), *lehitlahev* להתלהב (to become enthusiastic).

All of the following have the same vowel sequence (called *mishkalim*) and are referred to as *mipulpal*, along the same lines as *mishulhav*. A fascinating aspect of Hebrew is that old roots that began with only two consonants were doubled to portray repetitive actions as P-L-P-L פלפל (plpl), using four consonants so that the learner can immediately grasp that all the words below, with a doubling of the same consonants, indicate such repetitive actions.

gimgem stutter גמגם

iefef flutter עפעף

nimnem nod off, become drowsy (repeated sleep on and off) נמנם

gilgel roll over and over גלגל

bilbel confuse someone בלבל

tsiltsel ring over and over (telephone sound) צלצל

rishresh ripple (sound of flowing water) רשרש

dikdek to be exacting (constantly checking) דקדק

tetah to sweep טאטא

tzachtzeach to polish צחצח

One innovative author of a popular textbook recently invented her own word—*nishnesh* נשנש for "nosh" or "snack" (i.e., to eat on and off between meals!)⁵

Many compound words were directly copied from French: *pommes de terre* (apples of the earth), duplicated in Hebrew by *tapuhei-adamah* תפוחי-אדמה. Many similar constructs provided the format, which Hebrew copied, such as "teeth doctor" רופא-שניים for dentist.

But it was not only the most prominent *maskilim* who made suggestions for new words to be adopted for the many objects not found in the late nineteenth-century vocabulary before Ben-Yehuda led the campaign to make Hebrew a spoken language again. One example is the word needed for eyeglasses, which were invented sometime at the end of the thirteenth century in

Italy.⁶ The first Hebrew reference to them dates from 1404, as found in a dedication to a Bible written by Haim Ben Shaul of Saragosa. The term used was the equivalent of "glass seers between my eyes." A few decades later, another early reference appears in a dedication to a prayer book written by Isaac the Scribe in Ulm, Germany, in 1459: "*I am 61 years old and have written this prayer book without 'glass instruments' illuminating my eyes, which are called in German Brillen*" (the current German word for eyeglasses).⁷

Several different two-word phrases appeared in Hebrew in periodicals published in Europe to describe eyeglasses during the nineteenth century. The most popular of these names were *Batey Enayim* בתי עיניים ("eye houses") and *kley reut'* כלי ראות ("seeing instruments"). Then Haim Leiv Hazan, a teacher in Belarus, thought up a more original name in 1890—M*ishkafaiim*. He wrote a long article for the Hebrew daily *Hatzfira*, published in Warsaw, and explained the importance of making up new Hebrew words:

> No one will deny that it is better to use a single word than a multitude; and the instruments that are made by two equal parts—"moznaim" ("scales"), "melkakhaim" ("tweezers"), and in the Talmud "misparayim" ("scissors"), start with the letter mem and end with the pair-ending "ayim"; and since this instrument is made up of two equal parts, its structure is well portrayed in that name. "But why did I choose the root ŝ.k.f? I chose it because it is similar to the Greek word skepeo (I will see) that comes in words for seeing instruments in European languages such as telescope, microscope, kaleidoscope, and such."

His logic won the day and was undeniable. He did not have to consult with an academy or personally correspond with Ben-Yehuda. He was not a recognized scholar of international repute, but a Jew familiar with the basics of Hebrew grammar, and one who could follow the mechanics of new word derivation.

Ben-Yehuda made a careful study of Classical Arabic and Persian and found the basis for new words for which there was no immediate ancestral form of Hebrew that could serve as the basis for modern terminology. In Modern Hebrew, close contact with the local Palestinian Arabic and the English of the Mandatory regime, as well as retention of many Yiddish expressions, provided Hebrew with a fertile source of slang, curse words and profanity.

The tendency to "Hebraize" new words was carried to an extreme by some linguists and the official Academy of the Hebrew Language. They imitated Ben-Yehuda, who even proposed constructs derived from Hebrew roots for such widely accepted international words as radio and telephone. These terms never took hold and were removed from dictionaries after a decade or two. Many international terms were accepted, such as telegraph, although the essential consonantal root letters had to be expanded to four or five letters, such as T-L-G-R-F (telegraph) טלגרף.

Press and Radio Help Establish a National Standard

The rise in newspaper readership that followed journalists' usage of the new, more modern language, with its greatly expanded vocabulary, helped make it easier for the British Mandatory authorities to accept Hebrew as one of the three official languages of Palestine when they initiated the Mandate in 1920. A huge new wave of *aliyah* from Germany and Poland in the 1930s provided a much greater listening audience to regular radio broadcasts in Hebrew on the newly created "Voice of Jerusalem" service of the British Mandate. This service was avidly listened to because it set the model for correct pronunciation, eventually becoming "The Voice of Israel."

The "explosion" of the Hebrew press was due to the multiplicity of political parties and their subsidization in part by the various Zionist movements and the immense desire of new *olim* (immigrants) to master the written language of Modern Hebrew.[8] In rapid succession, *ha-Aaretz* (1923—independent) was followed by *Davar* of the Labor Movement (1925) and Revisionist *ha-'Am* (1931, but closed down by the British and later reestablished), *ha-Boker* (right wing—1936), and *ha-Tzofeh* (The Observer, 1936), which was established by the moderate and pro-Zionist Mizrahi religious movement. There was also *Yediot Ahronot*, an independent and evening paper founded in 1937, and in the 1940s there appeared *Al ha-Mishmar* (Far Left Zionist), *ha-Mashkif* (National Religious), *ha-Modia*, of the ultra-Orthodox and non-Zionist Herut (Herut Movement), *Ma'ariv* (non-party and eventually the largest in circulation), *Kol ha-'Am* (Communist Party—following the party line from Moscow), and *la-Merhav* (left-wing Zionist Party Ahdut ha-Avoda). By now, all of the party newspapers have folded, but they played an important role in increasing literacy and helping new immigrants become accustomed with conditions in the country.

The Academy of the Hebrew Language

The Academy of the Hebrew Language, which was founded in 1953 with its seat in Givat Ram in Jerusalem,[9] replaced the Hebrew Language Committee (Va'ad ha-Lashon ha-'Ivrit), established in 1890 by Eliezer Ben-Yehuda, who was its first president. It is an agency whose decisions are binding on the government. It publishes its rulings and deliberations as well as dictionaries and has coined thousands of words that are in everyday use. The Academy sets standards for grammar, orthography, transliteration, and punctuation based on the historical development of the language. An important part of its mandate is to create new words from roots and structures to replace loan words derived from other languages, but critics have argued that it has not pursued this goal vigorously and is too indecisive.

By comparison with such institutions abroad as the venerable state-run Italian Academy in Florence, the Académie Française in Paris and the Real Academia Española in Madrid, the Academy in Jerusalem is a modest enterprise in terms of its physical facilities, but it has a more demanding task in dealing with a language many centuries older and derived from diverse sources.

The number of Academy members range from 15 to 23. They are selected for life and are distinguished authors, poets, translators and researchers into the fields of language and literature of all time periods. There are both full-time members residing in Israel and honorary members, most of whom reside abroad. All proposals are brought before the general assembly for ratification. The Academy's decisions regarding transcriptions are of primary importance for researchers and involve three types: Hebrew to Latin letters, foreign languages to Hebrew, and Arabic to Hebrew.

The Academy of the Hebrew Language decides in matters of grammar dealing primarily with the conflicting forms inherited from different periods. Its stated policy is to find a middle ground between automatic adoption of current usage and rigid adherence to what was deemed "correct" in the past. It deliberates on the issues in depth and makes recommendations. These recommendations are then presented for approval by vote and acquire the weight of law.

The Academy's rulings have sometimes produced lively public debate regarding the various spelling systems, the introduction of newly invented everyday words and technical terms based on an authentic Hebrew root used in past eras. Often, the Academy's first choice is to find inspiration in the Bible, but it sometimes must resort to evidence from post–Biblical Hebrew, including oral traditions. The most recent trend is to give weight to currently accepted practices that have acquired legitimacy among the general public (unless they radically deviate from the structure of the language). The Academy regularly sends its rulings regarding grammar, syntax and new vocabulary to the state-run radio and television, the army and all government offices, which are "obliged" to abide by them.

The previous Committee for the Hebrew Language that began under Eliezer Ben-Yehuda adopted many words that never acquired legitimacy, such as the complex compound term *Sachrahok* (Distance Conversation) first used for telephone. Ben-Yehuda published several lists of the Language Committee's terms in his newspaper. Among the issues debated were the pronunciation and the principles in establishing new Hebrew terms to replace foreign words. The first published words included lists of plant names and terminology for dress, food, furniture, and geography.

Ben-Yehuda died in 1922, but the Committee continued and its quarterly publication, *Leshonenu* לשוננו (Our Tongue), was established in 1928, going on to publish many word lists and professional dictionaries covering some 30,000 terms in 60 professions.

After a considerable delay, the establishment of the Academy of the Hebrew Language was declared in January 1949 in the presence of Prime Minister David Ben-Gurion, and it was enacted into law in August 1953. The delay was comically due to the use of the name "Academia" itself. Ben-Gurion fancied himself as a great authority of the language and was against using a foreign word as the name of the institution. He had previously tried to set a personal example in changing grammar by ignoring the use of the marker את to indicate the direct object of an action. The committee members rejected his pressure and explicitly stated in the law that the institution had the right to name itself.

The most frequent interest among the public has been in the choice of new words or why the Academy didn't create replacements for modern words such as *technologia* ("technology"), *televizia* ("television"), *autobus* ("bus"), *elektronika* ("electronics"), *meteorologia* ("meteorology"), *psychologia* ("psychology"), and so forth. It currently creates about 2,000 new words each year for modern words by finding an original word that captures the meaning. The Academy's decisions are based on how rooted the term is already in everyday speech, whether it is easily pronounceable, whether the term also easily generates verbs and adjectives, and, of course, whether a Hebrew alternative would be catchy, convenient, and appropriate.

Noted journalist and linguist Moshe Atar, author of *Ivrit Safah Ḥaya* (Hebrew—A Living Language), had this to say about the Academy's policy:

> It is revealing that our educational institutions including the Academy of the Hebrew Language doesn't see anything wrong and only warns against overuse [of foreign words for which authentic Hebrew words already exist]. Thus the Scientific Secretariat of the Academy holds the view that a Hebrew word is preferable to a foreign (loazi) one only when there is no general agreement among the languages of culture and science regarding a particular term ... due to the fact that a majority of the country's inhabitants are not trained in our language, do not speak Hebrew as a mother tongue ... so that they are influenced by foreign languages in which they were educated and this influence is manifest in their spoken Hebrew.[10]

He views the Academy as suffering from a timid approach, fearful that traditionalists and those anxious to cater to the lowest common denominator will see too many radical neologisms.

Past Debates

Fortunately, the Academy was spared the most controversial issues and emotional debates that were decided by the public in Palestine during the early days of the first waves of immigration and during the period of the British Mandate. Neither Ben-Yehuda's personal whims and fancies nor the directives of the Hebrew Language Committee, nor even Ben-Gurion, could operate in a vacuum. In the end the public, the great majority of which was secular or non-traditional in outlook, proved to be the decisive arbiter about what to accept or reject.

Perhaps the most telling and humorous case was the debate over which word to choose for tomato—totally absent from the biblical flora or past Jewish experience. Tomatoes are an essential ingredient in the typical Israeli salad and much loved by the Arabs as well. The Hebrew word, *agvania* עגבניה, well known now, and accepted for several generations, nevertheless ignited a fierce debate. The plant is native to the Western Hemisphere and was first brought to Europe in the sixteenth century. Its deep red color, associated with blood, put off many Europeans who rejected eating it initially but found it attractive in their gardens as an ornamental plant.

The legend grew that tomatoes might be poisonous, like its relatives in the nightshade family, or that it was probably an aphrodisiac. It took at least another century and a half for the plant to become well known in Eastern Europe, and for some Jews its reputation made it suspicious, so that among Orthodox Jews, it was first called "*treyf* (non-kosher) apple." Nineteenth-century accounts report stories about Jews, notably rabbis who came to Israel at the end of the nineteenth and beginning of the twentieth century, who had serious concerns about eating tomatoes, but the locals convinced them they were not dangerous.

While the English word "tomato" comes from an Aztec name, the names that European languages provided convinced many Orthodox Jews that their suspicions were correct. The English term "love apple," the German *Liebesapfel* and the French *pomme d'amour* all highlighted the aphrodisiac connection. The Italians preferred *pomo d'oro* (apple of gold), copied by the French as *pomme d'or* and subsequently adopted as *pomodor* in Polish.

Rabbi Yechiel Michel Pines and his son-in-law Dr. David Yellin, distinguished personalities in the old Yishuv, opposed Ben-Yehuda's choice of *bandura* for "tomato," pointing out that it was not of Semitic origin. They coined a new word in 1886 that matched the European "love apple"—*agbanit* עגבנית, which later was changed to *agbaniya*, and then *agvania* עגבניה. The root as used in the Bible, עגב, means "to lust, desire," and it is also found in the root of the name for syphilis (עגבת). Even worse for orthodox sensibilities, the same root is used in the words for buttocks (עגבות *agavot*), reflecting the fruit's shape; lust (עגב); and coquetry (עגבנת *agvenet*). For Ben-Yehuda, this was all rather vulgar, and he tried unsuccessfully to prevent its use. In any case, *agvania* and its related words eventually won out.

5. How Hebrew Became a Modern Language

Moshe Leib Lilienblum was a Jewish author born in Kovno, Lithuania, in 1843. He was a Hebrew scholar and writer who also dabbled in astronomy. In his article on the Jewish question and Palestine in 1881, written in Russian, he clearly and soberly analyzed the precarious position held by the Jewish people among the nations and argued that only national independence could redeem them from hopelessness. Nevertheless, he expressed his skepticism that Hebrew could be "modernized" and wrote sometime around the turn of the century, before his death in 1910, "If, over time, this disgraceful, ridiculous language will really be accepted as a living language among our brethren in the holy land, then I seriously doubt if the language savants will appreciate this 'revival' and thank its initiators for doing well for our language." He could not have been more wrong.

Like other Hebrew scholars and writers visiting Palestine about the same time as Lilienblum's death Ahad ha-Am could already discern that spoken Hebrew in Palestine had made remarkable progress compared to his first visit in 1894, commenting that the dedication of the teachers had accomplished a miracle.[11]

A 1970 study of Israeli newspapers indicated that 60–70 percent of the vocabulary originated from the Old Testament and another 15–20 percent from Mishnaic Hebrew, with the remaining neologisms stemming from international words like *radio* and *televizia* at about 20 percent.[12] A similar study today would probably see the neologisms rise to close to 25 percent, excluding popular current slang, but linguists differ on exactly how to carry out similar surveys.

The Neologisms—In Danger? The Slowing and Occasional Reversal of Hebrew Roots for New Vocabulary

Modern Hebrew has derived much of its contemporary vocabulary from two sources: the one indigenous to the ancient language based on existing recognizable three-letter roots, and the other, international words. The many alternative words in the vocabulary of the average Israeli include terms that are easily recognizable by an international audience. Why would anyone need to use "situatzia" instead of *matzav* מצב, or "consensus" instead of *tmimut da'im* תמימות-דעים, or "faktim" instead of *uvdot* עובדות, words that have been in use in journalistic and radio Hebrew for the past 50 years? This way of thinking has led many Israelis to unconsciously prefer the international words in everyday speech.

This very lenient policy has long-term negative consequences, as can be seen in the many grotesque street and shop signs that use Hebrew letters to write English or "international words." The Academy has more than once issued statements to the effect that while the native Hebrew term is "preferable," it is left up to the speaker as a matter of choice. Occasionally one can see the same word appearing twice, such as "Galilee Investment-Mercaz Center" (*mercaz* and *center* are the same thing). The answer is that many Israelis still feel that they are somehow speaking to a more "sophisticated" audience that has knowledge of foreign languages.

The following word pairs of diverse origins are a few samples of this "dual vocabulary," and they reveal the diverse heritage of Modern Hebrew. The preference of a speaker for one or the other has been a matter ultimately decided by popular opinion, regardless of the official judgments of the Academy. The "indigenous" words below marked with an asterisk appear to have won out in most popular usage, since they appear frequently on public signs and are in constant use by the media. This is a dynamic situation and Hebrew speakers who return to the country after an absence of a decade or more are sometimes surprised to discover that words they considered part of everyone's common vocabulary are no longer regarded as such.[13]

Foreign (Loazi) / Indigenous	*English*
aggresivi / tokpani	aggressive
addict / mimukar*	addict
administratzia / minhal*	administration
adaptatzia / histaglut*	adaptation
alternativa / ḥalufa	alternative
breksim / blamim	brakes
illuzia / ashlaya	illusion
immunizatsiyah / ḥisun*	immunization
impulsivi / ḥapizut	impulsive
improvizatzia / iltur	improvisation
introvert / mufnam*	introvert
infekzia / zihum*	infection
situatzia / matzav*	situation
blondinit / tsahavonit	blond girl
helicopter / masok*	helicopter
dokumentatzia / tiud*	documentation
dinami / nimratz	dynamic
diagnosis / avḥana	diagnosis
defektivi / lakui*	defective

Foreign (Loazi) / Indigenous	English
standard / teken*	standard
piston / buchna	piston
radiator / makren	radiator
terminal / masof*	terminal
mikrob / ḥaydak	microbe
model / degem*	model

Many of the words based on original ancient Hebrew roots are still favored in intensive language courses taught in the ulpanim or as part of instructions, or at government facilities. However, the use of foreign words is slowly increasing and common among those with little previous knowledge of Hebrew who learned the language after arriving in Israel. This is all the more ironic, since these words were in use before the pioneering work of Hebrew linguists who were able to coin new words. There are well over a thousand such word pairs commonly heard today.

During the early "renaissance" from the 1880s to World War II, new words of Hebrew (or Arabic or Persian as indigenous to the Middle East) origin were coined, and the public was encouraged to use them instead of the internationally recognized words that have German or Russian suffixes. Today, many readers with a minimal grasp of the Hebrew language and not familiar at all with the written format can much more easily relate to the words of foreign origin. This explains their growing usage not only in the popular press, comic books and cheap novels but also among politicians who often cater to the lowest common denominator in their speeches.

The words most subject to this foreign trend are within the areas of medicine, automobiles, "teenage culture" and computers, where there are already substantial similarities in the vocabulary of most European languages. Many of these terms are spelled with a variety of weak consonant letters (*aleph*, *ayin*, *heh* and *yod*), functioning as vowels as in Yiddish. Their ungainly appearance is immediately recognized.

The period of 1880–1920 witnessed the greatest challenge and decisive triumph of clothing the skeleton of the ancient language with the new vocabulary and grammatical flexibility to make it into a vernacular.[14] By the 1920s, Modern Hebrew was no longer an experiment or desk project. It had been recognized as an official language and served as the language of instruction at the Hebrew University in Jerusalem, and outside that institution's walls, the Hebrew banter of children could be heard. It is today the idiom of a vibrant nation-state and dynamic economy, an accomplishment that met the most difficult challenge to the development of the language over the past 130 years.

6. Do the Israelis Speak Hebrew or Israeli?

In addition to the political difficulties involved in establishing a Jewish state, many linguists doubted that a language that had been "dormant" and persisted primarily in written form for centuries could meet the needs of a modern society. Modern Hebrew grew in power and prestige due to territorial concentration through immigration (*aliyah*) to Mandatory Palestine and was a better "fit" for achieving a national sense of identity for many immigrants from diverse cultural backgrounds than Yiddish or other languages.

The traditional view is that "Modern Hebrew" is a new version of the Classical Semitic language of biblical times that was revived at the end of the eighteenth century due in large part to scholars of the "Enlightenment" (*Haskalah*) in Eastern Europe and elaborated and refined by innovative linguists a century later. The monumental growth of the language has often been portrayed as a mighty plant with deep roots.

Largely unknown to most Jews in the Diaspora, a debate has been raging for more than a decade among linguists in Israel that deals with the most fundamental aspects of the rebirth of the Hebrew language. Even the term "rebirth" has been called into question by "Revisionists," who refer to the language spoken in the State of Israel today as "Relexified Indo-European," and prefer the term "Israeli" to denote what they call a "hybrid language" based on both Hebrew and Yiddish as well as other languages.

Regardless of the points of debate marshaled by linguists on both sides, practically all Israelis agree that they feel a direct historical continuity with the land and language of Israel. Ghil'ad Zuckermann is an Israeli linguist who has become the leading "Revisionist" proponent, claiming that the Hebrew spoken in Israel is really a "hybrid language." He prefers to call it "Yisraelit" (Israeli) and his polemical book, *Yisraelit, Safah Yafa*[1] (*Israeli—A Beautiful Language*), raised a storm of controversy and a running feud with many Hebraists.

Zuckermann has admitted that, whatever its faults and shortcomings, the contemporary spoken language of Israel has considerable and vibrant productive powers and a great expressive capacity. He nevertheless insists that although it is called Hebrew, it should more properly be called "Israeli" because of its hybrid Indo-European and Semitic origins, its immense debt to Yiddish and its essential newness. The spoken and written language today has undergone many changes from the model held up by the Academy. According to Zuckermann, "Whatever we choose to call it, we should acknowledge, and celebrate, its complexity."

He correctly points out that there was "no continuous historical chain of native speakers" that produced today's spoken "Israeli." The language was a vernacular that had been the language of a minor power—ancient Israel of the First and Second Temples. It had a life span that dated from the conquest of Canaan (ca. fourteenth century BCE) and ceased to be spoken by the second century CE, and was closely related to the neighboring Hebrew dialects of Moab and Edom.

The Residual Problems of the Classical Language of the Bible and Mishnah—The Alphabet, Conflicting Spellings, Sparse Vocabulary, Awkward Grammar

The many modern changes introduced since Ben-Yehuda began his work in 1880 for a largely European Yiddish- and Russian-speaking Jewish population inevitably had to contend with all sorts of problems "left over" from the ancient language written in an alphabet with separate symbols for consonants and vowels, a sparse vocabulary of only several thousand words, and other awkward and cumbersome grammatical problems for speakers of Indo-European languages that continue to hamper both learning and reading Hebrew.

In Zuckermann's view, although the words of what he calls "Israeli" are Hebrew, the sound system continues to follow the strikingly similar word order, phonetics and phonology of Yiddish, the native language of the original revivalists from the time of Ben-Yehuda who were attempting to speak Hebrew, with Semitic grammar and pronunciation.[2] They nevertheless retained an Ashkenazic mindset that was subsequently modified by speakers of Russian, Polish, German, Judeo-Spanish ("Ladino"), Arabic and English; therefore, the term "Israeli" is far more appropriate than Israeli Hebrew.

Opponents of this view contend that it makes no more sense to call Modern Hebrew "Israeli" than it does to refer to "American" as a separate language (rather than as "American English") and that Zuckermann's linguistic arguments mask a "post–Zionist agenda," designed to deprive Israelis of a historic continuity in their sense of nationhood and connection with the past.

In fact, it is obvious that no other so-called "modern language" changed less over such a long period of time. Any school child in the fourth grade in Israel can read and understand many parts of the Old Testament books that are more than twenty-five hundred years old, whereas for modern English speakers, the works of Shakespeare or Chaucer, only four and seven hundred years old, respectively, are very difficult, and anything older is impossible to understand.

This debate is so acute in Israel because the formal modern language taught in schools retains many difficult classical features from both the Biblical and the Mishnaic periods (endorsed by the Academy) that were "frozen" for centuries and today constitute problems for both native speakers and learners of the language.[3] For many new arrivals in Israel who learned Modern Hebrew without any previous "classical" or religious training in the ancient forms of the language, many features they learned were bent and "distorted" into the mold of the Indo-European languages—especially Yiddish, Russian, and Polish—so that the linguistic deviations represented a dilemma for educators as to how much leeway they should allow in departures from the recognized principles of formal grammar taught in school.

A number of difficult hurdles challenged the ideal of transforming a language that had been largely dormant for centuries. They were (and continue to be) characterized by the following:

1. The need to develop appropriate word derivations for a new vocabulary and the resultant search for indigenous "roots," the consonants that form the skeleton of Hebrew words.
2. The difficulties of a Semitic-based grammar with awkward, unfamiliar constructions for speakers of European languages.
3. An alphabet that is unable to properly represent vowels, creating serious problems in reading comprehension and spelling. Hebrew continues to be one of the few languages in the world for which there is not one single standard system for ordering words in the dictionary.
4. The narrow range of vowel sounds and the paucity of vowel combinations (diphthongs), as well as the elimination of several Semitic guttural consonants ('*ayin* ע and *het* ח), have made the spoken language sound very monotone. The result is a poor match between speech and spelling.

Regardless of the enormous success of Hebrew and its solid position as the "National Language" in the State of Israel, all of the above problems continue to present considerable barriers to literacy and the development of the language. Moreover, another threat intensifying the difficulties is the enormous appeal of English and its challenge as an alternative language of communication for a tiny elite in countries like Israel, whose languages have a small number of speakers and are spoken nowhere else.

The Great Spelling Dilemma

Although Hebrew won the dual battle of transformation into a modern spoken language and recognition as the official language of the State of Israel, a serious problem remains, one that has resisted "modernization" and constitutes a growing barrier to literacy and comprehension. The transformation of the ancient language into a modern idiom remains unfinished as long as the language continues to use the traditional "holy" square Babylonian letters introduced in the fifth century BCE, which replaced the original Hebrew-Phoenician alphabet.[4] The retention of this archaic alphabet has made necessary the retention of three spelling systems! The letters used in all of the systems are the same and represent consonants, but they differ on the representation of the vowel sounds and the two weak letters *vav* and *yod* that may be used as both consonants and vowels.

The first system, used in older dictionaries, shows just the "grammatical spelling" of the original consonants. This is the "bare bones," representing the skeleton of the word without the *nikud* vowel symbols below the letters. In the second system, in addition to the consonants, vowels are represented by a separate system of signs (*nikud*) above, below or within the consonants—as in the Old Testament, to which scholars added the *nikud* sometime in the ninth century CE. The third system in widespread use today, and approved by the Academy (called by the Latin term *plene*, or full), employs the weak consonants *vav* (o) and *yod* (y) to function as vowels as well as consonants (v and y, respectively), but does not use the special vowel signs.

The Bible has utilized another method since the ninth century of the Common Era, employing full *nikud* but omitting the weak consonants that also function as vowels; compare the original biblical spelling of the word for morning—B-K-R בקר—to the modern *plene* version—BoKeR בוקר. For those who wish to study Biblical Hebrew to better understand the New Testament, it is important to know beforehand that the authorized translation known as the "Septuagint" (from the Greek word for seventy—that is, the number of elder scholars involved who translated it from the original Hebrew without *nikud*) was created approximately 285 years before the time of Jesus, when the Greek language was the most widely understood "international language."

The Torah also has additional signs to indicate how the words are to be chanted. Full *nikud* is used in the Bible, prayer books, and children's works, as well as in poetry, where meter is important. *Plene*, known in Hebrew as *HaKtiv HaMaleh*, is now the standard in most dictionaries. A recent edition of a Hebrew-English dictionary, *Milon Megiddo Ḥadish*,[5] explains that *plene* spelling is now in use in literature, science, newspapers, most books, the press and general correspondence.

Only by using *nikud* and full *plene* spelling can the reader instantaneously (and correctly) read a given word. The lack of distinctive vowel letters creates considerable uncertainty regarding the identity of the word to be read. In Hebrew, there are many groups of homographs: words of two, three, four, five and more letters that even in *plene* spelling appear identical, like "read" and "read" (past tense), and can only be distinguished by full *nikud*. For example, the word mDBR without vowels may be miDBaR (a desert), miDaBeR (is speaking) or mehDaVaR (from a thing). In Hebrew letters, they all appear as מדבר

Are Israelis "The People of the Book?"

The alphabet poses difficulties of legibility due to the square shape of most letters, with none extending below or above the line. Tests have shown that whereas most readers can correctly read an English sentence that has been partially hidden by blocking out the top or bottom half of the line, this is impossible in Hebrew.

The difficulties the alphabet poses for literacy extend beyond the new immigrant population and explain why many veteran residents in Israel who get along quite well when it comes to spoken Hebrew are unable to read a daily newspaper, let alone enjoy a work of serious literature. This comes as a shock to many foreign observers, who still have an image of Israelis (Jews) as "The People of the Book."

An English reader who comes across the word "read" may encounter an initial doubt as to whether this verb is in the present or past tense, but by the time the reader approaches the end of the sentence, the context will make it clear which tense is intended. The Hebrew reader, however, is faced with hundreds of such choices (distinguishing between "homographs," different words that are spelled identically). Such "words" with multiple possibilities slow down reading considerably in the course of perusing a Hebrew book! For example, when the reader sees the three-letter combination *samech-peh-resh*, ספר, it may be variously read as *sefer* (a book), *sfar* (a border region), *sapar* (a barber), *safar* (the past-tense masculine third-person form for "he counted") or *sippear* (masculine third-person singular form meaning "he told").

Arthur Koestler, in his memoirs about the time he lived in Israel and acquired a knowledge of the spoken language, made this same point about the difficulty of learning to read Hebrew more than seventy years ago and was ignored. The great Hebrew scholar Werner Weinberg summarized the extent of the problem and the many reform proposals, including Latinization, in his excellent study *Tikun HaKtiv haIvri* (The Orthographic Reform of Hebrew).[6]

The difficulties are increased by the practice of "tacking on" prepositions and conjunctions (the words for "and," "that," "from," "in" and "on," "to," "when," and "at" are all represented by a single letter) to the beginning of the next word.

Since Hebrew has no upper-case or lower-case letters, these orthographic peculiarities make it difficult even for the fluent native-born speaker to immediately identify the word to be read. Unfortunately, printing everything in *nikud* is expensive and slows down reading considerably.

The "purists" argue that any distortion of the alphabet would obscure the word-building skeletal structure of the language that enables readers to recognize the essential root letters. As the Modern Hebrew vocabulary grows in complexity with maturity, this antiquated alphabet and its ambiguities create occasional uncertainty and slow down reading comprehension. There is no escape from this dilemma outside a major reform of the orthography, such as "Latinization" or the addition of new "true vowel" letters. There have been well over a hundred reform proposals for new alphabets and new letters.[7]

What is certain is that the traditional alphabet becomes more and more inefficient and cumbersome. It is the equivalent of maintaining Roman numerals for our modern civilization, and it retards literacy for a people renowned for their ability to adapt to modern times. With the traditional alphabet, no Hebrew reader can grasp how to pronounce foreign words unless they are written with full *nikud*, and even then there are difficulties in handling certain combinations of consonants so as to know the correct division of syllables. The challenges of the traditional alphabet are particularly critical in a number of modern fields of study, such as chemistry, in which it is absolutely essential to recognize whether, for example, a particular word is sulfite or sulfate.

The reform proposals have even included a Latinized Hebrew newspaper, *Deror*, begun in 1933 and edited by Itamar Ben-Avi, the son of Eliezer Ben-Yehuda. All such proposals ran into the determined and rabid opposition of most traditionalists, the Orthodox and even many secular Jews who would regard it as too radical a break with the past to surrender the archaic but "holy" square letters that are almost 2,500 years old.

Pronunciation

The relatively small number of phonemes (distinctive sounds represented by consonants, vowels and diphthongs) in Modern Hebrew using the Sephardi pronunciation common in Israel creates difficulties in the comprehension of the spoken language. Whereas English and French have approximately fifty such phonemes, and German and Russian about forty, Modern Hebrew makes do with only twenty-five! This makes the language sound quite undifferentiated and "dull," and it causes confusion because many words sound quite similar. This is accentuated by the failure of many Israelis today to pronounce the guttural "Semitic" letters. The result is even greater confusion due to the spelling system in use and its lack of correspondence with the way most people (particularly the population of Eastern European origin) pronounce words.

The Distortion of Classical Hebrew Grammar

To understand much of the Old Testament books, there are some necessary adjustments involving quite different grammatical concepts employed in ancient Hebrew (and other Semitic languages). The first and most apparent is the lack of tenses based on time and the employment of a grammatical device known as "consecutive *vav*" used in Biblical Hebrew. This difficulty had already begun to cause problems of interpretation by the time of the Mishnah and became totally obsolete in Modern Hebrew, which, like the Indo-European languages, has an exact structure to express actions according to time—past, present and future, as well as complex compound times and conditional tenses.

Students of Modern Hebrew who read the Bible often confuse the present and the past tenses because they originally represented a different aspect of intention—whether an action had been completed or was still in progress. No one can say that this aspect of the language is missed.

Much more significant is the growing loss, and probably eventual disappearance, of the gender-distinctive conjugation of verbs! The Semitic languages are notoriously concerned about sex—the sex of the speaker or subject of a sentence. This applies to the second-person pronoun "you," which is distinguished four ways: *atah, at, atem,* and *aten* (by gender, single and plural: אתן אתה אתם את). Nouns, verbs and even adjectives must "agree" and all require this four-way division (masculine singular, masculine plural, feminine singular, and feminine plural). It even applies to the command forms of the verbs. To give any command, one must recognize this four-way distinction regarding who is being ordered to do something! Such "extra baggage" is falling by the wayside as more and more speakers, even native ones, are following the trend of omitting such awkward forms. The plural feminine form was dropped as early as Mishnaic Hebrew (see Chapter 3) and is considered obsolete, although songs like *Tzenah, tzenah* צאנה (which utilized the biblical plural command form for girls to "go out") were popular during the Mandate period. It is a reminder that in the biblical language all such commands end in the *-enah* אנה form.

The grammatical marker *et* את, which indicates the direct object of an action, used to be stressed in grammar and advisory bulletins issued by the Academy of the Hebrew Language, but it is often omitted or, even worse, used when it is not required.

The same problem of misuse applies to the "construct state" סמיכות (*smichoot*), or dependence, the way in which nouns and their qualifiers are expressed. The more traditional way of expressing a concept such as "The City's Garden" was in the form of "Garden-the-city" (*Gan Ha'Ir* גן העיר). This is often replaced by the much "easier" use of all articles and prepositions that made its appearance in Mishnaic Hebrew (*HaGan shel Ha'Ir* = The Garden of the City הגן של העיר).

Nevertheless, an expression with two levels of dependence, such as "My mother's friend's garden," in the more elegant Hebrew is *Gan Haver-Immi* גן חבר אמי; while a bit literary, this sounds more sophisticated than the somewhat cumbersome, if colloquial, Hebrew, with its formal "translation" of every preposition, as in *HaGan shel haHaver shel HaImma sheli* הגן של החבר של האמא שלי (literally, "the garden of the friend of the mother of me"—every word, including each preposition, is represented by a separate word as in English). Talking this way (or listening) can easily become an arduous task. Even to those listeners not familiar with the Hebrew language, such frequent speech constructions with the many prepositions sound tedious, akin to "baby language" (the word "of" repeated three times).

Linguists don't use these terms, but they do distinguish between languages such as English that they call "isolating," in which all words stand apart, and those called "synthetic," like Hungarian or both Hebrew and Arabic to a lesser degree, in which the stem or base of a word is modified with all kinds of additional grammatical markers (this is what *smichoot* does) called prefixes, suffixes and infixes, which denote the relationship between words.

In ordinary conversational Hebrew almost all speakers today habitually use the "isolating" words "the mother of me" (*Ha imma sheli*) rather than *immi*; yet the latter is quite common in more polished speech, even though it harkens back to Biblical Hebrew, but also it is more demanding because many of the nouns and verb forms undergo subtle vowel changes.

Just as English underwent what for most of us is undoubtedly regarded as a process of simplification in its evolution from Anglo-Saxon, with its many case endings, to our modern tongue, in which each word is represented by the same letters without the use of affixes (like pre-, anti-, and counter- in front of words or -ity, -tion, and -ness at the end of some nouns). For example, the phrase "in the house" represents three specific words, but so-called agglutinative languages (notably Hungarian and Finnish, and partially Hebrew) make use of these morphemes to change words so that they also combine nouns, articles and prepositions, so that the Hungarian word for house (ház) has many different endings; "my house" is *házam*, "your house" *házad*, and *házunk*, is "our house."

Hebrew Literacy and Literature—The Problem of a Small Reading Public

The English-language biweekly magazine, *Jerusalem Report*, featured an article in 1993 under the headline "A Movable Feast,"[8] lauding the then-current state of Hebrew literature. The author, Hillel Halkin, a renowned translator and a neighbor and colleague of mine in Zichron Ya'akov when I lived in Israel, provided an upbeat judgment of the state of Hebrew literature, claiming that the Israelis indeed inherited the mantle of the historic Jewish People in the Diaspora as the "People of the Book." He cited the statistics that Israelis consume more books per capita than almost anywhere else (after Iceland, with its minuscule population of 250,000), but these "facts" warrant much close attention to determine whether the glass is really half full or half empty.

Halkin makes an assumption in his remark that "Finland has a population like Israel's but when did you last hear of a Finnish book?" This was obviously meant as a rhetorical question, but it deserves a factual reply that calls into question the notion that the Israelis are truly the "People of the Book" and raises issues on the relation between literacy and orthography.

Finland, with approximately the same population as Israel, can boast a best-seller titled *The Unknown Soldier* by Väinö Linna, which sold 600,000 copies, whereas the best-selling Hebrew novels have not reached anywhere near that number! Finnish Americans are a much smaller community than English-speaking Jews, and although an English translation of the Finnish novel exists, almost all readers of Halkin's article are bound never to have heard of the book due to a lack of interest in this historical saga of the 1940 Winter War.

Under the present system, the fact remains that a significant proportion of the adult Israeli reading public is not sufficiently literate in Hebrew to appreciate fine literature; only a handful of writers can make a living from professional writing and quite a few must finance their works through self-publishing.

The Hebrew alphabet poses a number of serious problems for literacy. It is not only the lack of a true alphabet with separate vowel letters but also the absence of capital letters, the attachment of prepositions to the words they relate to, and the similar shape of many letters, with only a few of them extending above or below the space of a line.

The statistics claiming that Israelis read more books than anyone else are also distorted by the discrepancy between titles and actual number of books sold. They do not take into account many prayer books destined for religious communities throughout the Diaspora and include many self-published titles.

This is not just a question of aesthetics. In an article titled "Revamping the Aleph-Bet,"[9] the columnist "Philologus" explains that although he is fully bilingual in Hebrew and English, when travelling along an Israeli highway, he instinctively prefers to look for road signs in English rather than Hebrew because it is easier to take in the information with the limited amount of time available. No less than ten Hebrew letters have the same slightly curved flat top, while in English the largest such group of letters has only four—the r, n, e and s.

Research cited by Robert Alberg supports the view that the eye moves faster to take in reading comprehension from left to right rather than right to left, as determined by comparative studies among native-born Israelis who have later become literate in European languages. Alberg, a Hebrew scholar,[10] maintains that there is indeed a connection between orthography and literacy. At his own expense, he has sent thousands of copies with his own proposal for a spelling reform to writers, Knesset members, the Hebrew Language Academy and many public figures in Israeli society. The response to his proposal was generally sympathetic with regard to admitting the difficulties involved with the traditional alphabet and conflicting spelling systems. Nevertheless, the general public has resisted any call for a new campaign after the failure of dozens of similar projects in the past, inertia and the opposition of devoutly religious Jews everywhere.

The Irony of Hebrew Pronunciation and Prejudice Towards Arabic

The relationship between Arabs and Jews, and their respective languages, is an asymmetrical one. Arabs distinguish between the social necessity and desirability of communicating in Hebrew for many practical purposes, even though their relationship to Jews and the State of Israel may be hostile. Most Jews have a negative attitude toward Arabic as a result of the two people's mutual animosity. This is apparent even among the children of Jews who are native Arabic speakers and were expelled from the Arab countries in 1947–1952.

The distinct pronunciation of the "guttural" letters of the Hebrew alphabet, ע (*ayin*) and ח (*ḥet*), functions as a guide for correct spelling. They originally had the same pronunciation as the corresponding ones in Arabic. What was once considered "correct Hebrew pronunciation" is now largely regarded by the Jewish majority as a marker of lower-class origin and Arab or "Eastern-Oriental Jewish" identity.[11]

Although many educated Israelis "violate" the rules of the classical forms of Hebrew and may, as Zuckermann argues, be guilty of "shortcuts" and bending the language in the direction of a hybrid vernacular, most Hebraists reject the notion that this warrants calling Modern Hebrew "Israeli." This debate has created a dilemma and a challenge for the future. "Purists" fear that unless the more traditional forms, and especially the alphabet, are preserved and the proper neologisms based on authentic Hebrew roots adhered to, the language will lose much of its authentic character and critical link with the past.

A recent and very welcome textbook that pays much more attention to the actual spoken language is *Modern Hebrew: An Essential Grammar*.[12] Author Lewis Glinert uses a much more innovative and novel approach than standard course textbooks, along with colorful contemporary dialogue and custom-built vocabulary. He rightly singles out for criticism the "unhealthy tradition of fussing over inflections" and the need to "teach students to understand and simulate the average educated speaker rather than sound like a newsreader or funeral orator."[13]

7. The Worldwide Rivalry with Yiddish

Visitors to Israel can scarcely appreciate the enormous difficulties that were involved in the restoration of Hebrew as a living language. The Hebrew-Yiddish conflict in Palestine took three generations to resolve. Without victory over Yiddish in this competition, Hebrew would not today be the official language of the State of Israel.

One hundred and thirty years ago, there were approximately six million Yiddish-speaking Jews.[1] No one then was a primary, habitual or native speaker of Hebrew. The battle to establish Hebrew as the national language of a future independent Jewish state would never have succeeded had it not won clear recognition as the only realistic candidate able to claim the loyalty of Jews everywhere. Nevertheless, the argument was effectively made by Yiddishists that this meant a betrayal of a "living tongue" in favor of a "constructed," artificial language, like Esperanto, that was not really anyone's mother tongue and thus unable to draw upon the wealth of Jewish folklore, prior literature and cultural creativity.

The Close Ties Between the Jewish "Hybrid Languages" and Hebrew

Although Hebrew ceased to be the spoken language of the majority of the Jews in their original Judean homeland between the second century BCE and the second century CE, it remained as the most important and prestigious language of religious observance and commentary and heavily influenced the "hybrid languages" that arose in the Diaspora, such as Yiddish (Judeo-German), Ladino (also known as Judezmo, or Judeo-Español), and several other varieties. These all still use the Hebrew alphabet. A parallel twin vocabulary also developed, in which words of Hebrew origin were used specifically to designate a concept, occupation, ceremony or item with Jewish content, as opposed to the parallel word of foreign origin: *emes* vs. Warheit (truth), *luakh* vs. calendar (calendar), *katsef* vs. fleysh-haker (butcher), *seyfer* vs. bukh (book), *levaye* vs. bugrebnis (funeral), *khokhme* vs. Weisheit (wisdom).

Many Hebrew words with a slightly different pronunciation and the accent put on an earlier syllable were absorbed by Yiddish to indicate specific religious beliefs and practices—*Shabbos* (the Sabbath), *milchumah* (war), *mishpucha* (family), *koiyach* (power), *zichronos* (memories), *melamed* (religious teacher), *Kaddish* (memorial prayer for the dead), *rachmanos* (mercy, compassion), *yomtov* (a holiday), *bris* (circumcision), *mikve* (ritual bath), *talis* (prayer shawl).

For a time, a lively rivalry existed between the two languages vying for the loyalty of several generations of literary figures, writers, playwrights, philosophers and political personalities. The largest Jewish party in Poland, the Bund,[2] cultivated an autonomous Yiddish culture, and until the late 1940s, the vast majority of Jewish immigrants to Palestine were native Yiddish speakers. On the eve of World War II, there were dozens of Yiddish newspapers in a score of countries and the Zionist movements carried on considerable propaganda in Yiddish.

Hebrew's growth was greatly aided by the circumstances of the increasingly difficult situation of the Jewish minorities in all the states of Eastern Europe and the rise of anti–Semitism in Germany. Territorial concentrations of Jewish emigrants in the 1920s and 1930s, many of them enthusiastic Zionists, learned Hebrew in Europe, and they were able to demonstrate their ability to speak the language proficiently and counter the Yiddishist arguments that it was an "artificial language."

Many individuals who possessed a love for both languages experienced a soul-wrenching dilemma over the necessity of "choosing sides" in the increasingly polarized atmosphere of the new society being built. For many committed Zionists, even those who grew up with Yiddish as their first language, there was a conscious identification of Yiddish with the ghetto experience and humiliations of Eastern Europe.

The American public, including millions of non–Jews, have become familiar with dozens of Yiddish words and expressions through dozens of films, plays and novels and the outstanding success of Leo Rosten's *The Joys of Yiddish* and *Treasury of Jewish Quotations*.[3] These two best-sellers further intensified the sense of complete identity among Jewish folkways, humor, and the Yiddish language.

For centuries, Hebrew was used as a means of communication between educated Jews travelling abroad where the native languages were unintelligible. It admirably fulfilled this role in the Middle Ages when Sephardi Jews (living in Spain and Portugal) maintained a wide net of commercial contacts in an alliance of merchants known as the Rhadanites (after the Jewish quarter in Baghdad). This link connected trade stations across the Mediterranean, the Sahara and the Abbasid and Byzantine Empires and beyond through a kind of secular-commercial Hebrew. It was in wide and respected use for religious commentary and as an eminent "high language" for philosophical, legal and even scientific texts by learned individuals who addressed themselves largely to a Jewish, but not necessarily Orthodox, audience. However, in Europe, for almost a thousand years, Yiddish was synonymous with Jewish—it simply meant "Jewish" in the Yiddish language.

The pioneering work of Eliezer Ben-Yehuda to make Hebrew a spoken language had its initial impact in Eastern Europe and then Palestine in the late nineteenth century. He drew upon the work of many advocates of the *Haskalah* (Enlightenment) across much of Europe who had written essays and literary works in a refined classical Hebrew since the middle of the eighteenth century. It was a linguistic form designed to establish an intellectual community of Jews thirsty for secular knowledge and expanded commentary on Jewish law and ethics.

Initially, Ben-Yehuda's efforts were looked upon as eccentric or regarded as impossible by most Jews with any amount of secular education living in Palestine and the Diaspora. Even Theodore Herzl, the founder of modern political Zionism, scoffed at the idea of reviving what was universally regarded as a "dead language," much like Latin and Ancient Greek. In his romantic novel *Altneuland* Jews were pictured as cosmopolitan multilinguists with knowledge of German, French, English and Russian.[4] At the first Zionist congress Herzl asked the rhetorical question, "Who among us can as much as ask for a train ticket in Hebrew?" It is likely that among those present in the audience, only a handful were aware that the Hebrew word for "train" had just recently been coined.

Nevertheless, Israel has succeeded in reviving the language and making it the dynamic vernacular of millions of Israelis and linking the fortunes of the new state to an ancient historic past more than three thousand years old, quite likely the most ancient language and literature of any ethnic group and historic civilization. In Herzl's *Altneuland*, there is no mention of Hebrew or Yiddish.

Yiddish reflected the folkways and religious life of the mass of European Jews and later was adapted to meet the requirements of sophisticated urban life and modern literature, but the Holocaust dealt it a death-blow as a spoken language (other than among ultra-orthodox Jews in scattered enclaves). Nevertheless, Isaac Bashevis Singer, a leading figure in the Yiddish literary movement in Poland transplanted to the United States, won the Nobel Prize in Literature in 1978, provoking a renewed flurry of interest in the language.

The Yiddish Claim as the Authentic Mame Loshen *(Mother Tongue)*

Yiddish partisans, or those very Orthodox Jews antagonistic toward Zionism, proclaimed that a distinctly secular Modern Hebrew vernacular was a desecration of the "Holy Tongue" and that only the "Mame Loshen" could create a proper social environment that might be re-created and relocated to Palestine. Only thus could they believe Yiddish literature and cultural creativity might continue to make progress. Several generations of great writers, poets and playwrights had won international recognition and would never feel at home in the Middle East, far removed from their familiar European environments.

In his opening address to the First Yiddish Language Conference in 1912, Nathan Birnbaum spoke of the great progress of Yiddish. His speech was also an attack on assimilation and a dismissal of Hebrew supporters as "lost wanderers" turning themselves into "ramblers, torn from home and nationality," and going off to a "desert wilderness." The argument, continually repeated, was that only Yiddish was the natural vehicle of expression for millions of Jews who had learned it at home, were fluent in it, and had already elevated it on the world stage. No other language could serve to express the needs and desires of an entire people. The other hybrid languages were never even brought into discussion, as if they were of no relevance to a future Jewish society in Palestine.

"Turning the Clock Backward"

Critics of Zionism pointed to the apparent absurdity of "trying to turn the clock backward" to an eccentric re-creation of an extinct culture thousands of years old. It was "nonsense" to struggle to learn an "ancient dead language" like Latin and attempt to make up for the loss of almost two thousand years of development. These arguments were "logical" but ignored the reality of finding a common language in the multilingual society of Jewish Palestine, with its substantial Sephardi and Middle Eastern population from Yemen, Turkey, the Balkans, North Africa, Persia, and the Caucasus region (Georgia, Azerbaijan and Uzbekistan).

Not only were Turkish and Arabic of prime importance for reasons of commerce and administration, but competing Zionist agencies and charitable organizations also encouraged the use of English, French, German, and Russian. By the establishment of the Palestine Mandate under British auspices in 1920, it was already becoming crystal clear that the huge and growing American Jewish community would contribute to the continued decline of Yiddish and growth of English.

It became increasingly obvious after Israel's independence in 1948 that the arrival of massive waves of new immigrants from the countries of North Africa and the Middle East fully justified the decision that only Modern Hebrew could appeal to them as the basis for a new sense of national identification. Many already had a basic knowledge of Biblical Hebrew due to their religious training, and the transition from Arabic was much easier than for the European immigrants. Hebrew and Arabic share many grammatical similarities and a vocabulary of many closely related words.

The Great Rivalry

Detractors of Modern Hebrew ridiculed both the halting speech of their native Yiddish-speaking colleagues unable to converse freely in Hebrew and what they regarded as the stilted character of Hebrew novels attempting to portray real conversations in a language that was not yet the vernacular of a community outside the struggling Zionist colonies in remote and backward Palestine. Yiddish speakers compared the artificial character of Modern Hebrew with Esperanto (see Chapter 3). This was at a time when both languages were in their infancy and could not rely on the broad social base of national existence in a homeland embracing two or more generations.

The arrival of tens of thousands of German-speaking Jews in the 1930s from Germany and Austria radically changed the balance of the language controversy in Palestine. The new immigrants, who had been proud of their fluency in German, became enthusiastic converts to Hebrew. They had always looked down on Yiddish as the "jargon" of Eastern European Jews and were determined to forge a new Zionist identity.[5] In Palestine, the language rivalry occasionally provoked street battles.

Hebrew's growth and prestige led to the decision of the British Mandate to recognize it as one of the three official languages of the country, and ultimately to recognition as the primary official language of the new Jewish state in 1948. Arabic is the second official language of the country, although Arab citizens contend that it is slighted.

Although Yiddish had reflected the folkways and religious life of most European Jews, Zionists correctly foresaw that Yiddish could never achieve the status of a "national language" linked to a specific territory or independent state anywhere, and would suffer an inevitable decline even though it had met the requirements of sophisticated urban life and modern literature in Eastern Europe. The organized Zionist movements did not, however, neglect the frequent use of Yiddish in their propaganda. Ze'ev Jabotinsky was not atypical in his categorical rejection of Yiddish, although, paradoxically he was a polished orator in the language, when he wrote the following words of advice after promoting the Sephardi pronunciation and denouncing the inflection of Yiddish speakers still apparent in their spoken Hebrew: "Do not sing when you speak. This ugliness is infinitely worse than every other defect, and regrettably, it is taking root in our life. Both the school and the stage are guilty: the first, out of sloppiness, the latter out of an intention to 'revive' for us the ghetto and its whining. The time of the ghetto is ugly because of its weeping tone which stirs unpleasant memories in us."[6]

The growth of resistance to the British Mandate encouraged the younger generation of Jews in Palestine to identify more with the ancient past and the use of a modernized and revitalized Hebrew to express nationalist sentiments in favor of independence.

Yiddish Under Pressure in Israel

Radio programs utilizing a model spoken standard Ivrit with proper pronunciation became a feature of the Israeli Broadcasting System, *Kol Yisrael*. They were avidly listened to throughout the Mandate period and in the years of mass immigration alongside news and culture feature programs in a dozen immigrant languages. Radio broadcasts in Yiddish declined from four hours daily (two directed to an Israeli audience and two by shortwave for consumption abroad) twenty years ago to currently 25 minutes each. Special courses in spoken Ivrit provided live-in facilities in kibbutzim and featured the *ulpan* method of teaching, using no foreign language assistance. Since then, Israelis have been fond of claiming that Hebrew is the only language that "the children teach their parents."

The language debate continued for two generations and reached the level of social ostracism, picket lines against Yiddish theater, polemical literature and boycotts of the rivals. In the years of mass immigration in the early 1950s, the number of native Yiddish speakers surpassed those fluent in Hebrew, and state officials as well as the Zionist movement took a harsh, discriminatory and vengeful policy against the use of Yiddish in the press and theater. In January 1951, *haMoetza Libikoret Seratim uMachazot* (The Council for the Criticism of Films and Plays), a government agency charged with approving the public showing of films and plays, issued its first directive banning presentation of a play in Yiddish in Tel-Aviv and threatened fines for the actors. To avoid creating the "wrong impression," the ban did not apply for special performances intended for Yiddish-speaking tourists from America or Europe. The Yiddish theater company published incorrect dates, times and venues for some performances, with the correct information being circulated by word of mouth in order to mislead the police! This cat-and-mouse game lasted for a year.

The Yiddish newspaper was only allotted very limited access to the government's control of the supply of paper and the editors had to resort to the black market, where the only paper obtained was yellow, green and red; a collection of such comical multicolored editions of *Letzte Nayes* was, for many years, on display in the newspaper's office until the final death of the paper in 2006, following the disappearance of the other foreign language newspapers in German, Polish, Hungarian and Romanian.

Even the "image" of Yiddish as painted by Ben-Gurion, contrasting it as "the language Jews took with them into Auschwitz and Treblinka" with the "Hebrew that Jews in Palestine took with them into the Negev when conquering it," was calculated to identify the language with the "Galut" (exile) mentality. An effective poster designed by the Cultural Department of the Israeli Army featured a fork in the road with one large sign pointing to a bright future in an idyllic landscape. The sign was marked עברית in bold letters. Aimed in the other direction were numerous road signs labeled with the half-dozen common languages of the Diaspora pointing back toward a grim past surrounded by barbed wire. This was, of course, deeply wounding to Yiddish-speaking survivors and ignored the examples of heroism and resistance during the Holocaust in Europe; yet it must not be forgotten that bitter memories remained among both secular and religious Zionists for the policies used in Stalinist Russia to strangle Hebrew by a generation of committed Jewish communists through prohibiting all cultural activity as well as teaching the language.

A television documentary,

Israeli army poster, Cultural Department, featuring road signs to the future and the past. Image from the 1950s (Lavon Institute for Labor Movement Research).

Mother-Tongue, Children-Tongue, on Yiddish produced in 2002 in Israel gathered together the former editors of the Yiddish newspaper *Lezte Nayes*; the *Kol Yisrael* Yiddish radio announcers; Shmuel Atzmon, director of Yiddishshpiel Productions; distinguished faculty including Chava Turniansky, then head of Yiddish studies at the Hebrew University; and veteran actors, who all berated themselves with guilt that they had not insisted on teaching their children Yiddish. They also made the point that the hope of some lovers of the language for its future—that it will continue to thrive among the most hardened extreme ultra–Orthodox circles—is totally misplaced. Now, in Meah Sha'arim, Israel, or Williamsburg in Brooklyn, unlike Jews in Eastern Europe and the Soviet Union before World War II, those who use Yiddish at home and bring up their children in that language have no contact and little interest in secular affairs, the modern world or innovative literature, art and music.

How a Base Society of Hebrew Speakers Was Created

When Eliezer Ben-Yehuda began his work, Hebrew lacked much of the simplest everyday vocabulary to deal with many domains and needs of modern society and technology. The problems were not simply those of a limited vocabulary but also lack of characteristic and habitual modes of speech to express spontaneous emotions or reflective thoughts and moods. It was still not spoken in any large settlement but only in small, intimate groups.

There was the one essential ingredient that Ivrit needed to take off, survive and grow, without which its fate would have been that of Latin and Ancient Geek or the many artificial laboratory-devised languages. The requirement is what Benjamin Harshav has called "a base society" that was formed from a "social desert,"[7] or the "social existence of the language." This meant a community of a sufficient number of speakers from all walks of life for whom the language is the essential tool of communication and information in all areas of human experience. A national and living language must permeate every social and institutional setting: the government bureaucracy, business and commerce, the educational institutions from grade school to university, the cinema, and other media of communication and all age groups.

The inauguration of the Hebrew University in 1925 made the world aware that Modern Hebrew had reached a level of maturity as a spoken tongue and could function as the language of instruction, research and scientific investigation. By 1968, Shmuel Yosef Agnon became the first Hebrew writer to win the Nobel Prize for Literature. Only when children who were educated in Hebrew schools began to hear Ivrit spoken by adults serving as policemen, shopkeepers, lifeguards, government clerks, and postal workers, rather than just their own parents or teachers in school, could they begin to imitate and even invent words and expressions that seemed "natural" to them in specific contexts.

THE IMPORTANCE OF THE HEBREW SCHOOLS, RADIO AND THE PRESS

Perhaps the most crucial early achievement that enabled high school graduates in Palestine to gain confidence was the realization that more and more schools would use Hebrew as the language of instruction for all subjects and provide a true framework in which students could expect to meet, court, marry, and raise families in a Hebrew-speaking environment.[8] This began to happen sometime between 1905 and 1912. This milestone served to establish a new Hebrew-reading and -speaking "base society."

The arrival of a new wave of immigrants with a more secular outlook and knowledge of Hebrew encouraged the growth of the press and the beginning of radio. By 1948, the lively Hebrew press reflected a multiplicity of views and appealed to a much wider reading public than in 1920.

Israeli stamp honoring "Herziliya," first Hebrew "Gymnasium" (academic high school); cornerstone laid July 28, 1909 (designed by Chaimi Kivkowitz) (courtesy Israel Postal Service).

Although Hebrew emerged the winner and increased its legitimate authority following independence as the country's official language, ultra–Orthodox circles have generally maintained a hostile attitude toward its modern role as a secular language. They insist that a vernacular, secular, profane and public Ivrit amounts to a sacrilegious and blasphemous transgression and can readily justify this view by pointing out how the modern language is used in advertisements for pornography, the football lottery, detective novels, or sensationalist and bizarre tattoos. On numerous occasions, demonstrators have defaced both the house in which Eliezer Ben-Yehuda lived and monuments to his memory.

In the 1990s, the Knesset passed the Yiddish and Ladino Heritage Law,[9] recognizing the languages' importance in Jewish culture and the need to preserve them. The law led to the creation of the National Authority for Yiddish Culture. Today, Yiddish is an optional subject in secondary schools and is held in high regard by all segments of the Israeli cultural establishment. Even the famous Habimah Theater now offers plays in Yiddish, and subsidies for cultural and scholastic endeavors in the language have been made available by the government, local municipalities and institutions abroad, notably from Germany.

Countless Yiddish expressions have entered popular Israeli Hebrew speech and it may be said to have risen from the bottom of the social ladder of languages. Nevertheless, a consequence of the great debate between Yiddish and Hebrew has been the growing gulf between the sense of Israeli nationhood and the traditions and values of the Diaspora that had been based on Yiddish and other Jewish hybrid languages.

The conclusion is unavoidable and confirmed by many studies that Yiddish as a vernacular "is still of low status and serves as an identity symbol for those who, because of their own (deliberate or unwilling) social aloofness from the public scene—the aged, or the low class Ashkenazim—feel less or not at all committed to the central cultural values."[10]

Although the Yiddish-Hebrew rivalry in Israel has abated, it is remarkable that it continues to be carried on in the United States on a low-level burner due to strong political divisions between Jews who have become alienated from Israel and the country's more traditional supporters. Among the many replies to Hillel Halkin's view of Hebrew's justifiable victory over Yiddish, as expressed in his book *Letters to an American Jewish Friend*,[11] the following is typical:

> I'd rather fight with tradition than lose its riches. Your tragedy is that you think that living in Israel makes you a Jew. Oh, you yourself are one all right, you grew up in the Diaspora but how about those children of yours for whom Zionism is so irrelevant. Are they and secularly raised Israelis like them any more than Hebrew-speaking goyim?[12]

Hebrew-speaking goyim is a term of disparagement used by some anti–Zionists, ultra–Orthodox Jews and those who continue to consciously cultivate Yiddish as if it were still the hallmark of Jewish identity and a proud symbol of Diaspora identity. Halkin responded to his critic as follows:

> When nothing is left to sustain the Jews of Israel but simple Israeli patriotism—no sense of being the revolutionary bearers of Jewish history, no higher Jewish mission—will that be enough? There are nations that stood their ground because simple patriotism sufficed, such as England during World War II, and nations that fell because it did not such as France, in the same war.[13]

Halkin's implication is clear: Israeli patriotism is sufficient—love of homeland as it was in Britain during the war, and not an idealized world mission that was linked closely with revolutionary idealism in the Diaspora to create an ideal society. This exchange continued to stir controversy in the pages of *Commentary* magazine and other Jewish forums.[14]

The Yiddish theater and singers have a devoted audience in Israel today and there is a host of degree-granting programs offered by Israeli universities and evening schools in Yiddish linguistics, language and literature.

Yiddish and Hebrew in the United States—The Census Figures

The continued decline of Yiddish and growth of Hebrew is also evident in the United States, where a new community of ex–Israelis (*Yordim*[15]) is now settled. From a pre-war (1939) population of more than nine million Yiddish speakers throughout the world, the number had been reduced to under half by the end of the war in 1945. The Yiddish press in New York City reached a high point in the early 1930s, when daily circulation was almost half a million. The number of speakers currently in the United States is rapidly dwindling and includes all those with a rudimentary knowledge. In Israel there are no more than 250,000, and in Russia there are today less than 100,000, almost all of whom are elderly, bilingual or multilingual in Russian and several other languages.[16]

The U.S. Census shows a steep decline among Yiddish speakers in spite of recent popular attempts to maintain the language. In data on mother tongue claimants collected by the U.S. Census in 1970, Yiddish still stood as the sixth most common mother tongue foreign language in the United States, with just over a million and a half claimants, behind Spanish, German, Italian, French and Polish. Most young people study Hebrew either because of religious obligations (often at the behest of their parents) or else as an identification with the vibrant Israeli society, usually as a result of a visit there. In contrast, few young people conceive of Yiddish as anything but a somber reminder of the Holocaust.

In a special study by American Community Survey Reports, made with the cooperation of the U.S. Census Bureau on foreign language use in the home, the 49.7 percent drop of Yiddish speakers from 1980 to 2007 was the largest of any of the languages recorded, and the total of number of Hebrew speakers (mostly *yordim*) was 214,000, considerably more than the 159,000 Yiddish speakers!

American Community Service Reports, U.S. Census Bureau. www.census.gov/acs/www. Languages Spoken at Home. 1980, 1990, 2000, and 2007. Number of speakers.

	1980	1990	2000	2007
Yiddish	316,000	214,000	170,000	159,000
Hebrew				214,000

Hebrew's Victory—There Was No Alternative

Hebrew's success was the result of a combination of factors and unique circumstances that other nations were unable to duplicate. Jews migrating to Palestine had no other common language, and no other argument could so successfully verify the Jewish attachment to the Land of Israel. Countless everyday documents, scrolls, archives, letters, tombstones, and monuments from past millennia written and carved on stone, wood, clay, papyrus and paper have been uncovered, all of which "speak Hebrew," confirming the Jewish attachment to the land. As Hillel Halkin put it so succinctly, "Any alternative to Hebrew would have meant the loss of Zionism's historical content, the political consequences of which would have been to degrade the movement into the mere colonizing enterprise its enemies always viewed it as being and so doom it in advance."[17]

8. Negation of the Golah (Exile) and the Hebraic Identity of a New Nation

As dissatisfaction with the British Mandate grew, a clandestine underground emerged and began to contest the official Zionist leadership. These movements made more and more use of the term "Ivri" (Hebrew) as an adjective to express their instinctive attachment to the language, soil and landscapes of the homeland, and their creativity in music, song, literature, dance, and humor, as nationally "Hebrew" rather than "Jewish."[1] Zionism amounted to a revolution in traditional Jewish life and the majority secular elements sought to include every aspect of social, economic and political life. This was the most ambitious response to a challenge and dilemma facing an oppressed people.

The term was used prominently in the biblical passage in which Jonah proudly asserts his identity: "IVRI Anochi" (I am a Hebrew!). Seeking to escape God's command to fulfill a mission, Jonah boards a ship bound for Tarshish. When the ship is struck by a storm, the sailors seek to discover why the gods have deserted them and threaten disaster:

> And they said everyone to his fellow, Come, and let us cast lots, that we may know for whose cause this evil is upon us. So they cast lots, and the lot fell upon Jonah. Then said they unto him, Tell us, we pray thee, for whose cause this evil is upon us; what is thine occupation? and whence comest thou? What is thy country and of what people art thou? And he said unto them, "I am a Hebrew; and I fear the Lord, the God of heaven, which hath made the sea and the dry land."[2]

The passage was deemed the most appropriate to inculcate a sense of pride in the new Zionist movement's attachment to land and language, imitating Jonah, who first tried to hide his identity. These passages are part of the book of Jonah, which is read in its entirety on Yom Kippur—an indication of its importance.

The Zionist movement embraced new cultural elements to separate and institutionalize a distinct Hebrew identity, starting with language[3] and liter-

Right: A 1958 Israeli stamp celebrating the 25th anniversary of the Makkabi Games (Jewish Olympics) in Israel, showing the hammer-throw event.

ature,[4] but extending to personal and family names and different attitudes toward male-female relationships, child care, courtship and marriage, work, clothing, sports, military training, seamanship, the home, a love of nature, the cinema,[5] the nature of a new national identity based on the biblical or pre-exilic past,[6] and even a different cuisine and cooking than in the *Golah* (exile), featuring eggplant, chickpeas, olive oil and citrus fruit.

Ben-Yehuda's Campaign and the Fierce Opposition

The Zionist "elite" emerged at the end of the nineteenth century to propagate Hebrew, teach it in primary schools, and follow Ben-Yehuda's pioneering work. They were all volunteers and "powerless" in the traditional sense of being without financial means, the support of the authorities, access to mass media, or organizational tools. Resistance from the Orthodox religious community in Palestine was immediate and determined.

The Orthodox in Jerusalem acted aggressively against Ben-Yehuda—they even refused to bury his children and denounced him to the Turkish authorities, leading to his imprisonment. In several of the agricultural colonies, teachers of Hebrew were threatened or expelled because they had gone too far by promoting Hebrew as the language of instruction in secular subjects.

Hebraization of Personal and Family Names

The renaming process started with Eliezer Ben-Yehuda himself, who had been "Perelman" before arriving in Palestine. Many new Hebrew speakers arriving in Palestine chose first names, not the traditional ones from the Bible but those symbolizing hope, optimism, wild animals and nature, such as Rina (Joy), Geulah (Redemption), Rakefet (Cyclamen), Narkis (Narcissus), Tikvah (Hope), Zohar (Shining Light), Tal (Dew), Dror (Freedom), Ŝaĥar (Dawn), Ilan (Tree), Nitzan (Bud of a Plant), and Ayal and Ayala (Male/Female Deer).

Some even selected the names of shady characters from the Scriptures not previously used by Jews in Europe, such as Nimrod (mighty hunter), Boaz, Ehud and Yoav.[7] In 1944, the Zionist leadership and the Jewish National Council proclaimed the "Year of Naturalization and the Hebrew Name" and published a booklet that contained guidelines on the creation of new Hebrew surnames.

Many immigrants to modern Israel changed their names to erase memories of the oppressive Russian, Austrian, and Polish "exile countries" where Jews had often been humiliated. Although certain "typical Jewish" names,[8] particularly those ending in -berg, -stein or –man, are actually of German origin, and those ending in -sky and -vitz are Slavic, they nevertheless came to be regarded as reminiscent of a humiliating past.

The switch to Hebrew surnames was spearheaded by the principal leaders of the Zionist movement, so Schneor Zalman Rubashov became Shazar, Yitzhak Shimshelevitz became Ben-Zvi and Golda Meyerson became Meir. It is interesting to note that the Revisionist/right-wing leaders within the Zionist movement, such as Menachem Begin and Joseph Klausner, did not change their names, and neither did Israel's first president, Chaim Weizmann.

After the establishment of the State of Israel, Ben-Gurion, in an order to the IDF soldiers, wrote, "It is desirable that every commanding officer (from Squadron Commander to Chief of Staff) should change his surname, whether German, English, Slavic, French or foreign in general, to a Hebrew surname, in order to be a role model for his soldiers. The Israel Defense Forces must be Hebrew in spirit, vision, and in all internal and external expressions."[9] A "Committee for Hebrew Names" was established to supervise the implementation of this order, whose task was to assist in the choice of a Hebrew name.

The Zionist movement not only pleaded for *Aliyah* (immigration to Israel) but also desired to create a new national identity in the image of a native Eretz-Yisraeli ("Palestinian Jew" in the language of the period 1920–1948), who would be different from the Yiddish-speaking Jew of the Diaspora and the image of the "non-productive" *shtetl*. Israeli banknotes in the 1960s featured a trio of muscular, young, healthy men and women engaged in the military, agriculture, fishing and industry as symbolic of the new Israeli nation, and traditionally regarded as "non–Jewish occupations."

It was no accident that many of the leading Hebrew writers who settled in Palestine or were born there and were active in the 1930s, 1940s and 1950s Hebraized their family names—Ratosh, Amir, Meged, Shamir, Tammuz, Yizhar, Bartov, Guri, Shacham, Aloni and Kenan. After the establishment of the State of Israel, there was still the attitude that the Hebraization of family names should continue, in order to get rid of names with a Diaspora sound. Israel's pre-state leader and first prime minister, David Ben-Gurion, was very committed to Hebrew names (he changed his surname from Gryn to Ben-

Top: Israeli ½ shekel banknote; female soldier from "Naḥal" unit of troops, who also receive agricultural training. *Middle:* Israeli 1 shekel banknote; Israeli fisherman. *Bottom:* Israeli 5 shekel banknote; industrial worker.

Gurion). He endeavored to influence many people to adopt "real" Hebrew family names and convinced Herzl Rosenblum to sign Israel's Declaration of Independence as "Herzl Vardi," a pen name (and later he changed it to his legal name). Nine more signatories of the document would later go on to Hebraize their names as well.

Yitzhak Ben-Zvi, leader of the Labor movement and historian and second president of the State of Israel, was a founding member of the Socialist-Zionist (Ahdut ha-Avodah) Party and active in the *Haganah,* a member of the Jewish National Council, and a signee of the Declaration of Independence. He expanded on Ben-Gurion's views:

> Our surnames are mostly of foreign origin, which cling to exile ... even names based on Hebrew first names were damaged and distorted from the original ... by German and English suffixes, like "son" or "sohn" and the Slavic "in," "ovich," "ovsky" and "shvili." These surnames fill the air and the pages of our newspaper, the posters and announcements in our streets and public squares ... it is indeed not really clear if the hardship of this inheritance which remained with us as a result of the Middle Ages and subsequent ghettoization should be tolerated.[10]

Even a number of rabbinic authorities encouraged Hebraic first names, but the movement also provoked opposition among those Jews who saw it as an act of erasing part of Jewish history and their origins. Some, including those who were committed Zionists, were, of course, emotionally attached to their Diaspora last names, and could not accept a dogmatic Hebraic-Zionist contention that such names would be out of place in the *Yishuv* (modern Jewish community in Palestine). One anecdotal story used as a joke to represent this view tells of an Israeli diplomat who told David Ben-Gurion, "I will change my name if you can find me one non-Jew named Lifshitz."

The debate over the issue of Hebraization of surnames continued during the Mandate period and in the formative years of the new state of Israel. For example, the famous archeologist and Israeli general Yigael Sukennik changed his name to Yigael Yadin and Levi Shkolnik, Israel's third president, became Levi Eshkol.

There is also an opposite trend under way that has been noticeable for the past thirty years—returning to one's roots just as in the United States (i.e., people re-adopting the name their family previously abandoned for the sake of "Israeliness"). These include Israeli writer Yitzhak Orpaz, who restored his family's original family name of "Averbuch." His decision is indicative of the dilemma of dual identities felt by many in Israel.

The vast immigration from the ex-Soviet Union during much of the 1990s of mostly Russian speakers has profoundly changed the Israeli cultural landscape with the number and variety of Russian-language publications, radio and a general weakening of the practice of Hebraizing names, as part of the marked tendency of these immigrants to cling to their specific Russian linguistic and cultural identity. A recent eye-catching and ear-catching example is the Israeli minister of tourism, Stas Misezhnikov. In spite of his right-wing nationalist (and anti-religious!) stand on many issues, Misezhnikov did not feel impelled to change his clearly Slavic first name and surname. There was no public pressure on him to do so, as there would have been on an Israeli minister during the country's early years.

The following principles were recommended by a committee for changing a foreign surname to Hebrew:

1. Change of vocalization where there is already a close Yiddish variant of an original Hebrew name: Leib becomes Lev.
2. Retention of the basic consonants of a foreign name that can be equated with a Hebrew word: Borg (originally meaning mountain in German-Scandinavian) becomes Barak (lightning in Hebrew).
3. Shortening by omitting a "foreign ending": Rosenberg becomes Rosen or Rozen.
4. Shortening a name with a Hebrew meaning by omitting the foreign suffix: Yakobovitch (Jacobowitz, Jacobowicz) becomes Ya'akovi.
5. Translating the foreign name into Hebrew according to the meaning: Abramovich (Abramowicz, Abramowitz—son of Abram) becomes Ben-Avraham.

With regard to first names adopted as surnames:

1. Name of a father or mother murdered during the Shoah: Bat Miriam, Ben Moshe (*bat* and *ben* are the Hebrew equivalents of daughter and son).
2. Son or daughter who fell in battle: Avinoam (avi = my father).
3. Brother or sister who was killed or fell: Achimeir (aḣi = my brother).
4. Beloved or admired biblical figure: Shaul, Davidi, Yitzhaki, Gidon (Gideon).

Names were also changed by using names of places, plants or sites in Eretz Yisrael—Hermoni, Eilat, Gilad, Yarden (Jordan), Negbi, Galili.

Some of the most common translated Hebraized names are as follows:

Goldberg = Har-Paz

Steinberg = Har-Even

Rosenstein = Even-Shoshan

Meyerson = Meir or Ben-Meir

Mendelssohn = Ben-Menachem (son of Menachem) (Yiddish diminutive: Mendel)

Davidson = Ben-David

Wilner = Vilnai (both meaning "from Vilna")

Often a name was chosen in Hebrew when it had approximately a similar sound or was a partial translation:

> Rosen becomes Shoshani; or Vardi from Vered, meaning rose.
>
> Shkolnik (a yeshiva student in Yiddish) becomes either Lamdan (a student or learner in Hebrew), or else the similarity in sound makes it into Eshkol, meaning "cluster of grapes." Thus we get Levi Eshkol.
>
> Feld becomes Sadeh (field). Israel's Palmach commander was Yitzhak Sadeh.
>
> Loewe becomes Lavi, meaning "lion"; Lempel, meaning "a little lamp" in Yiddish, becomes Lapid in Hebrew, meaning "torch."

Humor

How have Israelis managed to survive psychologically once again after so many conflicts, wars, acts of terrorism and threats of annihilation? Jewish humor, like every other aspect of life, was conditioned by centuries of existence as an outcast minority subject to scorn, rejection and, at times, ostracism from the rest of society. A special humor developed that was created by Jews for Jews reflecting, and often mocking, this fact of life, particularly for those individuals who could not simply accept with equanimity the notion that this was the price they had to pay for their "election" as a "chosen people" with a divine mission to bring the Torah as a "Light Unto the Nations."

Part of the Jewish means of adaptation was to develop a darker, more sarcastic kind of humor than other nations. Many scholars assert that this sense of humor helped them survive. Laughing at difficult situations became a defense mechanism that enabled them to endure. The underlying tenet of the humor was that Jews found themselves in a situation in which they had no power or weapons to change it. A favorite technique that became a staple of Jewish humor in both the Diaspora and Israel is to turn the tables on the enemy:

> Ezra, a Jewish gentleman, was sitting in Central Park one day, and his best friend Moshe came up to him and asked him why he was reading a particular newspaper. "You know, Ezra, that paper is anti–Semitic."
>
> Ezra replies, "I know, Moshe, but I love hearing so many good things that come out of this paper. They think the Jews control Hollywood, the government, the labor unions, big business, all are rich and live in beautiful homes with big cars and beautiful blond mistresses. It's great being a Jew!"

This kind of humor also reinforces two contrasting stereotypes widely accepted by Gentile society in spite of the fact that they appear to be mutually exclusive. These are a picture of the Diaspora Jews as (1) inept, clumsy, inhibited, naive or starry-eyed dreamers totally out of their depth, as demonstrated by the great number of Yiddish words such as *schlemiel, shmendrik, klutz, putz* and *schmuck,* typified by Woody Allen and Jack Benny, or (2) brash, loud, vulgar, aggressive, sarcastic and assertive, challenging the polite and often hypocritical niceties of Gentile society, as signified by the now thoroughly Americanized Yiddish words *chutzpah* and *mamzer,* as typified by the Marx Brothers and Mel Brooks. Milton Berle, Sid Caesar and Jerry Lewis were successful at playing both types simultaneously in what could be called "the aggressive schlemiel."

Just as the first type of humor became identified with Yiddish in the Diaspora, Israeli humor definitely tends toward the second type, but with the added dimension of the Hebrew language. Many observers find humor in Israel more aggressive, "dark," and intense, as befits a people who have thrown off the acquired characteristics of an oppressed minority expected to defer to the majority and forced in the past to use humor as the weapon of the weak.

What, then, has happened to humor in Israel now that the Jews are a sovereign nation there? Jewish humor as social satire was frequently used to deflate the pretensions and arrogance of the rich and powerful on behalf of the poor and has been transposed onto the national scene in a similar vein today, with Israel as the heroic David threatened by its enemies.

Some sensitive Jewish critics in the Diaspora find that Israeli humor has, however, gone too far and is too blunt, tough, and iconoclastic, even macabre and vulgar. They often miss out on the delightful playfulness of Modern Hebrew slang that often defies translation, and for the same reasons that Yiddish did. The language and humor are inseparable from the social and political environment. In Israel, life differs drastically from Jewish life elsewhere in spite of the common historical origin.

War and the intense anxiety produced by horrific acts of terrorism must be deflected somehow, and many Israelis face them head on, often shocking many religious and Diaspora Jews as grossly insensitive. Outsiders also find coarse jokes about the Orthodox, new immigrants unfamiliar with the Hebrew language, or Arabs offensive in the same way that Polish Americans found so-called Polish jokes demeaning. But perhaps these jokes represent a freedom for Jews to finally make someone else the "victim."

In peacetime, Jews in Israel cannot blame "the other" (i.e., the Gentiles or even the Arabs). Having lived there for several years, I found that the Israeli target for satire and even invective was well placed—the country's politicians, political system and maddening bureaucracy, often flavored by an explicit envy of American life, popular culture and personalities, much like an admiring distant cousin.

Self-deprecating jokes are still popular, although the sophisticated comedian often implies that Israelis aren't really proud of the way their lives have been forcibly shaped by the many problems and tensions that are part of daily life: for example, "An Israeli, a Russian, and an American are sitting in a restaurant. A waiter comes by and says, 'Excuse me, but we have a shortage of meat.' The American asks, 'What's "shortage?"' The Russian asks, 'What's "meat?"' The Israeli asks, 'What's "excuse me?"'"

Nevertheless, there are two important aspects of Israeli humor that set it apart from that of the Diaspora. The first stresses pride in Israel's accomplishments and a "can do" mentality in the face of overwhelming odds—precisely the opposite of the poor *shlemiel* stereotype. This trend began long before Israeli independence. Native-born Hebrew-speaking "sabras" have been represented in the public mind and literature of the early pioneer generations as strong, brave, somewhat coarse, and outspoken, although often gentle, childish, and uncultivated.

A collection of anecdotes in *Jokes and Witticisms* by Alter Duryanov tells the following story[11]:

> Tel Aviv, Herzl Street. A group of children pour out of the Herzlia Gymnasium (academic high school). Two famous Yiddishists are passing by, having come to visit Palestine [probably just before or after World War I], and the greater Yiddishist says to his junior colleague: "The Zionists boast that Hebrew is becoming a natural tongue for the children of Palestine. I will now show you that they are lying. I will tweak one of the boys' ears and I promise you that he will not cry out ima ["mother" in Hebrew], but mame [Yiddish]." So saying, he approached one of the boys and tweaked his ear. The boy turned on him and shouted: hamor ["donkey" in Hebrew]. The famous Yiddishist turned to his friend: "I am afraid that the Zionists are right."

The whole point of the joke is not simply the change in language but rather the change in a new generation in their own land and brought up to defend themselves. The image of brazen Israeli youth standing in sharp contrast to the traditional restrained behavior of Jews in the Diaspora became a staple in much humor. This gap between the generations was in part caused by the greater rapidity with which younger immigrants learned Hebrew. A popular poster pictured a father learning the language from his daughter!

The Hebrew School System Tarbut "in Exile"

Throughout Europe and in much of Latin America and South Africa, "Tarbut" (Culture), a vibrant Zionist educational movement and Hebrew school system, arose to create a new sense of nationhood distinct from those Jews who looked to traditional responses as their "solution" to the problem of growing anti–Semitism (including working for the cause of civic equality as citizens of the nation-states in which they lived, attempts at assimilation and rejection of any identification with any sense of a Jewish nationality or religious community, and commitment to some kind of cultural autonomy based largely on Yiddish culture). In the more liberal democratic states in the Baltic and in Czechoslovakia, and even autocratic, Catholic, and ultra-nationalist Poland, the presence of the Zionist political and Hebrew cultural alliance created a true Jewish "Palestinian Diaspora," demanding respect and acknowledgment from both the authorities and the local nationalist forces of a genuine modern nationalist–Jewish minority committed to a cultural transformation and emigration.

In his semi-autobiographical work, Israeli author Amos Oz recounts the close connections his family maintained with relatives in Europe and the sense of wonder, confidence, creativity and inspiration that infused the Zionist-Hebrew alliance among young Jews in Eastern Europe in coping with the prevailing sense of apprehension, depression and fear that increasingly paralyzed Jewish communities throughout the world.

> Nobody imagined what was really in store, but already in the twenties almost everyone knew deep down that there was no future for the Jews with Stalin or in Poland, or anywhere else in eastern Europe, and so the pull of Palestine became stronger and stronger. Not with everyone, naturally. The religious Jews were very much against it, and so were the Bundists, the Yiddishists, the communists, and the assimilated Jews who thought they were already more Polish than Paderewski.... But many ordinary Jews in Rovno in the twenties were keen that their children should learn Hebrew and go to Tarbuth ... and the echoes that came back to us from the Land were simply wonderful—the young people were just waiting, when would your turn come? Meanwhile everyone read newspapers in Hebrew, argued, sang songs from the Land of Israel, recited Bialik and Tschernikhowsky, split up into rival factions and parties, ran up uniforms and banners, there was a kind of tremendous excitement about everything national.[12]

The *Tarbut* תרבות movement was a network of secular, Hebrew-language schools in pre-war Poland, Romania and Lithuania. Hebrew was the main language of instruction at all levels. This network was established in 1922, when the first *Tarbut* conference was held in Warsaw. It operated kindergartens, elementary schools, secondary schools, teachers' seminaries, adult education courses, lending libraries and a publishing house that produced pedagogical materials, textbooks and children's periodicals.

By 1939, it had some 45,000 students enrolled in about 270 institutions, and these included about 25 percent of all students enrolled in Jewish schools

8. Negation of the Golah (Exile) and the Hebraic Identity

Top: Israeli 10 shekel banknote honoring Hebrew poet Chaim Nachman Bialik. *Bottom:* Ze'ev Jabontinsky on 100 shekel Israeli banknote.

in Poland. It comprised 9 percent of Jewish students in all Polish schools![13] The leading names in the Hebrew revival, such as poet Chaim Nachman Bialik and Zionist leaders Nahum Sokolow and Vladimir Ze'ev Jabotinsky, were active supporters and fundraisers. Miraculously, during the war years, a few schools (notably one in the city of Bukhara, Uzbekistan) continued to function under the auspices of the Soviet authorities, serving the large population of Jewish refugees from Poland in spite of Soviet rejection of the Polish government in exile based in London. The graduating students took high school matriculation exams and, as a result were able to continue their higher education after the war.

The school system's own publishing house produced *Shibolim* ("Ears of Wheat"), a Warsaw biweekly published during 1922–1923, which featured both vowelled and unvowelled text, making it suitable for children of all ages. It also ran *Olami*, a biweekly from 1935 to 1939, for grades 1–7, and much of its material included current events in Palestine alongside information about Jewish life in Poland.

A few similar schools continue to exist today, but they are few in number and a pale reflection of the pre-war movement, with its largely secular outlook.

In *A Tale of Love and Darkness*, Amoz Oz's aunt Sonja, a native of Rovno, tells in her own words what she and her sister felt after finally being able to leave Poland just before the outbreak of the war and what her "homecoming" to the Land of Israel meant after her many years in the *Tarbut* movement:

> Early one morning, I can even tell you the precise date and time ... it was exactly three days before the end of 1938 just after Hannukah—exactly before the end of 1938, Wednesday 28th December—it happened to be very clear, almost cloudless day.... And suddenly, almost in an instant, above the line of the clouds the winter sun appeared and below the clouds was the city of Tel Aviv; row after row of square, white-painted houses, quite unlike houses in a town or a village in Poland or Ukraine, quite unlike Rovno or Warsaw or Trieste but very like the pictures on the wall in every classroom at Tarbut.... So that I was surprised and not surprised. I can't describe how all at once the joy rose up in my throat, suddenly I wanted to shout and sing. This is mine! All mine!
>
> That evening Tsvi and Fania took me out to see Tel Aviv. We walked to Allenby Street and Rothschild Boulevard, because Ben Yehuda Street was not considered really part of Tel Aviv then. I remember how clean and nice everything looked at first glance in the evening, with the benches and street lights and all the signs in Hebrew; as if the whole of Tel Aviv was just a very nice display in the playground of the Tarbut school [page 193].

Do Hebrew Words Carry the Same Connotations for the Secular-Nationalist Israeli and the Traditional Observant Orthodox Jew in Israel?

As early as 1926, Gershom Sholem raised a provocative and sensitive issue relating to the modernization and secularization of the Hebrew language with Franz Rosenzweig, which touched upon the contradiction of such a trend with all the previous literary spiritual and messianic character of the Biblical, Mishnaic texts and the mystical trends in Judaism.

Sholem argued that, paradoxically, a Hebrew nationalism built on a "national language" could never really remain wholly secular. This contradiction can still be observed in the language employed by Israel's political spectrum, in which the "Right" includes both anti-religious, secular nationalists and those in Orthodox circles who envision an apocalyptic, messianic End of Days scenario. Sholem's views were formed by his life-long opposition to radical or extreme forms of nationalism, and he hoped that Zionism could escape this fate. He remained a committed secularist, and secularism played an important role in his views on Jewish history and the study of Kabbalah, but he remained very aware and sensitive to the "holy" character the language had acquired through millennia of history and tradition that had been "absorbed" by many words. In Scholem's opinion, the mystical, mythical and emotional components were at least as important as the rational ones reached by the rabbis versed in the Talmud and enshrined in the minutiae of the Halakha. These mystical and emotional trends such as Hassidism, the Kabbalah and Zohar paid special attention to what they believed was the "inherent" significance of Hebrew and even their numerical value (each letter in the alphabet bears a numerical value and words are thus "summed" to give a total result) according to the system known as Gematria, far beyond their purely utilitarian meaning as used by secular writers, the Zionist parties and nationalists. Similarly, for many devout Jews, the notion that Hebrew could become like any modern vernacular full of slang and profanity was an anathema.

As a result of his criticism of his father's German nationalism and bourgeois lifestyle, he was expelled from the family home and forced to seek the company of Eastern European Jewish immigrants in Berlin, among whom were many prominent liberal-minded Zionists. They had an important influence on his life, especially after he immigrated to Palestine in 1923.

During the Mandate (1920–1948), the dominant force in the Zionist movement was decidedly secular and aspired to create a national home or eventual autonomous community/state in which Hebrew would be the national language and devoid of any original religious connotation. This view changed considerably among the elite in the new state after 1948, who began to regard Israel in "apocalyptic" terms, not as a normal nation-state united by territory and language, but rather the Holy Land of all the Jewish people, "A Light Unto the Nations."

The first vision did not seek to make Israel the nation-state of all Jews— only those who Herzl had predicted would not be able or wish to assimilate. The strong Hebrew national character of the Jews in Palestine was a matter of choice and affiliation either with Herzl's original Zionist vision (a state of the Jews—'Medinat ha yehudim'—that is, only those who wished to establish it, whatever their motivation) **OR** with the exclusivist apocalyptic vision of the now current leadership in Israel ("A Jewish State"—HaMedinah haYehudit) that seeks to speak for all Jews worldwide and believes that they are destined to affiliate with Israel and eventually become its citizens. Obviously, the two terms have a different significance for non–Jews who are Israeli citizens. One asks them to regard the state as principally, but not exclusively, Jewish, whereas "The Jewish State" tells them that they cannot truly identify with it.

The Growing Gap Between the Diaspora and Israel— Another Dilemma

The disinterest in the Modern Hebrew language and the sometimes poor quality of instruction throughout the Diaspora are an unfortunate result of the decline in worldwide devotion to the national rebirth that Zionism sponsored. Three quarters of American Jews have never visited Israel and few Jews in the Diaspora are familiar today with such beloved singers as Zohar Argov,[14] Haim Moshe, Boaz Shar'abi, Yehoram Gaon, Shlomo Ber and even the old favorites from the era of 1948–1956 like Shoshana Damari and Yaffa Yarkoni. The Hebrew culture of Israel, especially in song, dance, popular music, design of embroidery, jewelry, and religious ornaments, has a major Sephardi-Mizrahi (Eastern), particularly Yemenite, component,[15] with many more metaphors and colorful language than most current pop songs.

In a national sense, the Hebrew language, so successful in Israel, has, in the Diaspora, retreated, following the disappearance of the dynamic atmosphere of the campfire, the pioneers and victorious Israeli army of 1948, 1956 and 1967 that produced dozens of wonderful songs.

There is much about contemporary Israeli society and its rough edges, as well as what has been called "post–Zionism,"[16] that made idealism wear thin: the litany of daily frustrations, the pressure of an intense hothouse atmosphere of constant tension, the political involvement of many ultra–Orthodox and their rejection of any other mind-set or alternative form of Jewish identity, as well as an aggressive, archaic, obtuse and obdurate bureaucracy that exerted a heavy toll on many Zionist idealists, becoming the "final straw" issue that drove them away.

In Europe and South America, more traditional Jewish communities (or older ones than the American community) devoted more attention and enthusiasm to cultivating a Hebrew-oriented secular and religious Jewish education. Along the lines of the Tarbut movement, schools continue to flourish in Mexico, Chile and Argentina, and in European countries such as France, Holland, Denmark and Belgium.

Jabotinsky's View on the Unity of Hebrew Nationalism and Language

Ze'ev Jabotinsky, charismatic leader of the Zionist Revisionist Movement, regarded as the "father figure of the political Right" in Israel, was a monumental literary as well as major political personality, a talented author and poet with a fantastic capacity to master languages. He stressed that it was the inherent right of the majority nation even in bilingual or multinational states to maintain its language and culture in a dominant position, while at the same time allowing loyal minorities to ensure that their own identity enjoyed a measure of state respect and acknowledgment. Acting with Jabotinsky, writer and editor Yechiel Heschel Yevin promulgated "Twelve Principles of the Constitution of Freedom." He provides the clearest intellectual link between the political nationalism as advocated by Jabotinsky and the messianic spirit of poet Uri Zvi Greenberg, who clearly foresaw and warned against the coming Holocaust as early as the late 1930s. The twelve principles recalled some of Maimonides' own "Thirteen Principles of the Faith":

> Principle Number 1—The transition from the Exile to Eretz Israel is not a physical move, but a move toward the concretization of the state concept on the territory requiring a radical and fundamental change in the thought patterns, feelings, approach and innermost structure of the soul of the individual and the collective. Zionism is THE HEBREW REVOLUTION.
>
> Principle 3—The adoption of the Hebrew language is not a mere change from one vernacular to another, but a manifestation of the new spiritual transformation, a concept based on the classical philological view that language is the innate expression of the soul and world outlook of a people.
>
> Principle 11—Hebrew visionary literature should guide the liberation movement and determine its goals.

The Canaanite "Heresy"

For approximately two decades, starting in the mid–1930s, a divisive, so-called "heretical" (by its detractors) cultural and political movement known as "Canaanism" rejected Zionism as insufficiently militant in the face of Nazi anti–Semitism and the British conciliatory policy toward the Arabs. It also sought to divorce itself from the two-thousand-year-old control of Judaism by the rabbinical authorities and called for the creation of a new "Hebrew Nation," based in part on the sovereign Hebrew identity and language of the ancient Israelite kingdoms.[17] It also called for the inclusion of the non–Jewish population in Palestine in a Semitic alliance, and for the beginning of a war of liberation from British imperialism.

This iconoclastic view regarded Israel and its ancient neighbors of Phoenicia, Moab and Edom as part of a great Semitic, non–Arab Mediterranean culture that was later submerged and obliterated by the Muslim conquests of the seventh century CE. In the radical Canaanite-Hebrew nationalist view, the ancient prophets of Israel had formed a traditional-agrarian reaction to the maritime and imperialist orientation of the Phoenician-Canaanite civilization (which included the alliance mentioned in the Bible between King Hiram of Tyre and King Solomon). Phoenician merchants and seamen paved a path across the Mediterranean and established colonies and various enterprises, mainly in mining, fishing and agriculture. Their major new center in Carthage eventually became the greatest power in the western Mediterranean and challenged Rome for supremacy.

The principal founder and advocate of these views was the historian, mathematician, sociologist and researcher in Semitic languages, Adolphe Gourevitch. Born in Kiev, and a graduate of the University of Paris, he took the pen name A. G. Horon and established close ties with the *ha-Aretz* journalist Uriel Shelach (writing under the pen name of Yonatan Ratosh), whom he met in Paris in 1938. Together, they formulated "A New Hebrew Consciousness." This ideology grew in popularity during the anti–British underground struggle and Israel's War of Independence, but it was submerged by the tidal wave of immigrants who arrived with little or no previous activism in the Zionist movement and knowledge of Modern Hebrew.

In June 1939, Horon wrote in the journal *Shem/Revue d'Action* that, in order to regain their homeland, Jews must become Hebrews and disassociate themselves from Zionist contentions: "One need not hide the birth pangs of a new nation behind a Jewish veil—in an attempt to convince the whole world that there is finally something happening in Palestine, when it is actually something Hebrew in Canaan that is finally taking place."[18]

As early as 1943, Ratosh issued a call to mobilize "Hebrew youth" in the midst of the Second World War to fight British imperialism and justify the struggle for independence, NOT on the basis of the 2,000 years of Jewish existence in the Diaspora, but rather the reality of the new Hebrew-speaking nation.

Although scorned and ridiculed by the Zionist establishment, the Canaanite ideology attracted a number of influential intellectuals and won converts among a small portion of the native-born Jewish population in Palestine or those who had arrived in the country at an early age and for whom Hebrew was their first language. Aiding the movement to win adherents was the terrible psychological blow of the Holocaust, which only the so-called dissident movements—the more militant "Stern Gang" (the Fighters for the Freedom of Israel, known by the acronym לח"י Lohamei leḤerut Yisrael; LEḤI) and those younger native-born Palestinian Jews who identified with the Canaanite movement—had accurately predicted. They argued that it was the product of the minority–Jewish existence of the Diaspora, with its extreme pacifist traditions that deprived the Jews of a national will to exist. Such views have been an anathema to the Jewish establishment in the Diaspora and the Zionist movement and have given added ammunition to the claim that many Israelis are "Hebrew-speaking *goyim*."

Religious opponents (both Jewish and Christian) ridiculed any attempt to separate Jewish ethnic identity from traditional Judaism and the Orthodox mocked these ideas as fanciful flights from reality and as a "pagan" affront. For most Arabs and Islam, they are an even greater abomination; yet no matter how long the Arabization of the Near and Middle East has had time to perpetrate the eradication of the authentic original cultures of Mesopotamia, Egypt, Lebanon-Phoenicia, Israel, Malta and the Berber-speaking peoples of North Africa, it is evident that roots of these cultures, languages and nations endure.

A small Canaanite circle of writers, journalists, historians and artists continued to be active, running a periodical titled *Aleph* and writing for the Hebrew press for several decades following the establishment of the State of Israel. One of them, Amos Kenan (Hebrew for "Canaan"), in reminiscing about the Canaanite movement and the sense of history and pride he felt it bestowed, wrote a revealing essay, "Envy Tyre," in the daily newspaper *Yediot Ahronot* in 1982:

> I always had an attraction to this wonderful phenomenon called Tyre and Sidon, and as one who was born on the sands of Tel-Aviv on the coastal lowland, I feel a closeness to all that was, is and will be on the eastern shore of the Mediterranean which I am a part of, and which is a part of me. The Hebrew language which is my language today was 4,000 and 3,000 and 2,500 years ago the language spoken in Jerusalem, and Tyre, in Shechem and Sidon, in Jaffa and Ugarit ... and in Carthage. Tyre and Sidon and Jerusalem were two axes of one culture ... the spiritual one of Jerusalem and the material one of Carthage. In those days when the prophets of Israel tried to create a universal code of morality, the seamen of Tyre established their colonies.... Why shouldn't we feel a sense of pride in our proximity to that ancient contemporary of ours who stamped his image on the area, gave to the world writing and once sent his elephants across the Alps under Hannibal's leadership and momentarily brought mighty Rome itself in danger of destruction?[19]

Horon wrote an influential pamphlet in 1970 following Israel's victory in the Six-Day War, *The Land of Kedem—A Historical and Political Guide to the Near East*,[20] calling on Israelis to annex the territories and grant full citizenship to all the inhabitants willing to accept equality in a Hebrew-speaking nation. These views remained a distinct minority view but one that is clearly unambiguous in seeking to eliminate and divorce all concerns about the role of Judaism in the Israeli national identity.

The Uneasy Relationship Between Zionism and the Movement to Revitalize Hebrew in North America—A Dilemma

The Zionist Organization of America (ZOA) was founded in 1897 simultaneously with the first Zionist Congress, but it was not until 1916 that the major organization to promote and popularize the Hebrew language, *HaHistadrut Ha-Ivrit*, began. From the start there was a formal declaration of unity and cooperation but, as time revealed, the relationship was often problematic. From its inception, the ZOA was designed to promote sympathy for the Zionist cause and the adoption of the Balfour Declaration in 1917 ensured that it was dealing with a practical program and not an idealistic dream.

Little effort was made to take practical steps to convince the public and then plan for immigration and settlement of American or Canadian Jews in Palestine. However, when the *Histadrut Ivrit* began, the great majority of its members were themselves recent immigrants or the children of recent immigrants from Eastern Europe whose first language was Yiddish and who were struggling to learn and master English. Although sufficient in numbers to support several newspapers and periodicals, and even the publication of original Hebrew literature by talented writers who had learned Hebrew in their youth while in Europe, the audience for these publications dwindled rapidly. They came to be dependent on subsidies from the much larger and more financially stable ZOA.

The success of Zionist diplomacy in first the creation of the Partition Plan and then the State of Israel produced a renewed wave of support for Hebrew-language programs. This primarily took the form of summer camps among Jewish youth, but by the early 1960s, before the dramatic events culminating in the 1967 Six-Day War, the most proficient Hebrew speakers in North America had already emigrated and settled in Israel, where they carried on their work.

Dedicated teachers continued to do noble work but their resources were insufficient and many Jewish parents became apathetic and unwilling to support Hebrew education beyond the need to be conversant with synagogue prayer and ritual.

In summing up the impact of *HaHistadrut Ha-Ivrit* in the United States on the occasion of the organization's eightieth anniversary, Dr. Moshe Pelli, veteran Israeli scholar and long-time resident in the United States, had this to say: "Even though the Hebrew movement has always been a minority group within American Jewry, it has catered to the cultural elite of writers, educators, professors, rabbis and professionals. As such, it set the cultural and literary tone among its followers and was instrumental in establishing the pedagogic values and cultural criteria in American Hebrew education."[21]

The Hebrew-Yiddish Controversy in American Politics

The popularity and impressive achievements of the revival of spoken Hebrew got off to a very slow start in the United States due to the close linkage between the dominant Yiddish press and the left-wing stance of most American Jews that intensified during the 1930s. The three major Yiddish newspapers reached a combined circulation of close to half a million. Although attentive to events in Palestine and the Zionist movement, they gave little coverage to the language issue. The Jewish daily *Forward* (*Forvaerts*) began life as a Yiddish-language Jewish American national newspaper published in New York City in 1897, originally edited and published by the Socialist Labor Party. The *Forvaerts* became a leading U.S. metropolitan daily and reached a nationwide circulation of more than 275,000 in the early 1930s.[22] The much smaller communist newspaper in Yiddish strictly followed the party line from Moscow. The *Morgen Freiheit* (Morning Freedom), with about one-tenth the circulation, was, nevertheless, the largest foreign-language communist newspaper and was openly hostile to the entire Zionist enterprise until the Soviet vote in favor of the partition of Palestine in November 1947. A third daily, *Der Tag* (The Day), which began in 1914, was sympathetic to Zionism and friendly toward the Democratic Party and labor union activity but not hostile toward Hebrew.

In 1927, Zalman Shazar visited the United States on a tour to promote the Zionist movement and influence public opinion. In his memoirs, he recounted the surprise and astonishment of prominent Jewish socialist leader Victor Berger upon learning that Hebrew was actually a spoken language in Palestine. Berger was an immigrant from Germany who had settled in Milwaukee (where Golda Meir lived in her youth). He led the American Socialist Party and was a representative to the American Jewish Congress. Berger had argued during his time as editor of the socialist newspaper *The Leader* against "the reactionary nature of Zionism," sympathizing instead with the European socialist Yiddish Bund movement in Europe that sought to establish regional cultural autonomy.

Berger found it unbelievable that the Zionist workers' movement in Palestine was so strong that it had established a viable daily Hebrew newspaper and an extensive literature. He confessed to Shazar that he had never received accurate information about the language situation, but he knew that Hebrew was always "associated with clerical circles" and could therefore not be a progressive force. Not until Shazar actually pulled out of his pocket a copy of *Davar*—the newspaper of the Labor movement—could Berger actually accept that he had been mistaken. Berger was thrilled and raced into the adjoining room with the newspaper and shared the new information with his fellow workers and party members about a language that had come back to life after a long sleep. He had to explain to them that the newspaper was not written in Yiddish, like the *Forvaerts*, but in what he called "Biblese!"

An hour later, Shazar addressed a public gathering attended by Berger, his wife (a counselor for cultural affairs for the city of Milwaukee), their daughter and other members of the Milwaukee *Leader*. Although Shazar's talk was not on their agenda, Berger warmly endorsed the movement to promote Hebrew among the Jewish workers in Palestine and their union activity.[23]

It is no wonder that many of the traditionalist Jewish communities in Eastern Europe speaking Yiddish (including the Orthodox religious segment, the Bundists who favored cultural autonomy and the communists) all realized how much of a challenge Modern Hebrew and Zionism presented to them, their way of life and their political views.

The modern renaissance of Hebrew created a national modern form of economic activity, song, dance, literature and other elements of popular culture drawing upon the ancient past that still bear radical secular and nationalist overtones. Nothing less could solve the growing dilemma and danger that faced the Jews of Europe on the eve of the Holocaust. Only a radical transformation that laid the groundwork of nationhood afforded what would have been an escape route for an entire people who were trapped by the Nazis' genocidal plans. Yet these drastic transformations have also increased the emotional distance between much of the Diaspora and the modern State of Israel and its dynamic Hebrew culture, a dilemma that continues to grow with each passing year.

9. Baltic Rebirth and the Zionist Staging Ground for a Jewish State

Lithuania: Zionist Staging Ground for a Jewish State

In no other part of the Diaspora was there such a vibrant full-blown cultural life in both Yiddish and Hebrew as in the Baltic States between the two world wars. What emerged was a decisive achievement—the formative period of the flourishing of Modern Hebrew language and culture, and official recognition of an educational system based on instruction in it. All Jews were subject to the decisions of *Va'ad HaAretz* (Jewish National Council) in Lithuania, and the country's Zionist minister of Jewish affairs, Max Soloveichik, often delivered speeches praising Jewish autonomy and declaring, "We are rehearsing here towards a Jewish state."[1]

The need of the Baltic States to mobilize international Jewish support for their independence and territorial claims, especially Lithuania's claim to its historic capital Vilnius (also known as Vilna in Polish, Russian and Yiddish), resulted in liberal constitutions guaranteeing minority rights and cultural autonomy. A Lithuanian delegation to the Paris Peace Conference at the end of World War I pledged that the Jews would enjoy full national-cultural autonomy. The promise was kept and in 1920 the Jewish community was recognized as a legal institution with the right to legislate binding ordinances. On a visit to Kaunas in honor of the local newspaper *Die Yiddishe Shtimme*, Chaim Bialik also added his appreciation of the rights accorded the Jewish minority and stated, "If Vilna is known as the Yerushalayim deLita [Jerusalem of Lithuania], then all of Lithuania should be known as the Eretz-Yisrael deGaluta [The Land of Israel in Exile]."[2]

The principal language of instruction in the main Jewish academic high school (gymnasium) in Kaunas (Kovno), the Lithuanian inter-war capital, was Hebrew. Students also studied Latin and Lithuanian. All courses—except for

Lithuanian language, literature and history—were taught in Hebrew. The school was named after Edward Azriel Chase (Eduardas Čais in Lithuanian), a famous philanthropist who grew up in czarist-ruled Lithuania but later immigrated to the United States. With his financial help, a new building was erected for the Hebrew Real Gymnasium[3] in 1930 in Kaunas. The formal inauguration took place on August 30, 1931, in the presence of the Lithuanian minister of education, Konstantinas Šakenis. This gymnasium had a very good academic reputation all over the country and was considered the equal of the best Hebrew-language high schools in Palestine.

It is a telling similarity that the rebirths of the Hebrew and Baltic languages are striking examples of an ancient cultural heritage that was restored and preceded the national sentiment for an independent homeland and reappearance on the world political stage. The tragic similarities, the shared fate of Israel and the Baltic nations as cultural isolates and the bearers of an ancient pre–Christian heritage, survived into the modern world and deserve recognition. The Lithuanian language can compete with Hebrew in terms of age. It is considered an archaic branch of the Indo-European family, and the one that has changed least in its development over the last three thousand years.

The story of the Baltic peoples is an inspiring one. The preservation of their ancient language and literature and its adaptation to the modern world, like that of Hebrew, would be key to their survival and renewed independence.

Like the Jews, the Latvians, Lithuanians and Estonians maintained a distinct and isolated cultural and linguistic heritage stemming from pre–Christian times; they likewise suffered the persecution of militant Crusaders (the Teutonic Knights considered it a holy task to Christianize or exterminate them from the twelfth to the fourteenth centuries). They were also victims of the intolerant designs of the Russian and German empires to assimilate "peculiar" minorities. Later, they enjoyed a late-flowering national renaissance based first and foremost upon the ancestral languages, sustained a far-flung Diaspora (for the Balts in Scandinavia, Canada, Australia and the United States), and strove to bring about reborn national states committed to democratic ideals but surrounded by aggressive and much more powerful hostile neighbors.[4]

The shared history of "Litvak Jews" (those resident in the areas ruled by Lithuania at its height of power and prestige in the seventeenth century) and the Baltic peoples was, however, tragically flawed by the Holocaust and the brutal subjugation and annexation of all three Baltic states by the Soviet Union. It is fitting to put these events in historical perspective in order to understand how and why Baltic-Jewish coexistence foundered.

Under the Commonwealth of Poland and Lithuania, Jews were invited to settle in the sixteenth century and enjoyed an unprecedented tolerance of ecumenical spirit that stood out like an island amid the vast ocean of religious intolerance provoked by the Reformation and Counter-Reformation. This was largely due to the Lithuanian element that had only a short time earlier abandoned its long devotion to the old pagan Baltic religions and accepted Catholicism as an expedient to avoid further bloodshed and rivalry with the rest of Europe. The Lithuanians, as the last people to be Christianized in Europe, were much less susceptible to the accumulated prejudices of the established state churches. Jewish, Russian Orthodox and Lutheran subjects all enjoyed the new order of tolerance that laid the foundation for the growth of the largest Jewish community in the world.

Lithuania became the most important center of Jewish Talmudic scholarship and a bulwark of resistance to the emotional populist appeal of Hasidism. Eliezer Ben-Yehuda, and many others who were active in the renaissance of the Hebrew language, were "Litvaks." Rationalist currents of thought among Lithuanian Jewry also welcomed the *Haskalah*[5] movement that sought secular knowledge and espoused democratic ideals while trying to remain loyal to Jewish traditions and make them more attuned to the modern world.

Under czarist domination, Lithuanian and Jewish nationalists worked together in a united front in the Duma (Russian parliament); yet this political cooperation never succeeded in bridging the enormous economic and social gap between the two peoples. The Yiddish-speaking Jewish masses formed a majority in Vilnius, and elsewhere they were concentrated in the *shtetls*, the market towns where they acted as middlemen for the produce of Lithuanian and Latvian peasants. German and Polish noblemen dominated large landed estates as well as the free professions in the cities, while a Russian elite of administrators filled the highest political posts.

Attempting to penetrate the urban middle class, both Balts and Jews adopted Russian and German to further their careers and assimilate with the ruling classes. Although Zionism and Hebrew culture became widely popular, the overwhelming majority of Litvak Jews were unable to appreciate or sympathize with the growing movement for Lithuanian and Latvian independence and the cultural reawakening of the Baltic peoples. Prosperous urban Jewish merchants and professionals invariably chose a Russian education for their children (German was preferred in East Prussia).

As little as 3 percent of Jewish elementary school students in inter-war Latvia studied in Latvian-language schools, as compared to 12 percent in German schools, over 50 percent in Russian ones, and about 33 percent in the Yiddish or Hebrew schools.[6] This was naturally resented by the native Baltic peoples, who had for so long considered the Germans, Russians and Poles the sources of their oppression. Unfortunately, this Jewish wish to be part of "prestigious" cultures was an ironic denial of the basis for Zionism itself, which urged Jews to return to their own heritage. It was only a handful of farsighted

Zionists, most notably Ze'ev Jabotinsky (himself an accomplished linguist and outstanding literary figure in multiple languages), who argued in favor of the necessity to cultivate Hebrew, even at great effort.

Jabotinsky's Support of "Minor Languages"

In the summer of 1932, Jabotinsky spoke in fluent Flemish before an enthralled audience in Antwerp on "The Flemish Language and Jewish Nationalism." In so doing, he openly sided with Flemish attempts to achieve equality with the dominant French-speaking Walloon society in Belgium. He saw the similarity of the national movements of small nations to Zionism and the danger of Jewish ignorance of these movements.

Jabotinsky specifically singled out *the Baltic States*. He agreed to look favorably on the proposals to use the Latin alphabet for a period of a few months to replace the square "Babylonian" letters with which Hebrew has been written since the fifth century BCE if it would aid literacy. This was a revolutionary step that even Ben-Yehuda's son tried in practice when editing a Hebrew newspaper.

Jabotinsky praised the national rebirth of the Latvian people during a visit to Riga and described Latvia as "an oasis" among the new independent states following World War I. He wrote:

> The world does not love small states. From time to time, when one of the great European newspapers mentions one of the small states, and especially those created after the war ... the writer's face gets all wrinkled and he curses why the world has become "Balkanized." Or else he puts on a serious scientific face and proves that the small states "are not able to exist," because previously when they were districts in one of the large states, they enjoyed a "hinterland" which they now lack.... If I had been the creator of the world I would have long ago decreed that all of the great kingdoms be divided up into tiny independent states.... My faith in small states has to do with this philosophy: the more capitals, the more culture. Indeed I remember Kovno, Riga and Reval [Tallin] from before the war. Their inhabitants complained about the boredom, exactly as they do today (to always be in Paris is boring like anything persistent); today each one of them is a laboratory of creative experiments: They are creating one of the greatest of God's miracles—the nations.[7]

An Appeal for Jewish and Small Nations' Rights

Although Jewish life in the *shtetl* (Yiddish for "small town") had evolved symbiotically with the Baltic peasants and small farmers in the countryside, there was nevertheless only limited contact between intellectuals and politicians among the two peoples, only a few of whom who saw an advantage in cooperating against czarist oppression. Not many Jews had Jabotinsky's insight. An anthology of Lithuanian literature in Hebrew translation summarizes Jewish cultural achievement, piety and attachment to a common homeland that was, however, for the great majority of Jews, bereft of appreciation and understanding for the rebirth of Baltic culture:

> There is a small nation in the North of the world which has distinguished itself by hospitality and an honest human relationship with the remote People of the Diaspora during centuries—the Lithuanian Nation. Its land has served us for generations as a storage place for the Torah, for wisdom and for the spirit of Israel. Here we have lived for hundreds of years, here we have created an original Hebrew culture, here our essence struck deep roots in the soil and here we adopted a second Mother Jerusalem—"Yerushalayim de'Lita" [Vilnius]. Here the study of the Torah flourished, here Yeshivot prospered and bloomed, here lived "The Gaon" and our great rabbis—the words of the Nation; here the cradle of our new literature stood, here lived our writers—the renewers of our tongue and those who breathed new life in us ... here arose the leaders of a renewed nation and here at the same time the living Hebrew language found a home and a network of schools brought forth a healthy living youth whose example one can only find in the Land of Israel. But behold, in spite of this, the literature of this people [Lithuanian] is locked for us with seven seals and entirely unknown to the Hebrew People.[8]

Independence without their historic capital of Vilnius was unthinkable for Lithuanian nationalists. Their claim was based on grounds of established tradition—an "immemorial possession" in spite of the city's Jewish majority. Polish nationalists, however, viewed the retention of Vilnius and Lvov (in the western Ukraine), with their large Polish populations and universities, as essential to the integrity of their own state. Lithuania's stated intentions of protecting minority rights and its less discriminatory attitude toward its Jewish population were used as arguments to sway public opinion abroad, and especially to influence the League of Nations. In the aftermath of the Russian Revolution and end of World War I, all three Baltic states were caught in the middle of a battleground between retreating German troops and a major conflict between Poland and Russia.

Nationalists in all the Baltic states viewed such minority rights as divisive. Their motives, however, were not based primarily on anti–Semitism alone but also on the view that the Baltic peoples should be given preferential treatment in raising their economic and social status, a process that inevitably would have to come about at the cost of the minorities.

The Jews, traditionally regarded as being without power, were initially viewed in a more favorable light than the disaffected minorities backed by hostile and powerful large states (Germans, Russians, and Poles), but Jewish economic preeminence, especially in trade, aggravated tensions. In 1923, there were 14,000 shops in Lithuania owned by Jews, and 2,000 by non–Jews; by 1936, the respective figures were 10,000 and 12,000.[9] With the growth of virulent anti–Semitism in Germany and Poland, anti–Semitic movements also won considerable adherents in Latvia and Lithuania, but they were tempered by fear of Nazi Germany using the economically powerful German minority as a fifth column.

Abolition of Jewish Autonomy

The Lithuanian Ministry of Jewish Affairs was abolished in 1924. The ostensible reason given for this decision was internal bickering between Yiddishists and Hebraists for control of the Jewish educational sector, but many observers held that this was actually the result of Lithuanian demands to assert their control of the state and cultivate the economic, social and political profile of the Lithuanian people. Although Lithuania eventually fell under an authoritarian regime (as did Latvia and Estonia), there was no mob violence against Jews or their property. Lithuania's toughening attitude toward aggressive pro–Nazi elements among the Germans in Klaipeda (Memel)[10] resulted in the trial and conviction of Nazi activists for treason, a step that infuriated German public opinion and instinctively evoked Jewish support around the world.

Jabotinsky and the Diaspora

We are three generations removed from Ze'ev Jabotinsky's proud declaration of a reborn Hebrew state sharing in the great gift of "the nations," one that still strikes many Diaspora Jews as anachronistic in spite of the Holocaust and the specter of nationalist turmoil and ethnic divisiveness almost everywhere.

For Jabotinsky, Zionism and the nationalism of other small nations were the accumulation of pride and sovereign self-respect, which for the Jews could only be obtained in the face of an immensely hostile Gentile environment. It was a revolutionary call for Jews to shoulder all the obligations of nationhood and take up the sword in self-defense. This meant doing all the dirty work of soldiers, jailers, farmers and street cleaners instead of preaching to Gentiles on how these affairs should be properly managed.

Borrowing from the vision of Italian nationalist leader Guiseppe Mazzini (Jabotinsky had lived and studied in Italy for three years), he proclaimed that each and every nation makes its own contribution to human culture within the sovereign body of nationhood in order to fulfill its task and mission.

For Jabotinsky, *hadar* (an explicitly Hebrew concept that he tried to inculcate into every member of the worldwide Zionist youth movement of Betar) was and remains fundamentally at odds with the century-long attraction of many Jewish intellectuals to the illusion of socialism and their false sense of *noblesse oblige* for the "masses." The essence of *hadar* is untranslatable. Literally, it means shine or glow, but for Jabotinsky it implied chivalry in conduct and lifestyle, a combination, as he defined it, of "spiritual beauty, respect, self-esteem, immaculate grooming, politeness, faithfulness and integrity." *Hadar* consists of a thousand trifles that collectively form everyday life.

In forming Betar among Riga high school students in 1923, Jabotinsky influenced the everyday lives of hundreds of thousands of Jewish children from the ghettos of Eastern Europe with a spirit of *Malchut Yisrael* (Jewish nobility) that their people had not known since the dispersion 1,800 years earlier. Like the Baltic and Polish intellectuals he had come to know and emulate, Jabotinsky gave forlorn youth a sense of being a proud part of not only a bright future but also a glorious remote past. He taught that the fate of the Jewish people is linked only with one -ism—ZIONISM, undiluted and untainted by any other "*ism*."[11]

Caught Between the Hammer and the Anvil

The Holocaust and Soviet annexation of the Baltic States left behind a deep traumatic residue of pain that obscures the previous centuries-long coexistence and suffering of both peoples. A tiny but vocal and dedicated minority of Jewish communists had, from the outset of the Russian Revolution, cast their hopes upon the Soviet regime. For them, the old attraction to Russian culture and disdain for the Baltic languages and customs were increased by the added magnetic pull of the center of world socialism. Jewish autonomy, the promise of a future Soviet Jewish republic and a thriving Yiddish culture were all idealized. The crowning achievements of the Jewish educational systems (the Hebrew secular *Tarbut* and the religious *Yavneh* schools) were denigrated, and Lithuanian Jewish communists even adopted the reformed spelling of Yiddish current in the Soviet Union.

These Jewish communists welcomed the arrival of the Red Army and the annexation of the Baltic States to the Soviet Union in 1940. Until the German invasion of 1941, the new Soviet regime decimated the ranks of the Baltic intelligentsia, thoroughly eliminated private enterprise, destroyed all independent institutions, exiled tens of thousands of civilians suspected of any nationalist or democratic sympathies (including Zionist activists, stamp collectors and Esperantists), and thoroughly wiped out every vestige of Jewish culture, including both Yiddish schools and the Hebrew ones.

Before the outbreak of the war, Jabotinsky had praised the Baltic nationalists and the human capital and sacrifice they invested in restoring national pride and sovereignty, and he linked the fate of these small European nations with that of the Zionist movement. Between the two world wars, the Jews of the independent Lithuanian state demonstrated a high level of patriotism and motivation, including their readiness for military service. Many fought with distinction in Lithuania's war of independence and against Polish and German irregulars during the border strife that followed. More than 3,000 Jewish war veterans were organized into 33 branches throughout the country.[12]

Even after the annexation of Lithuania and its absorption into the Soviet Union as a constituent republic in June 1940, the newly formed Lithuanian units of the Red Army included many Jewish soldiers who, although in no way sympathetic to communism, were aware of their historic opportunity to resist Nazi Germany on the battlefield even if it meant fighting under the banner of the hammer and sickle. A massive wave of voluntary enlistment in the Red Army followed the German invasion of the Soviet Union in June 1941.

At least 15,000 Jews managed to escape the German occupation of Lithuania and find their way into the interior of the Soviet Union, where many were mobilized into the 16th Infantry "Lithuanian Rifle Division" in spite of the fact that a very large percentage had been active in the Zionist youth movements, including the right-wing Revisionists and the religious Mizrahi organization. Many rose through the ranks to become officers and won numerous decorations, including that of "Hero of the Soviet Union." These included General Wolf Vilensky, whose autobiography[13] tells the remarkable tale of the heroic Lithuanian 16th Division of the Red Army comprised of many soldiers who secretly remained proud Zionists and/or had supported Lithuanian independence prior to the war.

Of Jews serving in Vilensky's unit, approximately 25 percent were graduates of Zionist youth movements and fluent in Hebrew. Normally Soviet policy would have made these soldiers suspect because of their "counter-revolutionary past"; yet the authorities were aware that precisely these Jews would have the best anti–Nazi motivation, and the best military-like training from their familiarity with physical exercises, long hikes, camping, and the technical skills acquired in their Zionist education.

Born in Kaunas in 1919, the son of a baker, Vilensky was raised in a Zionist household where he received a traditional Jewish upbringing. He studied in the Yavne high school and finished his studies in the ORT school. He worked in a Chalutz farm, preparing for *aliyah*, his Zionist dream. He was drafted into the Lithuanian army in 1939, and when Lithuania became a Soviet republic in June 1940, he was sent to an officers' course in Vilnius. Because of his courage and leadership skills, he quickly rose in the ranks and became the commander of the Third Battalion of the 249th Brigade, and then its brigade commander. He was loved by his men and achieved the rank of brigadier general.

Jews accounted for at least 30 percent of the Lithuanian Division, whose battle record includes liberating 646 settlements, inflicting 30,000 casualties upon the enemy and taking 12,000 prisoners of war.[14] The Division was still active after the war until it was finally dissolved in 1956, after which many of its Jewish veterans immigrated to Israel. Numerous Israelis who only had perceptions or memories of Jewish passivity during the war and Holocaust were amazed to hear these veterans recount their experiences in the Red Army, stories of singing Yiddish and Zionist Hebrew songs while marching or sitting around campfires during the bitter winter nights.

Nazi propaganda lost no time in singling out the Jews for revenge when the Baltic States were overrun. Nationalist extremists in the three countries wreaked their vengeance on the Jews (most of whom were not communists and had taken no part in the Soviet regime). This collaboration in helping the Germans commit atrocities on an enormous scale has been officially condemned by the current leaders of the Baltic republics since regaining independence, but many Jewish survivors suspect that it is largely cosmetic "window dressing." The misdirected revenge of Baltic nationalists against the Jews remains a bitter legacy of events in which both peoples were the victims of totalitarian states.

Following their renewed independence following World War II, the leaders of the Baltic States issued appeals calling for renewed contacts and friendly cooperation with the Jewish people. The Baltic States all have full diplomatic relations with the State of Israel. They resemble those of the early 1920s that won the sympathy and admiration of Jabotinsky. It is therefore all the more regrettable that there are still those in all three Baltic states who wish to absolve themselves of any collective guilt for the ghastly atrocities against the Jews committed by local collaborators with the S.S. by focusing attention away from the Jewish victims toward those Lithuanians murdered and exiled during the Soviet occupation.

The idea of regaining independence for the Baltic States, or even a cultural and literary revival, struck many observers as a fantastic notion in spite of much lip service by American foreign policy spokesmen regarding the illegality of their incorporation into the Soviet Union in 1940. The individuality of the three peoples, and especially the revelation that the archaic Latvian and Lithuanian languages, the former Baltic pagan religion, and Baltic legends and folk customs were all survivors of the ancient Indo-European or Aryan prehistoric culture, reinforced the analogy of "turning the clock back thousands of years," just as Zionism had sought to do by reestablishing a Jewish state and reviving the Hebrew language.[15] The re-emergent Baltic States captured world attention more than any other region within the disintegrating Soviet Union. This was certainly not a factor of their size and population, especially compared to the much larger Ukrainian and Byelorussian Soviet republics, but rather due to their previous strategic role as independent states in Europe between the two world wars.[16]

This shared sympathetic interest evoked by regaining their independence and recalling the brief interim between the two world wars when the Jews enjoyed an unprecedented cultural autonomy in all three independent Baltic republics led to the establishment of diplomatic relations between them and Israel.[17] The saga of the Baltic peoples and how they managed to maintain their ancient and isolated cultural heritage is remarkable, and their rebirth amid the disintegration of the Soviet Union immediately calls to mind the protracted struggle to establish a Jewish homeland after centuries of statelessness. The record of Lithuanian Jewry should be common knowledge and an antidote to those in the Diaspora who are ambivalent, ignorant, unmindful or disparaging of Jewish pride. It was an achievement that provided a microcosm and staging ground for the Hebrew state to emerge from the ashes.

10. The First Modern Hebrew Textbooks Set in Palestine

Language textbooks often try to present the cultural aspects of a tongue in its homeland as well as the formal training in the various learning skills of speaking, listening comprehension, reading and writing. Obviously, since languages such as English, French, Spanish, or Portuguese[1] are spoken in many different lands with quite distinct literatures, dialects, social relations and a wide range of national idiomatic expressions, these textbooks often provide clarifying footnotes regarding varying usage. If the language is spoken only in a single nation, such as Danish, Latvian or Hungarian, there may be more space to help the student understand the history of the linguistic homeland and its national traditions, music, and culinary specialties.

In the case of Hebrew, which had previously served for many centuries only as a liturgical language, without a single homeland for speakers in which the language was the spoken idiom from birth, textbooks with national content were entirely lacking.

A Hebraist movement, parallel but not identical to the Zionist movement, spread across the map of Europe and took inspiration from the work of Ben-Yehuda and the successes achieved by the growth of the spoken language in the Zionist pioneer colonies in Palestine. It also leaped across the Atlantic and took root in the United States, Canada and Latin America. For the first time textbooks appeared that sought to teach the spoken language and create dialogues that a visitor might expect to hear among the new Hebrew speakers.

Daniel Persky (1887–1962)[2] was the most influential member of this movement in North America, although he was born in Minsk, Russia. He spent six years in Palestine and Europe (1927–1933), and for the remainder of his career, he taught at the Herzliah Hebrew Teachers' College in New York. He published a major article in each issue of the Hebrew weekly *Hadoar*, which enjoyed the greatest popularity among American published journals in Hebrew, and he also wrote several textbooks, including *Ha-Medabber Ivrit* (Spoken Hebrew, 1921), *Ivri Anokhi* (I am a Hebrew! 1948), *Dabberu Ivrit*

(Speak Hebrew! 1950) and *Lashon Nekiyyah* (Pure Language, 1962), and even a book on humor, *Ẓeḥok me-Ereẓ Yisrael* (Laughter from the Land of Israel, 1951).

Persky corresponded with Hebrew writers all over the world, and his travels expressed his life's work in a single sentence: "I am a slave of Hebrew forever." His long-term vision that the Hebrew language could serve as a bridge to draw the Diaspora closer to Israel, however, remained elusive and unrealistic. Nevertheless, probably no one else has better expressed how the Hebrew language and literature powerfully encompass three thousand years of Jewish history and identity for those Jews who cannot identify with religious doctrines or reside in Israel:

> An ordinary Jew like myself who does not believe in religion and who does not keep the commandments. Who does not stand on the soil of his national homeland, and for whom abstract concepts of Judaism hold no appeal—what remains real and palpable for him of all the achievements of his people, if not only for the extraordinary and eternal Hebrew language? For such an ordinary Jew, nationalism is incorporated by the language, which fills his entire being and to which he will devote his entire life.[3]

My favorite however, is another book that captured the transition from scholastic textbooks in telling the story of modern Israel and its language, by presenting a story with dialogue between characters whom the reader can follow throughout the lessons, which also emphasize the cultural aspects of a tongue in its homeland rather than the Diaspora. This book, *Everyday Hebrew*,[4] was written by Chaim Rabin, a German-born scholar of Oriental languages who later immigrated with his parents to Palestine and then settled in Britain. For many years, he was a distinguished professor of Hebrew at Oxford. The book was first published in 1943, and a second edition appeared in 1948 almost simultaneously with the establishment of the State of Israel.

The "twenty-nine conversations" of this textbook follow Simon and Rachel, a newly married couple, on their way to the Land of Israel by ship to visit family and friends. Rachel is from England and Simon is a native-born *tsabar* (named for the local cactus plant called *tsabra*). From the very first conversation, the Jews define themselves as "proud Palestinians" and call "Palestine" their homeland.

Textbooks for the study of Hebrew published earlier for use in the Diaspora often featured dialogues set in Biblical times or that dealt with legends and folklore from the East European *shtetl*, medieval Spain, or the Israel and Babylon of Talmudic times. One exception that may have been influenced by Rabin's *Everyday Hebrew* is *Ivrit ḥayah* (Modern Hebrew) by Harry Blumberg and Mordechai Lewittes. In its earliest forms (1946, 1948), it also used a Palestinian/Israeli setting to follow the adventures of two characters, both teenage

American boys, journeying through the Land of Israel and to provide the reader with some insight into the geography and culture of modern Jewish society, but these characters are two-dimensional "stick figures" with no personality or personal history. They are simply observers rather than participants in the vibrant Zionist enterprise of the new state, and almost all the chapters are set in a nondescript neutral setting.

In the Hebrew text of Rabin's book, the term used for the country is "Eretz-Yisrael" (The Land of Israel); for those Jews born in the country or long-term residents, "Eretz-Yisraeli" (male) and "Eretz-Yisraelit" (female) are used. For the English-reading audience in Great Britain or the United States, or even South Africa, there was nothing unusual or contradictory in the use of the terms "Palestine" and "Palestinian" in a Jewish and explicitly Zionist connection; they had been in universal use from approximately the time of early Zionist activity in the 1880s and understood to apply to Jews only.

Under the British Mandate, Arabs in the country were generally reluctant to define themselves as anything but "Arabs," and all the UN resolutions, including the partition plan, spoke only of Jews and Arabs. Ironically, the term "Palestinian" was in general use only for the Jewish segment of Palestine. Yiddish radio stations in the United States frequently played what they called "Palestinian folk songs" to refer to the native popular Hebrew tunes describing Jewish pioneers (*halutzim*) working the land. Even Tin-Pan Alley Jewish songwriters like Irving Berlin employed the term "Palestine" to refer to the country's Jewish identity and associations. One such big hit from 1920 was "Lena Is the Queen of Palestina," played to a Klezmer tune and even sung in a Yiddish version.

Rabin faced a dilemma and resolved it by creating characters who typified ideal types of veteran and new Jewish arrivals in Mandatory Palestine for his conversations that reflected the sense of the Zionist mission in their adaptation to the new chosen homeland. The characters' dedication, enthusiasm and love of the Hebrew language enabled them to overcome the hardships of family separation. The language of the conversations in both Hebrew and the English translations are somewhat stilted, overly polite and formal, as might be expected from a distinguished Oxford professor.

The "official grammar" outlined in the textbook definitely makes the book outdated and would mark anyone using it in ordinary conversation today as a time-traveler (or worse). A notable example is the admonition not to use the simple word *lo* (*lamed-aleph*) to negate sentences. Instead, the reader is told,[5] "In colloquial style, 'lo' is often used instead of 'ayn' when meaning 'is not' and as negation of the present. This is however still considered ungrammatical and should not be imitated." The reverse is true today, and anybody using the *ayn* construction would be regarded as an eccentric pedant.

Even more stringent is the "prohibition" against using the grammatical marker "et" to indicate the direct object with the expression meaning "to have" (possess). The readers are admonished that the expressions "to have" and "not to have" are *not* verbs, but since they are treated as such in all the European languages spoken by many new Jewish arrivals, the end result is that today this "rule" is almost universally ignored, although the practice has been constantly criticized by the Hebrew Language Academy and "forbidden" in grammar lessons. Nowadays, many Israelis insert this unnecessary "et" into their dialogues constantly.

Rabin struggled with the problem of trying to produce a manual with all the traditional rules of classic Hebrew grammar that would also serve as a modern textbook with a colloquial and contemporary "Jewish-Palestinian flavor." The modern Israeli scholar Benjamin Harshav[6] has traced the creation of the modern Israeli-Hebrew idiom as a fused style of "fossil elements" from the past, reorganized and invigorated by the base language of the pioneering society of Zionist settlers and the spoken language created by a new generation of journalists and educators in newspapers, on the radio and in schools, and by an age cohort of highly motivated individuals, divorced from their original family and childhood social surroundings.

As Rabin begins his little tale of new arrivals in the country, he is at pains to explain to the reader much of the new social environment of Jewish Palestine and the prevailing British administration. In chapter one, Rachel proudly exclaims to her Palestinian-born husband upon their arrival that "I have been a full Palestinian for a fortnight, ever since I was married to you."[7] She is questioned by the customs officer at the Haifa port of arrival in the following chapter: "Is this your first visit to Palestine, Madam?" to which she responds, "Yes, only it's hardly a visit. I've come to stay," prompting the response, "That's the right spirit!"[8]

Simon, Rachel's husband, offers a generous "tip" (*bakshish*) of one piaster to a cab driver. The book offers a footnote explaining that the Palestinian pound is "divided into one thousand mills, one-tenth of which is a coin referred to as a 'grush' or piaster, i.e., a two pence farthing and that half a grush (5 mills) is roughly a penny."[9]

While sitting at a restaurant enjoying lunch and waiting for their bus to Jerusalem, Simon presses Rachel for her first impressions of the country. She exclaims, "It's marvelous! The sun and these colors! It's like a dream. I always thought people were exaggerating when they spoke so enthusiastically of the beauty of Palestine, but now I see that the reality is far better than the description."[10] Right away, her attention is diverted to the menu because she has never seen one in Hebrew, and she admits that she hardly understands a word of it, although she studied Hebrew abroad. Simon calmly reassures her, "No wonder.

It's not so easy to get the hand of practical Hebrew outside the country. Your Hebrew conversation is fluent enough, but you will still have a lot of difficulties in the kitchen and in the shops."[11] Here, Simon is basically introducing the reader/learner to the new colloquial Hebrew in their homeland and not the dry-bones language found in hundreds of books, brochures and teaching aids spanning centuries of use in prayer and religious services. Readers were made to follow the daily routine of characters in older language-learning textbooks, who, apart from their typically Jewish names, were divorced from any identifiable culture and society.

The first negative mundane remarks of everyday life are those of the alert Simon, who calls upon the waiter "to give us another fork, please, this one isn't clean. Also we have no napkins."[12] The English version of the conversation is thoroughly British, with expressions like "We shan't be able to explore Tel Aviv before we leave," and when meeting a friend, "Well, if it isn't Gabriel, you've got so fat. How are you, old man?" and "after all, I mayn't get the job."[13]

In Jerusalem, Rachel is impressed by the tall buildings, which she imagines have "an American appearance," and by the lovely gardens, which, Simon clarifies, are the result of hard labor (he comments that all the land Rachel sees between them and the Kiriyat Shaul neighborhood was a "stony wasteland" when he left Palestine a few years earlier).

The couple is welcomed by Simon's mother, who calls them "my children" and summons a maid to prepare dinner. She immediately offers Rachel an orange from "my orchard in Ra'ananah." Obviously, Simon belongs to a tiny affluent minority of the country's Jewish population who own their own plot of productive agricultural land at some distance from their primary residence. The mother then assures them that her health has improved since she took the "water cure" at the hot springs in Tiberias. Like any good language book today, Rabin finds a way to introduce important aspects of the country's geography and institutions in his storyline.

Rachel next urges Simon to get a new suit for an upcoming job interview, and that it should be a light linen one suitable to the climate. The salesman assures the couple that the material is the "first quality Palestinian fabric and that you can't find such quality even in imported goods."[14] Then the reader encounters a scene showing the great cultural vitality of modern Hebrew culture and the Zionist enterprise—the Habimah Theatre in Jerusalem (located today in Tel-Aviv), which is putting on "Danton's Death" and "Your People." Both plays are nearly sold out, so it is difficult to get tickets. Simon is, however, ready to pay the exorbitant price of ten piastres to get seats together.

Suddenly, Rachel is taken ill and it is necessary to call a doctor. She has a mild fever, but the wise doctor calms her, explaining that it is only a mild illness from which many new immigrants suffer. It will pass in three or four days, and he recommends natural light food, such as semolina pudding, rusks and weak tea. (I actually had to look at the Hebrew text to find out what is meant by "rusks" [cinnamon].)

Rachel intends to visit her sister in Hadera, and the reader gets a brief geographical picture of the journey via coach to Lydda and then onward by train. We learn that the sister actually lives in a kibbutz near Hadera and it is referred to as "The English Kibbutz." Simon is careful to address the members of the kibbutz as "comrade." It consists entirely of huts and tents. The sister, Elizabeth, works in the chicken run and is training to take part in settling a new kibbutz on "our land in the Beisan Valley." Rachel is thrilled by the way her sister refers to "our land," although security considerations require leaving the children for the time being in the care of others. Rachel admits she is jealous and that, from the moment she arrived in Haifa, she has experienced the marvelous feeling of speaking about "our country" and she envies her sister the privilege of "upbuilding the country."

Even Rachel and Elizabeth's mother in England, who was greatly disturbed by their immigration to Palestine, is so affected by her daughters' enthusiasm and the prevailing good feelings and prosperity that she, too, is considering settling there. In this way, Rabin smoothes over the pain and anguish that was caused to so many Jewish parents in the Diaspora by their children's decision to embark on the treacherous journey and the dangers of life in Palestine. The Arabs are only briefly alluded to in several remarks, the most important of which is "Our relations with our Arab neighbors are excellent just now, it's true, but who can tell? One must be prepared for any emergency."[15]

The first edition of the book was published at a time of good will in the country due to prosperity and the demand provided by the British forces in the Middle East, as well as the large number of recent Jewish arrivals from Germany and Austria and the skills they brought with them. Three of the photos show a recruiting office for young Palestinian Jews and Jewish volunteers in the British forces marching through the streets of Tel-Aviv. British Army recruiting posters in Hebrew stressed the urgency for Jews to demonstrate their patriotism and "Defend Your Homeland." Other photos dramatize Jews working in agriculture and industry, including a woman in a knitting mill. The text was probably nearly finished sometime shortly after the surrender of the French Army in 1940 and the prospect of a possible German or Italian push through Egypt to Palestine.

In chapter 26, "A Political Conversation," a friend, Mr. Keren, speaks to Simon about the possibility of Italy entering the war (Tel-Aviv was actually bombed several times during 1941–1942 by Italian planes). He reassures Simon that the number of Civil Defense volunteers is growing and that "we have a fine system of shelters"; when queried about whether he is afraid of an Italian invasion, Mr. Keren asserts that the Italians may try, but "It's pretty certain that the English will give them a hot time." When Simon voices his apprehensions about the suffering war would cause, Mr. Keren (an older and even more convinced Zionist, apparently, than Simon) explains, "After all, our fate as Jews depends on the victory of the democratic powers. If fascism should win, which God forbid, what good will it be to us that we were not directly affected by the war?"[16]

Of course, the thread running through the entire book is one of naive wishful thinking and optimism, as well as devotion to the Zionist ideal. All problems and hardships are minimized. This was the spirit of the time, which enabled the construction of a Jewish homeland and the victory of the reinvigorated, dynamic, earthy Modern Hebrew language. The book is a delightful illustration of how students were offered both a novel textbook for language learning and an introduction to the pioneering spirit and rebirth of the Hebrew nation in its old-new homeland.

11. The Soviet Persecution of Hebrew

For over half a century, authorities in the Soviet Union followed an ideological policy of condemning Hebrew as a "reactionary tool" of the upper classes, the ultra-religious and Zionism. In this view, only Yiddish could be considered the legitimate mother tongue of those "toiling masses" of Jews interested in maintaining a national existence. This resulted in an almost total prohibition of any expression of thought and cultural creativity in the Hebrew language, amounting to a ban on the publication of books, newspapers, magazines, films, public lectures, theater performances, poetry readings, educational courses, or radio and television broadcasts in Hebrew apart from research in restricted university libraries on the Semitic languages available to a handful of graduate students among the Communist Party faithful.[1]

The Zionist movement and the progress of Modern Hebrew faced their greatest challenge and dilemma in Soviet policy that closed the gates of *aliyah* to Palestine and forbade the continued progress of Modern Hebrew in what had been its birthplace. Nowhere else and against no other language (except Esperanto in Nazi-occupied Europe) was such a policy invoked by any regime to strangle a language into total silence.

Jewish communists organized in their own "national section" of the Communist Party of the Soviet Union (the *Yevsektsia*) took an unremitting hostile view toward Hebrew, insisting that its ultimate demise was demanded in the new socialist society of workers and toilers. Thousands of Jews would be imprisoned based on nothing more than the suspicion that they had offered instruction of the Hebrew language in their own homes. This was regarded as ipso facto proof of subversive and counter-revolutionary tendencies, leading to the search for other evidence to bring more serious charges and condemn the guilty to years of hard labor and imprisonment, often combined with exile to Siberia.

The language dispute between Yiddish and Hebrew had preceded the communist "October Revolution" of 1917 by many years. In the official czarist census of 1897, 96.8 percent of the 5,125,000 Jews in the Russian Empire (including Poland and the Baltic region) declared Yiddish to be their "mother tongue," although many were bilingual in Yiddish and Russian, or even trilingual in Hebrew as well. The competition between these three languages exacerbated the political division.[2]

It was assumed (too simplistically) that any active support in the public sphere on behalf of Yiddish was linked to the Bund, the Jewish socialist party in czarist times, a "workers' party" in favor of socialism and cultural autonomy in those districts where they formed a significant part of the population. Likewise, support for Hebrew was considered a corollary of belief in Zionism, emigration to Palestine and a rejection of Marxism and the class struggle. This view simply ignored the more complicated facts that several political groups existed that favored the "wrong" language. These included young intellectuals with a far left revolutionary attitude that supported the Soviet regime and espoused Hebrew, even founding a publication titled "The Hebrew Communist."[3] In so doing, they demonstrated their revolutionary zeal and opposition to religious orthodoxy and its attempt to maintain Hebrew as a purely sacred tongue to be used only in the synagogue.

Another left-wing Jewish party known as *Poalei-Zion* (Workers of Zion), and especially a splinter group *Poalei-Zion Smol* (Left Workers of Zion), espoused Zionism and Marxism—with the objective of creating a Jewish workers' (Hebrew-speaking) state in Palestine. Although they carried out much of their activities in Yiddish, they accepted Hebrew as the future

A 1936 political poster of the far left Socialist Zionist movement *Poalei-Zion Smol*, with the inscription "Long Live the First of May! To the battle—Down with English Imperialism! Down with Antisemitism and Fascism! For Unrestricted Immigration to the Land of Israel! For a Socialist Land of Israel!" (courtesy Palestine Poster Project Archives [PPPA]).

language of a Jewish workers' society in Palestine. By 1926, they, too, were forced to cease operations.

The growing use of Russian among many Jews as a first or habitual language was regarded as a vital step on the road to acculturation and then assimilation into Russian and Orthodox Christian (after 1917, Communist) society. In reality, however, the issue of language preference cut across ideological lines and many individuals had a deep attachment to Russian, Yiddish and Hebrew.

At the great Czernowitz Yiddish Language Conference in 1908, held from August 30 to September 3 in a city at the eastern edge of the Austro-Hungarian Empire but attended by many Russian Jews, Yiddish was declared a "national language of the Jewish People." Advocates of Yiddish desired above all to win respectability and prestigious status for their language, which had long been regarded as a dialect or "jargon" by many linguists. Both Russian and Austrian officials regarded the Jews of their countries as an unassimilated and troublesome minority and looked askance at the conference.

Quite unexpectedly for many of the participants, a vociferous anti–Zionist and anti–Hebrew element used the conference to win points by designating Hebrew as an elegant lady, a sort of aged grandmother, who, having lived her life to the full, should, in all fairness, hand over the keys to the younger housewife (Yiddish). The latter would show her respect by arranging an honorable funeral for her grandmother when the time came.

In spite of the hostility expressed by many in the Bund, a majority of the conference participants were eager for some sort of compromise and stopped short of proclaiming Yiddish "The SOLE Language of the Jewish People." Instead, the conference issued a statement resolving that Yiddish be regarded as "a national language of the Jewish People," and that every member attending the conference had the freedom "to relate to the Hebrew language in accordance with his personal views." Although seemingly a compromise, tensions between the two rivals increased.

Due to the disruptions caused by hostilities in the Ukraine and White Russia during World War I, many Jews fled from these areas known as "The Pale of Settlement" into Russia proper, where only relatively few Jews had previously been permitted to reside. The need to accommodate the children of these refugees in new schools led to an intensification of the language conflict.

Yiddishists insisted that pedagogic principles demanded teaching young children in the language of the home and their parents (Yiddish). Chaim Bialik and other Hebrew writers argued that Jews indeed faced a dilemma in making the language of the soul (Hebrew) a spoken language. By the time of the communist takeover in November 1917, the educational authorities had reached a compromise, with instruction in Yiddish and language courses to learn both Russian and Hebrew offered most schools in predominantly Jewish areas. The concentration of a number of wealthy and successful Jewish businessmen in Moscow who had become patrons of Modern Hebrew literature made the city a world center of Hebrew cultural creativity. This was later used by the *Yevsektsia* as proof of the reactionary and counter-revolutionary tendency of Hebrew.

In the first issue of the Jewish communist newspaper in Yiddish, *Emes* (Truth), the author speaking for the editors stated, "In these times, every Jewish worker must be on his guard. Weapon in hand, a soldier of the revolution, he will stand on his guard to the end.... In these times, we should not forget that we have a Jewish street of our own—a dark reactionary street, where we must conduct a bitter and protracted struggle, where there awaits us a great battle against traditional reaction, which is nurtured and cultivated by our bourgeoisie and petit bourgeoisie."[4]

Jewish support for the first revolution in March, which overthrew the czar and established the democratic regime of Kerensky, unleashed a great enthusiasm for a Jewish national and cultural identity that openly looked upon the Zionist settlements and achievements in teaching Hebrew in Palestine with great favor.

The progress made in schools and at public meetings, lectures, and journals, along with Jewish support for Hebrew, was astounding and confounded the Jewish communists. According to Marxist theory, Hebrew, always referred to as an "ancient" or "dead language," had ceased to exist as the spoken vernacular of any national group and could not be revived. It could only thrive as a mask for religious reaction or as a bourgeois hobby. Yet by November 1917, 188 schools had been established by the secular *Tarbut* movement dedicated to Hebrew: 119 kindergartens, 5 high schools, teachers' seminaries and two popular universities in Odessa and Kharkov. However, the *Tarbut* schools were closed by government order in 1919.[5]

The communist revolution in November 1917 that brought Lenin to power meant the *Yevsektsia* could argue successfully that the Yiddish-speaking Jewish community supported communism in the "here and now" while the Hebraists longed to create a future "then and there" (in Palestine).

Hillel Zlatopolsky of *Tarbut* argued in support of his position that in the small Central Asian area of the Caucasus Mountains, home to approximately 2 percent of the Jewish population of the Russian Empire, residents were totally ignorant of Yiddish. They were instead influenced by Turkish and Persian culture and had long used Hebrew as a national language, and not just a liturgical one for the synagogue services. It would be totally improper to impose Yiddish upon them. The delegates from Samarkand used an "Oriental"-sounding Sephardi pronunciation that resembled the new form of the language being taught in Palestine by a majority of teachers.

Zlatopolsky exclaimed, "If you give us two languages we will be separated from you forever and we will never be able to understand and know one another.... In our city of Samarkand there are twelve thousand Jews and all of them are Zionists, and I believe that all of the Jews of Turkestan are Zionists. We did not even know that in Russia there are Jews who are not Zionists and are not in favor of the Hebrew language."[6]

From 1917 until at least 1956, the official status of Hebrew in the Soviet Union was in limbo. Although no document or law specifically forbade Hebrew, the use of the language in all official areas was prevented. It was burdened in every way by massive red tape and the threat of punitive measures. Soviet apologists would continually argue that every nationality, including Jews, had the right to instruction in their own national language if they so wished, but "Hebrew was not the mother tongue of anyone" and parents would be endangering their children's future employment and career chances if they received instruction in a "dead language."

Officials became used to rejecting any application for Hebrew books, newspapers and journals (all the Hebrew presses had been seized after the revolution and were under government control), proclaiming that there was no need for such publications and the language had always been the tool of anti-Soviet "reactionary," "clerical" and Zionist elements. They argued that no workers really needed or used Hebrew. Moreover, experts in the Yiddish language were required to change the orthography so that words did not resemble the original Hebrew spelling from which the Yiddish terms were derived. Even the final Hebrew letters that are not used in Yiddish spelling were eliminated, and many printing presses previously used to publish Hebrew books were seized.

For a few years, sporadic efforts to teach Hebrew to adults at private night schools continued after the revolution, but were eroded and finally ended by 1926 with the argument that no officially sanctioned Soviet textbooks were available, which meant textbooks from czarist times had to be used. In public schools in Jewish areas, "where parents demanded it," some teaching time was allotted to approved teachers for instruction in Hebrew (in the old Ashkenazi pronunciation) from the 2nd to the 6th grades, but this, too, lasted only a few years.

In the field of Modern Hebrew culture, however, the regime, unmoved by the *Yevsektsia* arguments, supported the enormously successful *Habimah* Theater, all of whose works were in Hebrew. It often played to non-Jewish audiences as well, which were provided with Russian-language translations. Press reviews on the professional achievements of the theater were enthusiastic.

To a considerable degree, this hostility was fostered and encouraged by

Jewish communists who had long nurtured hostility toward Hebrew. The ultimate irony of this crusade is that for an initial period of eight years (1918–1926), the idea of a Hebrew Renaissance as an expression of Jewish national culture found among its strongest supporters non–Jews who were sympathetic to the new communist regime, such as Maxim Gorky. This same writer who was hailed by Soviet propaganda as "The Conscience of the Era" often condemned anti–Semitism in the Soviet Union as a leftover of the czarist regime and a disgrace to the Russian people. He even learned some Hebrew and exerted his influence to allow the leading Hebrew writers (mostly in Odessa) to receive permission to emigrate to Palestine in 1921. These included the person initially regarded as Modern Hebrew's greatest poet, Haim Nachman Bialik. In a rare anthology of Hebrew literature that the regime allowed to be published in 1926, *Bereshit* (In the Beginning), Gorky wrote that "Bialik is for me a great poet, the perfect and rare personification of the spirit of his people, like Isaiah, my favorite prophet, and like Job, who wrestled with his God. He expresses his sorrow and his anger in wrathful outpourings of a prophet, but he is no stranger to the simple human word; when he wishes, he is a magnificent lyricist."

Gorky would later become intimately involved with a veritable Hebrew Renaissance in the Soviet Union when full state support was given to the *Habimah* Theater in Moscow until 1926. During this initial period, the theater presented successful plays and toured Russia and the Diaspora. It was eminently successful and received rave reviews even from committed non–Jewish communists and theater critics who knew not a single word of Modern Hebrew. Sergei Radlov was such a critic whose review of "The Dybbuk" had this to say: "The play is performed in the Hebrew language, which is ostensibly a dead tongue like Latin, i.e., not even understood by most of the audience in Moscow and Leningrad. And nonetheless, you absorb the isolated words and the sentences, the blood-course of the language.... Suffice the sound, the resonance, the movement of the body, which are the focus of the theater's flame ... only in Habimah, the Hebrew theater, is there no duality, no barrier between the spectators and the audience."[7]

The universal praise accorded *Habimah* and its support by Makim Gorky represented an embarrassment to the *Yevsektsia*. The regime, however, found it useful to be granted recognition abroad for its efforts to sponsor *avant-garde* art and theater before Stalin's heavy hand eradicated all creativity. Ironically, no successful Hebrew-language theater had got off the ground in czarist times. *Habimah*'s success stemmed in part from the enthusiasm of the highest actors, directors and designers for a Modern Hebrew theater. Raphael Zvi, one of the *Habimah* founders, proclaimed that the communist revolution had set off a revolutionary storm that had "ignited our Hebrew rebellion."

The theater evinced no hint of any anti–Soviet activity; on the contrary, it was a showcase for the regime. Amazingly and ironically, there was no national Yiddish theater at the time in the Soviet Union that could compete with it; yet in the libraries and schools, Hebrew had already been extinguished and labeled as reactionary.

Zionist Labor Party leader David Ben-Gurion recalled this fleeting contradiction that seemed to him so improbable during a trip to Moscow in 1923. He visited the theater that proudly bore the huge Hebrew-lettered signs "*Habimah*" and "*Kupah*" (box office in Hebrew) on its marquee. He wrote in the Labor Party's journal upon his return to Palestine, "Does all this exist in the Moscow of 1923 where the state library does not allow Hebrew newspapers and conceals many of its Hebrew books, where study of the Hebrew language is not permitted? A sense of miracle grips me, a feeling of wonder, of rebellion against the laws of reality. Can it be? This acting, this stage, under these conditions, in our time, in the Russian Communist Moscow among the Yevsektsia?"[8]

It seemed almost mystical to many that the *Habimah* directors and crew of actors decided that the theater would adopt the Sephardi-Oriental pronunciation of Hebrew (pronouncing the letter *tav* as *t* instead of *s*, and changing the vowel *kamatz* from an *aw* to an *ah* sound), then only tentatively accepted by most teachers of Modern Hebrew in Palestine. This move facilitated the essential unified character of Modern Hebrew.

All this time, the *Yevsektsia* apparatus was gritting its teeth, confident that this aberration would not last. Yet, in spite of internal divisions and immense pressure to also perform plays in Yiddish, and in so doing tour the Soviet Union as well as the Yiddish-speaking Diaspora, the theater refused. R. Ben-Ari, a leading actor of *Habimah*, wrote about the decision to remain a purely Hebrew-language theater:

> We were acting in Hebrew not in order to create provocation but because this was our mission ... to bring to the stage a language which, despite all that has happened, has not died out over thousands of years. We must revive it. We must learn how to express in this tongue, ideas for the entire world, not only for the Jews. It is, of course, easy to swim with the current, but we want to express our thoughts in language emanating from our national struggle.[9]

The abrupt end came in January 1926 when the theater troupe left for a tour of the Diaspora. All those who had come to the railway station in Riga to see the actors off sensed they would not return and this was the end. Days before, the theater had performed its three hundredth performance of "The Dybbuk" in Moscow to rave reviews. The choice not to return was taken abroad and caused much soul-searching. The decision to locate to Jerusalem (and later Tel-Aviv) meant not only the realization of the Zionist goal and a great transfusion of European culture to Palestine but also the end of the "twilight zone." After this, the Soviet Union turned its back on Hebrew language and culture for fifty years and henceforth regarded it as a sign of dual loyalty.

No such policy existed toward any other language—certainly not toward German, the language of the ethnic minority of the Volga Germans and a language of major importance for scientific research and classic literature. The Hebrew-language Communist Party daily newspaper in Israel, *Kol ha-Am* (Voice of the People), began in 1949 and was heavily subsidized from Moscow; yet never once did it find it necessary to explain to its readers, including native-born Israeli Jews whose only language was Hebrew, the absurd contradiction that in the Soviet Union, the authorities maintained a policy denying Soviet citizens the right to study or teach Hebrew at any recognized institution of learning. All the party's activities in Israel were carried out in Hebrew and Arabic, and the party maintained its image in all electoral campaigning of a bi-national institution. During the "honeymoon" with the Soviet Union (1947–1949), the separate Jewish and Arab sections of the Palestinian Communist Party were instructed to unite and support the UN partition plan and the Israeli war effort to repel the Arab invasions of the country, even encouraging the army to drive on toward the Suez Canal and hand British imperialism a "stinging defeat."

In spite of a half-century of persecution, the underground teaching of Hebrew persisted and came out into the open in the 1970s as the life blood of the "Refusenik" movement,[10] helping to educate and train more than a million emigrants to the State of Israel. Prominent in this campaign was Natan Sharansky,[11] who endured nine years of imprisonment, with long periods in solitary confinement designed to make him lose his mind. He was hailed everywhere as a symbol of Jewish pride and human rights. He and his wife finally arrived in Israel in February 1986, forcing the Soviet regime to recognize that its attempts to strangle Hebrew culture had been in vain.

Soviet Yiddish Competitor to a Hebrew State—Origin of the Jewish Autonomous Region—The Birobidzhan Experiment

Let us imagine for a moment that the idealism of communists who wished to retain a sense of Jewish ethnic identity had persisted, that a geographically and climatically more suitable territory (such as the Crimea) had been chosen, that the Holocaust had not occurred and that the Soviet Union had welcomed large numbers of Jewish immigrants anxious to escape the Nazi regime and anti–Semitic societies in Eastern Europe, and that Birobidzhan has received massive charitable support, as did the Zionist movement, from world Jewry—admittedly a set of miraculous hypothetical assumptions.

This thought experiment leads to the inescapable conclusion that, under these imaginary circumstances, no one would doubt today that more than one Jewish nationality would exist in the form of two sovereign nation-states, Israel and a Soviet Jewish Republic (Birobidzhan or the Crimean Peninsula), both "Jewish" in the same sense that the United States, Canada and Australia are separate nation-states of "British origin." Both would correctly claim to be Jewish "national states," a scenario used in the 2007 novel *The Yiddish Policeman's Union* by Michael Chabon.

The remaining "Jews" of the world probably would still be referred to as "Jewry" and regarded wholly as a religious community—groups of families belonging to a wide range of religious congregations, split by doctrinal differences, and equally loyal to the lands of their birth and citizenship. By 1930, Soviet plans were declared to establish a Jewish Autonomous Region in Birobidzhan along the Amur River on the Soviet-Chinese border in Manchuria. Birobidzhan thus offered a competitive alternative to Zionism and Palestine in an area with absolutely no connection to any Jewish religious or historical memory.

The Birobidzhan experiment of the Jewish Autonomous Region was ultimately pathetic and comical. Migrant Jews coming from the United States, Argentina and Western Europe as well as the European parts of the Soviet Union had absolutely nothing in common with the local Mongol population. The selection of this territory, one without any Jewish connection in a remote corner of the Soviet Union in the Far East bordering China and Mongolia, was due to Soviet hopes that settlement there might serve their security needs and lessen the appeal of Zionism, thus killing two birds with one stone.

Even as early as 1938, just prior to the Hitler-Stalin Non-Aggression Pact, Jewish communists throughout the world were instructed to play on Jewish anger at Nazi Germany to win increased support for the Soviet Union and the communist parties. Moissaye Olgin, the veteran editor of *Freiheit* (Freedom), went to such lengths to follow the new line from Moscow that one could imagine him repenting at Yom Kippur services for all his past animosity to the cause of Jewish self-determination in Palestine (denounced as reactionary Zionism by *Freiheit* for the previous twenty-five years): "We managed to alienate the Jewish masses. More than that we managed to convey an idea that the Communists are hostile to Jewish national aspirations. We fought Zionism which was correct, but in fighting Zionism we forgot that many progressive elements of the Jewish People were Zionistically inclined. We forgot also that the craving, the desire for nationhood is not in itself reactionary, although Zionism is reactionary."[12] He ended his confession-diatribe with an appeal that the Jewish communists repudiate "national nihilism," but learn not to scoff at religion and be the "inheritors of the best in Jewish culture" (Communist Party National Convention in New York, 1938).

Although Marxist theory held that Jewish immigration to Palestine had been fostered by "romantics" or "religious circles" or "bourgeois nationalists," all under the reactionary banner of Zionism, the Soviet press now stated that in Palestine, a new Hebrew nation had been created that deserved the right to self-determination. Curiously, the Soviet propaganda machine even praised the "far right" underground groups of the Irgun and "Stern Gang" for their campaign of violence against the British authorities.

Soviet support for the partition of Palestine and the military aid (through the agency of the communist Czech government) rendered to the beleaguered Israeli state fighting for its life in 1947–1949 furthered a pro–Soviet position among many American Jews who gave considerable support to the far-left candidate, former vice president Henry Wallace of the Progressive Party, in the 1948 election. During this period, Jewish communists around the world took up the new party line favoring Israel.[13]

End of the Honeymoon

The brief Soviet foreign policy initiative in 1948 supporting the partition plan and offering active military aid helped the new Jewish state to survive.[14] It thus raised hopes that the Soviet leaders had finally acknowledged the existence of a Jewish nationality based in part on the Hebrew language. Nevertheless, just prior to Stalin's death, a new wave of suppression, including the murder of leading Yiddish writers in the Soviet Union, made it clear that Jews were still suspect of disloyalty. This was followed by the infamous "Doctors Plot" trials in 1952–1953, in which an anti–Semitic trend was evident, and yet the trials were supported by the Israeli Hebrew-language Communist daily newspaper *Kol ha-Am*. In summary, the "achievements" of the Jewish Autonomous Region were meager by any measure and ignored by Soviet foreign policy considerations. The classic Stalinist explanation of Marxist theory regarding the Jews was that they had lost the national characteristics of a people speaking their own language and residing in their own territory (even though the Soviet Union had supported the original 1947 UN partition proposal dividing Palestine into Jewish and Arab states).

In 1958, Khrushchev admitted the failure of the region and blamed it on "Jewish individualism." Today, the region has begun to recover and has even attracted some former residents who had migrated to Israel but couldn't find satisfactory jobs and make the transition to Hebrew and adapt to a totally dif-

Israeli troops complete the conquest of the Negev and raise their homemade flag over Eilat in March 1949.

ferent climate. Decades of Soviet intimidation that challenged the very foundation of Jewish identity were insufficient to quell the national movement that began with the demand to teach and learn Hebrew.

On June 25–26, 2012, Russian Prime Minister Vladimir Putin met with Israeli leaders in Jerusalem; this was his second visit and he encountered warm receptions wherever he went. The Israeli leader, Benjamin Netanyahu, in his remarks referred to the "vast human bridge" of more than one million recent Russian-speaking Israelis who had, in a few short years, contributed to making relations between the two countries warm and friendly. Both Putin and Netanyahu praised the close relations and spoke positively of the more than five hundred thousand Russian tourists (many of them non–Jews) who visit Israel annually. Putin recalled the service of half a million Jews who fought in the ranks of the Red Army to defeat the Nazis. These relations heralded the prospect of even closer ties in the future.

The Russian leader has encouraged excellent ties with the Jewish community and enjoys a close friendship with several Jewish leaders, especially Rabbi Berel Lazar, one of Russia's two chief rabbis. ORT, the Jewish educational agency, cites its cooperation with the government in running educational programs such as Moscow ORT Technology College, which opened in 1996 and has 4,000 students, and the ORT Gunzburg Jewish School No. 550 in St. Petersburg, which has won the President's Prize, the most prestigious national award for innovation and excellence in education.[15]

Hebrew schools flourish throughout Russia and the former Soviet republics. Sixty years of active persecution of the language achieved none of its objectives. Vibrant Russian- AND Hebrew-speaking communities now exist in both countries, something the activists of the old *Yevsektsia* could never have imagined in their worst nightmares.

12. Arab-Israeli Use of Hebrew

Many Jews in the Diaspora, even those who pray daily from the traditional prayer books, are unable to read or speak Modern Hebrew, whereas a majority of Israel's Arab citizens are competent in it, or may actually prefer Hebrew, especially in professional occupations. A recent study indicates that as much as 60 percent of the adult Arab population in Israel is proficient in the language (compared to 90 percent of Jews).[1]

The issue of language and its relationship to national identity presents several ironies and remains a dilemma for the State of Israel and its Arab citizens and resident non–Jews.

Israel, like Finland or Belgium or Canada, is bilingual, but the relationship between majority and minority is much more problematic and emotional.[2] No matter how sympathetic Jews in the Diaspora may be toward the "Jewish state," the majority do not define themselves as sharing the same "nationality," and the overwhelming majority are unable to experience the reality of Israel firsthand even if they have been there a number of times, thus missing out on a considerable content of jokes, word-plays, popular songs and literature.

As a fundamental tool of communication, Hebrew is taught in all public schools attended by Arabs from the age of nine during ten school years for 3 to 5 hours a week as a compulsory subject. The Israeli Hebrew syllabus for them involves grammar, reading comprehension of various texts in prose and poetry from different periods (including the Old Testament, the *Mishnah* and contemporary literature), and formal composition. Pupils are basically taught in Arabic, with increasingly more Hebrew conversation and instruction as they progress. Hebrew idioms and words are often introduced through their literary Arabic equivalents. The most common mistakes are omission of the grammatical marker "et" for the accusative form to introduce the direct object of an active transitive verb, incorrect "gender" of many nouns and disagreement between subject and predicate, all reflecting subtle grammatical differences between the two languages.[3]

Language—The Medium of Discourse for a Common Citizenship

It is largely language, the common medium of discourse, that transforms legal abstractions such as citizenship into a living flesh-and-blood community. We then are able to relate to our neighbors; the books, magazines and newspapers we read; what we listen to on the radio and television and in the cinema; the games we play; the social life we lead; and even the jokes we tell and the history we revere. People who do not have this common language must rely on intermediaries and translations.

About forty years ago, before the widespread acceptance of colloquial American expressions (even the term "movies" was frowned upon by the BBC, which insisted on always using "the cinema"), British tourists told their American hosts that they had "knocked up Mary that morning" and were immediately reprimanded that they shouldn't say that to mean they had simply knocked on the door of her house to check if she had been home.

Even among English speakers in the United States, Australia, Canada, and New Zealand, there are obvious and immediately apparent differences that reflect diverse origins of the population and distinct habits, histories and social conventions. The same applies to Brazilian and Portuguese speakers of Portuguese; French, Ivory Coast, Canadian and Haitian speakers of French; Argentine, Mexican and Spanish speakers of Spanish, and so forth. We do not laugh at the same jokes, nor is the political map identical to the language map.

The Difficulties of Literacy for Speakers of Arabic

The language issue should not be underestimated for precisely the reason that, in the Arabic-speaking world, there is a catastrophic deficiency of translations from other languages that would make the fruit of other civilizations comprehensible. The Greeks or Swedes, with a population of just over ten million people each, have more literature and news, economic, political, cultural and scientific information reports translated into their "minor languages" than almost 300 million Arabs.[4] In most Arab countries, there is a huge percentage of illiterate women, and regional dialectical differences make the standard literary Arabic learned in schools (*fusha*), referred to in Arabic as *fuṣḥā l-'aṣr* (Modern Standard Arabic) and *fuṣḥā t turāt* (modeled after the Koran but with modern vocabulary), an artificial medium, so that even among the diverse Arab peoples, there is little intercommunication.

The statistics below, taken from the most recent posting on the Internet by Index Translationium[5] and collected by UNESCO, tell a remarkable though unbelievable story. The number of books translated into the target language shows, for example, that a "minor language" like Danish is still major in the sense that it makes available to the Danish-reading public of less than six million people a "universe" of 64,864 books and articles, putting it in twelfth place, whereas Modern Standard Arabic, with a supposed official number of readers in excess of 300 million, was the target language of 12,700 works, just barely ahead of the less than 7 million speakers of Hebrew who could read 10,965 works in a translation! On the basis of per million potential readers, the Hebrew-speaking audience has at its disposal roughly 1,500 foreign works, and that of the "Arab World" only 44!

The Number of Books Translated in "Target Languages" Since 1979, as Compiled by UNESCO

"TOP 50" Target Language

1	German	301,880		26	Slovenian	18,692
2	French	239,968		27	Catalan	17,972
3	Spanish	228,492		28	Lithuanian	15,389
4	English	156,001		29	ARABIC	12,700
5	Japanese	130,638		30	Turkish	11,908
6	Dutch	111,267		31	Farsi, Western; Persian	11,105
7	Russian	100,698		32	HEBREW	10,965
8	Portuguese	78,838		33	Norwegian, Bokmål	9,944
9	Polish	76,697		34	Serbo-Croatian (to 1992)	8,273
10	Swedish	71,206		35	Latvian	8,151
11	Czech	68,919		36	Albanian	6,720
12	Danish	64,864		37	Icelandic	6,536
13	Chinese	63,113		38	Ukrainian	4,604
14	Italian	59,914		39	Indonesian	4,440
15	Hungarian	55,214		40	Macedonian	3,914
16	Finnish	48,311		41	Basque	3,902
17	Norwegian	35,158		42	Moldavian	3,739
18	Greek, Modern	30,457		43	Hindi	3,535
19	Korean	28,167		44	Welsh	3,186
20	Bulgarian	27,457		45	Uzbek	2,781
21	Serbian	23,731		46	Armenian	2,531
22	Estonian	20,508		47	Kazakh	2,465
23	Romanian	20468		48	Gallegan	2,357
24	Croatian	19,727		49	Georgian	2,189
25	Slovak	19,644		50	Belarusian	1,919

The database contains cumulative bibliographical information on books translated and published in about one hundred UNESCO member states since 1979. It totals more than 2,000,000 entries in all disciplines—literature, social and human sciences, natural and exact sciences, art, history and so forth—and is updated regularly. By publishing this list, UNESCO provides the general public with the valuable tool of referencing bibliographical inventories of translations on a worldwide scale.

The 57 members of the Organization of the Islamic Conference (OIC) appear to be united in their crusade against "Zionism," which serves as the whipping boy and repository of all blame to explain away their failure as nation-states. These attitudes have been shared in large part by the Arabs in Israel but are also the result of intense pressure applied against them by neighboring regimes to prevent any tendency to seek accommodation. Israel is a state in which language is a powerful factor, encouraging acculturation to values and norms traditionally ignored or despised in the Arab-Muslim culture of the Middle East, such as freedom of conscience and expression, women's rights and religious liberty.

Israeli linguist Eliezer Ben-Rafael[6] emphasizes that the native Palestinian Arabic dialect in current and popular usage in Israel differs substantially from the literary form (Modern Standard—the *fusha*) used by those with a higher education for entertainment, reading, education, and listening to the media. He explains why many Israeli Arabs find it easier to use Hebrew textbooks in many subjects rather than those from Arab countries, which the Ministry of Education is thus reluctant to import and are in the literary form of Arabic.

For many Arabs, the State of Israel is conflated with Judaism, regarded as a powerful ally of a militant "expansionist" Judaic civilization, which Muslims are taught that Islam had successfully confronted in the seventh century under the leadership of Muhammad. For several decades of the twentieth century, "Zionism" has been regarded everywhere in the Arab Middle East as the equivalent of a powerful mythical international conspiracy identical to the notorious "Protocols of the Elders of Zion," a scam-forgery endorsed by the czarist regime in Russia at the end of the nineteenth century.[7]

Nevertheless, the obvious signs of brutality and the violation of human rights in Gaza by Hamas and in Syria, Tunisia, Egypt, and Yemen (where the "Arab Spring" triumphed) and the growing instability in Iraq, Lebanon and Jordan have not been lost on Israel's Arab population, who have begun to critically rethink their role in the country following a near collapse of Arab nationalism.[8] The latter has given way to the vision of a triumphal Islamism and the stated goal of restoring the caliphate, a view certainly not embraced by many Christian Arab, Druze[9] and Circassian[10] segments of the population, who understand that cooperation and coexistence in Israel is an essential and inevitable part of any desirable (and peaceful future scenario.[11] It is no accident that few Arab Israeli men seek marriage partners among women from the West Bank, who are much more conservative, not likely to work outside the home, and not proficient in Hebrew.[12]

According to a report in the *Jerusalem Post*[13] under the headline "West Bank Hebrew Language Study Is Growing," more and more private schools in the territories under the rule of the Palestinian Authority are offering courses in Hebrew, but none in official "state schools." One example is the Mohammed bin Rashid Bin Al-Maktoum School in Al-Bireh, next to Ramallah, where many students in grades 7–10 have opted to study the Hebrew language.[14] The director of this private school, Samer Nimer, explained, "We want to know what is going on in Israel first hand, not what others are saying about Israel." What is truly surprising is that the curriculum used is that supplied by the Israeli Ministry of Education. The school, with the approval of the parents, decided to offer Hebrew rather than French because of its utility; many of the students have visited Israel and spoken Hebrew with Israelis. They also frequently use Israeli websites in Hebrew.

Jihad Zakarneh, the director general of curriculums in the Palestinian Ministry of Education, justifies the refusal of Palestine Administration (PA) schools to teach Hebrew because it is "not a language that is used outside of Israel, and the demand for this language is not high. Students who want to study abroad seek German, French, or Russian language because it will help them."[15] He also revealed that approximately 200 private language and translation centers operating in the West Bank under a license of the PA's Education Ministry have permission to teach Hebrew. Most of those adults seeking to learn the language work in imports and exports, finance, insurance and customs. In the Gaza Strip, the Hamas-controlled Education Ministry does offer Hebrew to its students in the public schools, out of necessity, since Israel is the only outlet to the outer non–Arab world.

Progress of Hebrew-Language Education in Egypt— What It Portends

Similar views have been endorsed by the Egyptian educational authorities. It comes as a surprise to many foreign observers that nine of fourteen universities, including Al-Azhar Islamic University, offer courses in Modern Hebrew, with approximately 20,000 students, more than are studying the language in the United States! These students are majoring in Middle Eastern studies. Mounir Mahmoud, an Egyptian journalist, told the Israeli daily *Ma'ariv* that between two and three thousand students graduate each year with bachelor's degrees from Hebrew studies courses. He explained that Egyptian students "are exposed to Israeli culture and history, and unlike their colleagues who see Israel as only a source of hatred and conquest, they learn about it from a different angle altogether."[16]

In a journalistic scoop, on July 2, 2013, Israeli reporter Guy Zohar interviewed Egyptian woman journalist and political activist Heba Abu Seif on Israeli live television.[17] Her perfect Hebrew surprised many viewers and is an optimistic sign. Just as Israelis can now view events with direct commentary from on-the-spot sources in their own language, in the future, Arab opinion about Israel will no longer rely entirely on its own traditional and highly biased accounts. These Egyptian students who are fluent in Hebrew can now consult the historical record to view how Israelis saw and acted upon events, and they can also regard Zionism and relations with the Arab peoples in a different light.

Israeli Arab Writers in Hebrew

Successful Arab authors writing in Hebrew, such as Anton Shammas, Atallah Mansour, Emile Habibi, and Sayed Kashua,[18] deserve to be regarded in the forefront of modern Israeli literature and journalism, but they are in fact nonentities and register a blank stare among many observers in the Diaspora.

Even when these authors have been ultra-critical of Israeli state policies, they have nevertheless been attacked by most Muslims and Arabs outside of Israel as traitors—the equivalent of Benedict Arnold. The late Emile Habibi, a Christian Arab and a long-term communist member of the Knesset, was awarded Israel's highest literary prize, as well as being the first Israeli Arab memorialized on an Israeli postage stamp, a move denounced by some Israeli Jews and many Arabs abroad. As a veteran communist, Habibi could point to his support of the 1947 partition plan to build his reputation as an "Israeli patriot" and at the same time a principled and determined fighter for Arab rights and equality. His novel, *The Secret Life of Saeed, the Pessoptimist*,[19] written in Arabic and translated into Hebrew by Anton Shammas, presented a sophisticated and highly literate Israeli Hebrew-reading audience for the first time with the full extent of the frustrations and daily compromises of the Arab minority in Israel.

Shammas, the author of the novel *Arabesques*, is a Christian Arab, widely acknowledged as a talented author, proficient in poetic Hebrew and known for his love of the landscapes of his childhood in Galilee. His work is not as caustically critical of Jewish society as Habibi's, but he eventually found it more comfortable to leave Israel and settle in the United States in a small Midwestern town. Moreover, the fact that Shammas is a Christian from the Galilean village of Fassuta, and that his parents were subject to considerable humiliation, ostracism and pressure to conform to the nationalist line during the Arab Revolt against the British Mandate authorities in 1936–1939, has produced some speculation that *Arabesques* is partly directed against the intolerance of general Palestinian Muslim opinion as well as the Jewish and Zionist authorities. Nevertheless, more than other previous Arab authors writing in Hebrew, Shammas has indeed forced a Jewish Israeli audience to look in the mirror and recognize the bitterness of life-long humiliation, alienation and displacement experienced by many Israeli Arab intellectuals.

Sayed Kashua, a Muslim from the border village of Tira in The Triangle[20] area, is only 36, and his three novels in Hebrew deal perceptively with the dilemmas of Arab intellectuals in Israeli society who are able and tempted to "pass" as Jews. His book, *Dancing Arabs*[21] captures the same precarious position of a minority under pressure as Shalom Aleichem's *Fiddler on the Roof*. It is a positive sign that Kashua's characters avoid blatant stereotypes and that there is a less overtly hostile treatment of Israeli society than in the novels of Habibi and Shammas.

The Israeli Arabic Academy's Complaints

There is no single Academy of the Arabic Language. The only one to operate outside the "Arabic-Speaking World" of independent Arab majority states is located in Haifa, Israel. It was established in 2007 and maintains a website at www.arabicac.com. Its objectives follow the design and law establishing the Academy of the Hebrew Language, and its major task is preserving, elevating and standardizing the use of the language in Israel, where many Arabs regard it as being a poor cousin to Hebrew in spite of its standing as an "official language."

The organization is particularly concerned with ensuring the use of Arabic on public signs and preventing what it considers the knee-jerk preference for Hebrew even in Arab municipalities and in shops that send out letters to their clients and constituents in Hebrew. Because Israeli Arabs with university ambitions can only choose among institutions of higher learning in which Hebrew is the language of instruction, they set their sights early on mastering the language of the majority.

Professor emeritus of Arabic literature at Tel Aviv University, Sasson Somekh, who is a member of the Arabic Language Academy as well as a former secretary of the Academy of the Hebrew Language, has remarked many times on the decline in the level of both spoken and literary Arabic among Israeli

Arab students entering universities in Israel. In a recent interview,[22] he explained how much Hebrew has gotten into Arabic: "There is a very strong interference of Hebrew, especially for those who go out of their communities and mingle with the Jewish population. From there on, every new thing they learn is in Hebrew. The Arab intelligentsia is irked; their newspapers are full of complaints about Hebrew infiltrating Arabic but they can't do anything about it. Meanwhile, the written language is weakening and disappearing. The Israeli Arabs have a feeling of losing their cultural basis."

There is no remedy for this situation as Israeli Arabs continue to improve their education, enter the professions, seek to integrate more successfully within society and serve a wider clientele. Hebrew is much more important, whereas the diversity of Arabic dialects would make even their Palestinian mother tongue of limited use outside the country.

Israel's Presidents Strongly Encourage a Bilingual Israel (Hebrew and Arabic)

Two of Israel's former presidents—Haim Herzog (born in Ireland) and Yitzhak Navon (born in Jerusalem and a direct descendent of the exiles from Spain in 1492)—cogently but gently argued for more Israeli Jews to learn Arabic as an important step in helping to reduce tensions and balance the increased knowledge of Hebrew among Israeli Arabs. In November, 1976, the Knesset's Educational Committee held several sessions on the implementation of a policy requiring compulsory study of Arabic in elementary and high schools. The barriers to implementing such a requirement are, however, significant—first and foremost, the existence of a wide discrepancy between the spoken vernacular of the local Arab population and the classical language, as well as the low "prestige value" of the wide diversity of Arabic dialects that were used "at home" by the parents and grandparents of many Mizrachi Jewish students.

An important study conducted to follow up the Educational Committee's suggestion in 1990, *Social Psychological Factors Related to the Study of Arabic Among Israeli Jewish High School Students* (Tel Aviv University; School of Education), found that among Jewish tenth graders who had studied Arabic as a voluntary subject for several years, a huge majority were in favor of Arab-Jewish youth contact and most believed Arabic study should be compulsory to help foster more Arab-Jewish contacts.[23]

Upper- and Lower-Class Hebrew

Ever since the days of Ben-Yehuda, researchers have searched Arabic for the source of many new Hebrew words and "correct" Hebrew pronunciation, which is now largely regarded by the Ashkenazi segment as a marker of lower-class origin and Arab or "Eastern-Oriental Jewish" (Mizrachi) identity.

Another irony of this situation is that failure to pronounce the guttural letters correctly leads to frequent spelling errors by the "upper-class" and largely Ashkenazi (European origin) Jewish majority. It also gives the language very little variety in terms of distinctive sounds.

One amusing anecdote of this situation is the solution found to the Hebrew translation of the great musical and film *My Fair Lady*.[24] How would the translators deal with Eliza Doolittle's lower-class "Cockney" accent and dialect, and her struggle to learn "proper" (upper-class) English? How to render these differences in Hebrew for an Israeli audience? The first attempt was ridiculous because a proper pronunciation of Hebrew in the "ears" of the purists meant imitating the "lower-class" pronunciation of Hebrew employed by most Arabs and many Oriental Jews (especially the clear enunciation of *ayin* and *ḥet*)! A solution was eventually found to make the Hebrew of the lower-class Eliza a sort of baby Hebrew, with several letters transposed.

Hebrew and Arabic Literature in Translation

The first tentative step taken toward intercultural exchange between Israel and the Arab world was the 1978 translation of an anthology of Hebrew literature. Several translations of Hebrew works into Arabic had already been made, but the novelty was that, for the first time, Israeli writers were able to reach the Arabic-speaking world without comment or censorship. Unfortunately, this took place using English as an intermediary language. No Israeli Arab fluent in Hebrew was brave enough to participate in the first initiative.

Subsequent translations made directly from Hebrew to Arabic were published in Egypt. These included the works of Amos Oz (*My Michael*), David Grossman (*The Yellow Wind*), Amos Kenan (*The Road to Ein Harod*) and Sammi Michael. Michael was born in Iraq and made the transition from being a successful writer in Arabic to one in Hebrew in the 1950s. He has published what might be called the classic "Romeo and Juliet" Israeli story calling for Arab-Jewish coexistence. It is the love story of a new Russian immigrant, a musician who plays the trumpet and speaks a crude, limited Hebrew, and a highly educated Christian Arab woman from Haifa who works in a travel office and is fluent in Hebrew and a devoted fan of Yehuda Amihai, considered by many to be Israel's greatest modern poet.

The book, *Hatzozra baWadi* (Trumpet in the Wadi),[25] in spite of its message of tolerance (or perhaps because of it), was not deemed appropriate by the Egyptian authorities, who hindered the publication of the Arabic translation. It is a very poignant story of prejudice and role reversal, and a commentary on the nationalist aberrations that make language, a political tool. The couple in love move across the barriers of nationalism, religion, and language but a tragic end is inevitable because of the prejudices held by their Arab and Jewish families, friends and neighbors.

The Hebrew works that the Egyptian authorities allowed reflect a critical view of Israel from the political left, particularly with regard to the status of the Arab minority. Since then, many additional Hebrew books have been translated into Arabic by both Jewish and Arab Israelis, but they are not allowed to be imported into any Arab country.

One fascinating aspect of the influence of education in Israel among Arab writers is their familiarity with biblical motifs and some of the early Zionist poets. This is particularly evident in the works of the poet Mahmud Darwish, who left Israel, and the late long-serving communist member of the Knesset, Arab writer Emile Habibi.

Hopefully, in the event of a more stable and overall peace agreement, bilingual Hebrew and Arabic writers among the Israeli Arabs will form an important bridge in cultivating a new age of cooperation and mutual respect between these two ancient cultures and languages.

The "Arab" Communities

In 2012, the official number of Arab residents and non–Jews in Israel was almost 1,600,000 people—almost 20 percent of Israel's population of eight million. This figure includes approximately 300,000 Arabs in East Jerusalem, under Israeli control since 1967. About 82.6 percent of the Arab population in Israel is Sunni Muslim (with a very small minority of Shia), another 9 percent is Druze, and around 9 percent is Christian (mostly Oriental Orthodox and Catholic denominations).[26]

East Jerusalem residents are increasingly becoming integrated into Israeli society, with growing numbers of applications for an Israeli ID card, more high school students taking the Israeli matriculation exams, and greater numbers enrolling in Israeli academic institutions. Also very significant are the rising number of East Jerusalem youths volunteering for national service, a higher level of satisfaction according to polls of residents and increased use of Israeli health services.

A survey showed that, in a final agreement, a not insignificant number of East Jerusalem Palestinians would prefer to remain under Israeli rule. There are 10 schools in East Jerusalem that specialize in preparing East Jerusalem students for Israeli universities and colleges.[27] When a survey carried out by

Pechter Middle East Polls asked if Arab residents of East Jerusalem preferred to become a citizen of Palestine, with all of the rights and privileges of other Palestinian citizens, or a citizen of Israel, only 30 percent chose Palestinian citizenship—as compared to 35 percent who chose Israeli citizenship. Another 35 percent either had no answer or declined to provide it. To most observers, this last group is really in favor but dares not express such views openly.

The number of East Jerusalem Palestinians requesting—and receiving—Israeli citizenship rose sharply between 2004 and 2010, per new data obtained by *HaAretz*.[28] According to officials, the stream of applicants for citizenship has intensified in the past two years. However, owing to various obstacles and bureaucratic hindrances, there has been mounting criticism that the government is relectant to offer incentives. Israeli Interior Ministry data report that from 2001 to 2011, 3,374 Palestinians obtained full Israeli citizenship. From 2004 there has been a steady rise in the number of Palestinians who were naturalized.[29] Current residents of East Jerusalem—numbering over 350,000, or 38 percent of the city's total population—shop at Israeli malls, use Israeli services, frequent Israeli restaurants and bars, send their children to study at the Hebrew University of Jerusalem, and receive Israeli social and health benefits. These trends are completely ignored by the world media.

For decades, the wholesale community-based exemptions from military service for both ultra–Orthodox Jews and most "Arabs" have rankled mainstream Jewish and Druze Israelis. That arrangement, generally known as the Tal Law,[30] has intensified the raucous national political debate.

The Tal Committee was established back in August 1999 to deal with the special exemptions from mandatory military service in the Israel Defense Forces (IDF). Based on its recommendations, the Knesset passed the temporary Tal Law in July 2002, authorizing a continuation of the "temporary" exemption for yeshiva students, providing alternatives after a "decision year" at age 22 to do one year of civilian service or a shortened 16-month military service. This legislation was due to expire after five years but was subsequently renewed, kicking the can down the road. The percentage of ultra–Orthodox individuals of military age who have received exemptions has continually risen since the beginning of the state.

In the end, no democratic society can continue to tolerate different classes of citizens with different rights and obligations. That prospect is now less likely than in the past and has exacerbated growing public dissatisfaction. Arab citizens and some ultra–Orthodox Jews who cultivate Yiddish have an equivocal, almost schizophrenic relationship with the state, its symbols, and the majority Jewish population.

Several opinion polls paint a somewhat more optimistic picture among the Arab population wishing to retain Israeli citizenship after the signing of a final peace agreement and establishment of a Palestinian Arab state. This reality may even lag behind the two-year-long civil war in Syria—once the proud "defender" of Palestinian rights, but now widely regarded among all Israelis, including many Muslims, as a despotic and oppressive barbaric regime.

The Declaration of Independence and Its Promises

Israel's Declaration of Independence and the statement of Prime Minister David Ben-Gurion in addressing the seventh gathering of the first Knesset on March 8, 1949, explicitly proclaimed that complete equality of rights and obligations are assured for all citizens regardless of differences in religion, race and "nationality" (*leum*). The term "Republic" was considered but dropped out of concern that it implied a full equality of all citizens in terms of both rights and obligations that might lead to demands for a "bi-national state."

For more than sixty-five years the same "state of suspended animation" has existed, leaving most non–Jews in Israel in limbo. Are they citizens? There is no doubt according to Israel's Declaration of Independence.

Jewish-Arab Collaboration Across the Political Divide

The history of the Palestinian Arabs under the British Mandate is replete with the violence of extreme nationalism as well as numerous assassinations and attempts on the lives of suspected "collaborators"; yet, without their help, advice and cooperation in facilitating land sales and the provision of vital intelligence to the Zionist settlements and Jewish Agency officials, it is likely that a Jewish state would never have succeeded.

Recent scholarship utilizing original sources, long kept secret, has confirmed the profound help afforded the *Yishuv* by Arab agents, sympathizers, collaborators, call them what you will.[31] It behooves Israel not to put symbolic obstacles in the path of those who do not identify with the enemy. This should necessitate some attempt to find the kind of compromises that foster identification with the state and lower barriers to full participation in society, but without insisting on acceptance of all aspects of Jewish identity.

Many observers who are aware of the unrelenting hostility of a majority of Arab Knesset members and many prominent figures in public life among the Israeli Arabs do not give sufficient recognition to the prevailing opportunism that characterizes the political culture prevalent in the region. This means there are no real political parties, no free press or independent judiciary—hence the expression "The Arab Street" (i.e., the opinion shaped by the inability to confront the power of intimidation exercised by the prevailing majority and conventional wisdom). Questions and issues of policy are not debated. They are manifested in street demonstrations, almost always orchestrated. In stable states with strong governments, the "people" support the government. In weak states, extremist religious and political groups capable of using force, coercion and the threat of violence hold sway because they promise greater pain and punishment than the rewards offered by the government.

Serious Problems but Not an Apartheid State

Do Israeli Arabs live under apartheid conditions? A simple answer must be a categorical NO. Many among Israel's non-Jews have held, and continue to hold, important positions in the Israeli Knesset, the police force, the army, the diplomatic corps, the arts, literature, cinema, sports, entertainment, the universities, medicine and science, and they are engaged in countless business partnerships with Israeli Jews.

Serious problems and discrimination do exist, especially in the areas of career choices and jobs, as well as a pattern of segregation in residence and elementary education that goes back to conditions prevailing in Palestine under the British and Turkish administrations. Like charges of discrimination practically everywhere else, historical reasons for this state of affairs cannot be ignored and must be put into perspective before any final judgments can be made.

Much of the criticism claiming that Israel is a "racist" or apartheid state is totally misplaced. Israel is by no means the only state that favors certain groups of foreigners with a priority status in immigration and acquisition of citizenship. Countries such as Greece, Norway, Spain and Ireland also provide an easier path to citizenship for those who can prove their grandparents were citizens of those states. Ironically, Spain even grants a favored priority to Jews who can prove that they are true Sephardim—that their ancestors were expelled from the country in the fifteenth century! Approximately ninety Bosnian Jews took advantage of this legislation to seek Spanish citizenship following the break-up of Yugoslavia, and tens of thousands of Sephardi Jews received protection from Spanish and Portuguese consular officials in World War II.

What is difficult and anachronistic and increasingly shameful and reprehensible to accept is that religious affiliation as determined by the orthodox tenets of the rabbinate in Israel should be the criterion to determine "who is a Jew" and the only path to full citizenship. Israel cannot force Hamas or the

Palestinian Authority to negotiate and reach a realistic compromise. But what it can do within its own borders is promote a common denominator of citizenship that will allow non–Jews to participate in Israeli society and be proud to sing a national anthem that relates to them as well.

The Promise of a "Hebrew Republic" and the Israeli Arabs Who Have Taken This Prospect Seriously

In December 2006, a highly pessimistic report by a group of prominent Israeli Arab "intellectuals" and politicians offered a "Future Vision for the Palestinian Arabs in Israel," written at the request of the Countrywide Committee of the Heads of Arab Local Councils in Israel.[32] They identified themselves as Palestinians—"obliged" to bear an Israeli citizenship but profoundly inimical to the Zionist project that created the state. Yet these self-proclaimed community leaders and "intellectuals" stand in contrast to many rank-and-file examples of Arab-Jewish cooperation in everyday life in thousands of joint enterprises and examples of Israeli Arab patriotism.

A resident of Nazareth, Azmi Nasssar was one of Israel's great football (soccer) coaches. Nassar was married to Ruthy, technically Jewish according to rabbinical definitions and labeled as a Jew under both categories of religion and nationality in her I.D. card until her marriage to Azmi when she was 18. Ruthy herself is the daughter of a mixed marriage between Ya'akov Kashlawi (an Arab Christian from Bir Zeit) and Rachel Cohen (a Jew from Petah Tikva). Due to Israeli marriage laws, Ruthy had to convert to her husband's religion of Christianity.

Nassar led the team *Ahei Nazereth* (Nazareth Brothers) and also *Beni Sachnin* (Sons of Sachnin), a team that had Muslim, Christian, Druze and Jewish players. He was a star in his own right as an Israeli footballer and guided his team to several titles. Due to his immense popularity, he coached a Palestinian "national" team and received special permission from both sides to commute back and forth from Nazareth to the territories on the West Bank. The Eretz Israel Museum in Ramat Gan staged an exhibition (summer 2012) of "A Hundred Years of Israeli football"—a colorful multimedia display of posters, banners, videos, uniforms, flags, newspaper and magazine headlines, and stories of the sport. In a video, Azmi is featured embracing fellow players in ecstatic joy: "We are all together—we love and embrace each other—Muslims, Christians, Druze and Jews!" This is not an ecstatic outburst from an eccentric, but rather part of the reality of fruitful inter-communal relations and a vision of the future without an I.D. card that puts citizens in a box.

Khaled Abu Toameh is a distinguished multilingual journalist who was born in the West Bank city of Tulkarem to an Israeli Arab father and a Palestinian Arab mother. He grew up in the large Arab-Israeli town of Baqa al-Gharbiyye and received his BA in English literature from the Hebrew University. He now lives in Jerusalem with his wife and three children. He is a defender of freedom of speech and has criticized the Palestinian Authority numerous times for arresting and harassing journalists in the West Bank, and he admits that there is no freedom for them to do their job under its grim rule. In 2009, he stated that "Israel is a wonderful place to live and we are happy to be there. Israel is a free and open country. If I were given the choice, I would rather live in Israel as a second class citizen than as a first class citizen in Cairo, Gaza, Amman or Ramallah.... If there is a Jew who would like to live in Palestine he is welcome, and if there is an Arab who would like to live in Israel he is also welcome. In an ideal situation, peace means that people can live wherever they want."[33]

Abu Toameh has also been forthright in criticizing the opportunism of Israeli Arab Knesset members in supporting extremism and calling Israel a "state of apartheid" rather than trying to improve the lot of Israel's Arab citizens. At the Durban conference, he refuted their constant harping as victims: "And then they come here to tell us that Israel is a state of apartheid? Excuse me. What kind of hypocrisy is this? What then are you doing in the Knesset? If you are living in an apartheid system, why were you allowed, as an Arab, to run in the election? What are you talking about? We do have problems as Arabs with the establishment here. But to come and say that Israel is an apartheid state is a big exaggeration."[34]

Dr. Suheir Assady, the newly appointed head of the nephrology department at the Rambam Healthcare Campus in Haifa, is the first female Muslim Arab physician in Israel to head a department at a major hospital. There is no Arab woman so young in such a prestigious medical position in the entire Arab world! She graduated from the School of Medicine of the Hebrew University, Jerusalem, and completed her residency in internal medicine and fellowship in nephrology at Rambam Medical Center. She is fluent in Hebrew, Arabic and English. In addition to her various clinical duties, Dr. Assady is active in basic scientific research and teaching both medical and nursing students. Her accomplishments amount to a total refutation of the campaign to paint Israel as a racist or apartheid state.[35] Dr. Assady was born and resides in Nazareth. She is also the author of a chapter in the prestigious book in her field titled *The Kidney*, edited by B.M. Brenner.

Ghaleb Majadla is Israel's minister of sport and the first Arab Muslim to serve in the Israeli cabinet in the country's sixty-year history of the country, an appointment that drew criticism from some right-wing Jewish Knesset members. Majadla rose to prominence in the Hapoel (sports association belonging to Israel's Histadrut labor union).

Qassem Ziyad, a veteran teacher of Arabic who taught the language to thousands of Jewish students in the kibbutz educational movement, decided to rally Arab regional leaders against any proposal for an exchange of territory with the Palestinian Authority more than two decades ago when he said, "No one will prevent us from identifying with our people and their suffering and fighting on its behalf in legitimate ways. To the same extent, no one will take away our Israeli citizenship which is citizenship that we are entitled to and was not granted to us as a favor. We are part of the social fabric of the country and that's a fact. We serve in it in the most positive sense of the word so don't tell us to go to hell."[36]

No memorial existed for fallen Bedouin servicemen killed in uniform while serving in the IDF until the construction of one (at his own expense) by Yousef Juhja in Arara, a hilltop village in the Wadi 'Ara. The memorial plaque is housed in a modest red-roofed edifice adjacent to Juhja's home. Two large Israeli flags fly at its entrance, and the side wall is embellished with marble memorial plaques—in Hebrew and Arabic—for eight soldiers, Muslim and Christian, killed between 1989 and the present. Two more monuments for Druze soldiers have been constructed with some government support.[37]

In the immediate aftermath of Sgt. Juhja's death, scores of soldiers, ministry officials, and even Israel's then-president Moshe Katsav paid calls of respectful mourning to the house. A number of Knesset members have since visited the memorial—but none have been Arab. This is because Juhja sent three sons to the Israel Defense Forces—a rare and deeply unpopular choice made by at least a few hundred Arab youths every year.

After years of dispute, the plaques were finally paid for in 2010 by the Defense Ministry, which agreed to recognize the site as an official monument and to reimburse Juhja for 50 percent of the cost of its construction. A belated memorial stamp honoring fallen Bedouin servicemen was issued in 1999.

Boshra Khalaila is a Muslim, but largely secular, independent-minded 24-year-old Israeli Arab woman who defies stereotypes. She grew up in the Arab village of Deir Hana, in the Galilee, and enrolled at Haifa University when she was 18. There, she had to speak Hebrew for the first time. She proudly represented Israel in a team of five people at an international conference in South Africa designed to slander Israel by comparing it to the old apartheid regime. She made her point in a dramatic way: "I study in the same educational institutions, ride the same buses, shop in the same supermarkets. Everything that they say is absolutely false. And I do feel that I belong to my country."[38] In Deir Hana, where she grew up, political activists from the communist and Arab nationalist parties published flyers and articles saying that she had sold out her people and had been brainwashed.

Aatef Karinaoui is a Bedouin from the Negev town of Rahat who began to form the first demonstratively pro-Israel Arab party, *El Amal Lat'gir*—"Hope for Change" in Arabic—for the Knesset elections of January 22, 2013. He is a "traditional Muslim" of the same type that was most frequently involved in cooperation with the Jews during the time of the Mandate. Karinaoui has openly criticized the "Arab spokesmen" in the Knesset and intellectuals who continually question Israel's legitimacy:

> Arab members of Knesset are setting a fire. They feed off of the politics of division and don't represent the Arab public. The Arab Knesset members do nothing to educate them or advance their situation.... But [at present] there is no alternative to the current leadership. Our leaders have defrauded us for 60 years. Give us a single Knesset mandate and we will do more for the people in four to five years than they have done in 60.... We want to prove that we are loyal and faithful citizens. And we also need more attention and support from the state.... I'm a proud Arab and a proud Israeli too. I'm not Palestinian.... Look at Syria. Look at Egypt, look at Libya, look at Tunisia, and look at Bahrain: the problem is not Israel, it's the Arabs.[39]

Karinaoui is married with five children and serves as the chairman of the nonprofit organization Social Equality and National Service in the Arab Sector, encouraging Arabs to take on part of the national service burden. "If the Jews were to leave the country," Karinaoui has said that the result "would be another Syria." Usually, the Arab sector elects 11 Knesset members and Karinaoui ambitiously projected a prediction that his new party could win several seats. Although disappointed by the results (his party got less than 1 percent), he has not been deterred.

The lack of an appropriate framework and symbols through which the Christian and Muslim population can identify with the state, rather than a specific grievance based on prejudice, is a problem that Israeli educators, philosophers and politicians have not sufficiently addressed. Knowledge of Hebrew is much greater among men and those who work in the Jewish sector of the economy outside of the village. Hebrew is needed for higher education; as there is no university in Israel wholly based on Arabic language with a curriculum developed by Arab scholars. The shortage of appropriate skilled jobs for Israeli Arab university graduates has always been a primary factor in antagonism and resentment toward the state.

Caught in the Middle

Although the Intifada and open expressions of disloyalty have dismayed many Jews in Israel, demonstrations of loyalty and even heroism by Arabs are often ignored. One case in September 2002 that made headlines was that of

17-year-old Rami Mahamid, who informed police of a suicide bomber by mobile phone just in time to prevent many fatalities at the bus stop in the Arab village of Umm-el-Fahm.[40] One policeman was killed and Rami seriously injured by fragments of the explosion. Rami was given a police citation by Brigadier General Dov Lutzky, for "saving life with great courage and initiative," and celebrated for his "good citizenship." He was originally shackled to his hospital bed until his story was checked out due to fear that he might have been an accomplice.

Rami described himself as Israeli, as opposed to Palestinian, but he spoke with some bitterness about the reality of the Arab minority. "I feel always under suspicion," he said. "You don't feel free in your own country." This is the great dilemma of Israel's Arab minority. They are under constant suspicion as disloyal. The way forward is to recognize and reward those who are loyal and make them feel that Israel is their state too.[41]

In January 2013, Father Gabriel Nadaf, 39, a Greek Orthodox priest from Nazareth, was excommunicated by the Orthodox Church Council after he expressed his belief that Christian youths in Israel should fully integrate into Israeli society and serve in the IDF or in the National Service. Since then, he and another Nazareth Orthodox priest, Father André Alamiya, have been the target of scurrilous attacks from "Arab nationalists."[42] The heretical view expressed by the priests is simply part of the reality easily observed by any unbiased observer—that Israel acts as a refuge and an anchor for the Christian Arab minority. "The religious council" is overseen by Dr. Azmi Hakim, a member of the Israeli Communist Party, and the two offending priests are now forced to move around with bodyguards.

In one YouTube clip, Nadaf is dubbed "a Zionist agent, a traitor, insane, who pursues money and tries to enlist the youth in the army of occupation." The council and the Arab nationalist parties, as well as the communists, have compiled a blacklist of Christian religious authorities, Christian IDF officers and Arab members of the security establishment who support Nadaf's ideas. Pictures of youths who participated in a recent IDF event were published in the local Arab press, resulting in an ugly wave of harassment at schools, in social media and in the streets.

Christians have been reduced from a healthy majority in Bethlehem to a cringing, fearful minority, and the same process has been under way in Nazareth for some time. Bishara Shlayan, 57, spokesman for the forum, told the Tazpit News Agency that the exodus of Christians leaving Nazareth has intensified lately: "Many have even left the country. We feel we are being forced out of the city."[43]

Shlayan and Nadaf's efforts have, however, had an impact. During the summer of 2013, 90 Christian high school graduates joined the Israeli armed forces (IDF). This number, small as it is, represents a tripling compared to the volunteers of past summers. Nevertheless, it has evoked an enraged outcry from Muslim community leaders and politicians.[44]

It is more than a shame that many Israeli Jews have shown little support for such brave pro–Israeli "Arabs" who are willing to serve their country. Still, Nadaf and his followers have found a few supporters within Israeli society and the likelihood is that more will follow, as Israel remains the last safe haven in the Middle East where Christians can practice their religion freely.

A poignant documentary film[45] about the life of Shadya Zoabi, a young teenage Muslim Arab Israeli girl, was produced by the Israeli Ministry of Culture and Sport in 2006 and exposes the many conflicting opportunities and traditional restraints that compete and impinge upon the country's Arab minority. Shadya, at the young age of 15, won the gold medal in the World Shotokan Karate Contest held in Durban, South Africa, in 2003. She grew up in the conservative Galilean village of Tamra, but her father, Mazen, was an independent, modern and successful businessman who had the audacity to take pride in his identity as an Israeli Arab, as well as encourage his young daughter to break the traditional taboos in Muslim society and strive for success in a field that was regarded by the rest of her family, friends and neighbors as a violation of the proper code of behavior for a young woman. She was friendly with the Jewish members of her team and even embraced the Israeli flag upon winning her championship in Durban, an act that was viewed as provocative and heretical. In spite of the backing of her father, however, Shadya could not openly oppose the selection of her husband-to-be and the enormous pressure put on her to become a stay-at-home mother and adopt the caustic anti–Israeli views of her brothers.

Another milestone on the long road to greater integration of Israel's non–Jewish citizens was the completion, at the end of October 2013 of the IDF's demanding Tank Commander's Course by the Bedouin corporal Mustafa Tabash, age 19. In an interview on the IDF website, he exclaimed, "Being the first Bedouin in the armored units is awesome, because I am the first to take part in the course, everybody is looking at me and it is a chance for me to show off my abilities."[46] Tabash always defined himself as an Israeli patriot. Initially, he served as an ammunitions loader. As a volunteer, he felt a strong motivation to provide an example to other young Israeli Muslims, and especially the Bedouin community. His family and friends have expressed pride in his accomplishments—especially his little brother, who wishes to follow in his footsteps.

These individuals are not alone. They represent a segment of Israeli Arab society, the proverbial "tip of the iceberg," seeking the full promise of equal citizenship. All of them used their excellent command of Hebrew as an initial tool to demonstrate their capabilities in a variety of fields and as a key to unlock the door of prevailing skepticism and cynicism.

New Examples of a Multicultural Society—Food

Up-market Arab restaurants are flourishing as never before in Israel. In 2007 the chefs and brothers Husam and Nashat Abbas, who own the fashionable El-Babur near Umm al-Fahm (a town that has almost always been portrayed in the Israeli media as a center of extreme Sunni Muslim practice), which is now rated by many critics as the best Arab restaurant in Israel, opened a second branch in northern Israel in the entirely Jewish town of Yokneam, followed by a third in Akko in June 2013. (Akko [Acre] is a mixed town catering to both Arabs and Jews.) Between them and three other brothers, Husam and Nashat own nine restaurants in the north of Israel, and the family proudly claims that it has taught many Jews to be more discriminating and not simply classify "Arab food" as the staple dishes served in many restaurants at the cheapest end of the spectrum. Three other mixed towns Haifa—Jaffa and Natzeret (Nazareth)—have a score of Arab restaurants that are similarly patronized by a Jewish clientele.[47] Food and music are indeed international languages that bring people closer together, but language is the most essential medium in which this cooperation flourishes, and that is almost entirely in Hebrew today.

Two Israeli writers, Amos Oz and David Grossman, have been particularly outspoken in welcoming the participation of new Arab authors writing in Hebrew, and they have actively campaigned for full equality for Israeli Arab citizens. Oz interviewed Atallah Najar, a senior reporter of an Israeli Arab newspaper in 1983, and asked him if he would prefer to move to an independent Palestinian state to be established in the future. Najar responded, "No way, I am an Israeli. It's a matter of a sense of identity. Even though I am discriminated against in Israel, a third-class citizen, I consider myself absolutely Israeli."[48]

They must, however, be given encouragement and a new framework to emphasize that their status is not an ambivalent one. Most of all, recognition of loyalty should be rewarded and common citizenship stressed instead of the deterministic division of society into "Jews" and "non-Jews."

Are the biographies presented above anything more than random and anecdotal "cherry-picking?" Objectively speaking, they are much more, and an indication that there is significant support for a Hebrew Republic—not in order to make the State of Israel "less Jewish," as its critics fear, but to make it more "Hebrew," so that an Israeli Arab loyal to the country and its institutions and flag will no longer provoke astonishment.

This is still a dilemma for many Israeli Jews. In his debate with Anton

Shammas, the prominent Israeli Hebrew author A. B. Yehoshua admitted that he sees a "threat" in the contribution of Arabs to Israel's cultural life. In an interview with Bernard Horn, Yehoshua confessed that he is anxious about the fact that "for the first time in Jewish history, a minority is penetrating deep into our culture. It is very embarrassing that they speak perfect Hebrew.[49]

Shammas responded to this as follows: "A certain Hebrew writer ... recently urged me to take my belongings and move one hundred meters to the east, to the Palestinian state to come, if I wish to fulfill my whole national identity.... But he does not realize that his left hand is already part of my Israeli being just as at least one finger of his right hand is one of mine."[50]

The outcome of this debate and prospects for the future will only be decided if Israelis can overcome the dilemma posed by the modern concept of nationality combined with their reluctance to abandon an exclusively Jewish identity with regard to the full participation of all citizens. Everywhere in the Diaspora, most Jews live with a sense of a dual identity, sharing participation in society with their fellow citizens and cultivating a particular heritage. The same should be possible in Israel for both Jews and non–Jews.

13. From Jewish State Toward a Hebrew Republic?

Language has played a central role in the nationalist movements of many peoples who realized that it, together with a common territory, is the basis for a nation. In Israel, this realization has been long delayed but is slowly emerging as memories of the Holocaust and Jewish homelessness fade, and it has been facilitated by two converging forces.

The first is the inability of a modern nation-state such as Israel to continue to rely on an outmoded religious definition of "who is a Jew," an intractable religious controversy and one that has already produced enormous frustrations among the hundreds of thousands of new Israeli citizens from Russia and the former Soviet Union who are "not Jewish" according to *halacha* (Jewish rabbinic law). The second is a growing realization among many "Arabs" in Israel that, like the Druze and Circassians, there is no realistic alternative to full integration and equal rights as well as responsibilities.

Israel has long been defined and regarded as simply a "Jewish state." Its national anthem, *ha-Tikvah* (The Hope), sings of the "Jewish soul" (*Nefesh yehudi*) yearning to return to "Zion." Israel's Arab citizens are between a rock and a hard place and "damned if they do and damned if they don't." Another dozen such aphorisms accurately describe the dilemma of non–Jewish citizens, among whom are many vociferous critics, some of them nothing less than a disloyal "Fifth Column," while others cannot express their loyalties and sentiments openly for fear of being targeted by extremists and sympathizers of the two recent uprisings (*intifadas*). Many observers sympathetic to Israel (let alone those who are hostile) commonly despair that any meaningful formula can be found to integrate the Arab minority.

There is also a growing realization that those who have cast stones at Israel live in an even more fragile glass house in which there was never an authentic "Syrian," "Iraqi," "Libyan," "Afghan," "Palestinian" or even Egyptian nation, but only a mosaic of sectarian, religious, tribal communities at each other's throats and subject to the whim of shifting mafia-like coalitions of families. Druze, Greek Catholics in Lebanon and Syria, Coptic Christians in Egypt, Chaldo-Assyrian Christians and Kurds in Iraq, Armenians, Turcomans, Marsh Arabs, Berbers throughout North Africa, and the minority communities of Shi'ites in Saudi Arabia and Sunnis in Iran all currently have less chance of being treated as fully equal members of their homelands than the Israeli Arabs.

Would a Hebrew Republic Necessarily Be "Less Jewish?"

Opposing any separation of the religious character and official state-supported rabbinate in Israel is the frequent and emotional use of the straw man argument made by many politicians who claim that the Palestinians must recognize the "Jewish character" of the State of Israel as a pre-condition of peace negotiations.

Even if a Hebrew Republic were established along the lines of the United States, with a clear separation of "church and state" formally expressed in a constitution, it would not sever the deep emotional connection still felt by those in Israel and abroad who would continue to view it as a historic continuation of three thousand years of Jewish history. No other state would continue to view its heroes as those who fought in the Warsaw Uprising, at Masada and during the Bar-Kochba Revolt, nor emblazon the symbols of the Star of David and menorah (the seven-branched candelabrum) on its institutions and flag. No other state would seek to glorify the armed uprising and heroism of the Haganah,[1] Irgun[2] and Leḥi (a.k.a. Stern Gang[3]) against the British Mandate that put an end to colonialism.

A nation, said the French philosopher Ernest Renan, is "a soul, a spiritual principle."[4] Czechoslovakia, Yugoslavia, Cyprus, Sudan, Lebanon and Pakistan all failed as nations, breaking apart into their original ethnic fragments. They never could call on a common sense of nationhood. Elsewhere in Europe, in countries like England and France, diverse peoples of different tribal origins and speaking mutually unintelligible dialects eventually achieved a higher sense of community through generations of rule under a royal authority that imposed national standards—weights, measures, currency, educational systems, devotion to a flag and the cultivation of a myth that they shared a primordial link with a common past and aspirations for the future.

In other, bi-national states, such as Canada and Belgium, diverse ethnic elements continue to be at odds over their individual sense of nationhood and perception of history, but at least they can agree to accept the same flag (or change it to one that is neutral) and resolve to continue in some kind of national fellowship, even if strained. The monarch in Belgium is never referred to as king of the country but rather as king of the Belgians. This title was bestowed to ensure that the king must gain and keep the trust of his subjects, who in reality are not Belgians but Walloons (French speakers) and Flemings (Flemish speakers).

Like the early citizens of the United States, Canada, Australia and New Zealand, who began as colonists from Great Britain and forged a new identity by either revolution or historical development, the residents of the State of Israel are on a similar but more painful path toward a new sense of nationhood based on territory and language that is not identical to those of the religious communities that adhere to one of several forms of Judaism and/or other religious denominations and ethnic groups.

A growing identification of the younger generation with radical ideas of a secular Hebrew nationalism and the vision of a secular republic were in part continued by the crusading journalist Uri Avnery[5] (born Helmut Ostermann), and his informative and sensationalist weekly periodical *ha-Olam ha-Zeh* (This World), arguing for the end of a Zionist state and bureaucracy and in favor of equal rights for all Israelis without discrimination, and in favor of Israel's support for the worldwide struggle for national independence of the remaining African and Asian colonies.

Uri Avnery, iconoclast and courageous Hebrew writer and journalist, for many years the editor in chief of *Ha-Olam ha-Zeh*. Avnery.

"The Fighter's List" (Leḥi) ran candidates in the first Israeli election in 1949 and elected one member to the Knesset (Nathan Friedman-Yellin), although all the Zionist parties, and especially Labor Party leader David Ben-Gurion, originally threatened to prohibit the party's participation in the election because it stood outside the Zionist consensus. The party won more than 5,000 votes (1.2 percent of the electorate). The results proved that Leḥi was indeed correct in claiming that in spite of all the attacks against it as a "fascist" or "ultra-right" party, it won its strongest support in the poorest neighborhoods, the same areas that had been its underground strongholds during the campaign of violence to end the British Mandate and achieve independence. Two cardinal points of its 18-point manifesto were as follows:

16. Power: The Hebrew nation shall become a first-rate military, political, cultural and economic entity in the Middle East and around the Mediterranean Sea.
17. Revival: The revival of the Hebrew language as a spoken language by the entire nation, the renewal of the historical and spiritual might of Israel. The purification of the national character in the fire of revival.

When it failed to gain Arab support beyond a handful of votes, much of its earlier doctrine of absorbing the Arab minority was replaced by a call for a population transfer against the view of Uri Avnery and *ha-Olam ha-Zeh*.

The Modern State of Israel Was Never Envisioned by Zionism as an Exclusive "Jewish State" in Religious Terms

The originator of modern political Zionism, Theodore Herzl, and many of the "founding fathers" envisioned a state that would be a refuge and new political organism only for those Jews who sought to preserve their identity or were unable/unwilling to be integrated into the nation-states in which they lived.

Throughout the ages, the use of myths about the past has been a potent instrument in forging a nation. The Zionist movement is not unique in propagating a simplified and varnished version of the past in the process of nation-building, but it does provide a strikingly successful example for the dual purpose of promoting internal unity and enlisting international sympathy and support.

What is becoming clear is that many non-Jews in Israel are also evaluating what citizenship has afforded them, what problems and issues need to be resolved for them to feel like equal citizens, and how this long-term prospect compares with the ugly and brutal disregard for elementary human rights that is a daily spectacle in the surrounding Arab states.

Even friends of Israel are usually unaware of the very high casualty rates suffered by Druze, Circassian and Bedouin veterans of the IDF.[6] This contrasts with the non-participation of segments of the Orthodox Jewish population, who are exempt from national service of any kind. These facts, of course, do not sit well with the proclaimed image of Israel as a "Jewish state."

The Internal Israeli I.D. Card

It is obvious that loyalty is not determined by birth or what is stamped in an I.D. card.[7] Israel is a successful state that has flourished in spite of incredible hardship and challenges, but it is not yet a true nation. Internal Identity cards list separate categories of nationality and religion, although all citizens are "equal before the law." No one can omit the category of religion, and Jews who are not observant have no alternative but to list their religion as Jewish. The children of many Russian immigrants whose mothers are not Jewish are listed on their I.D. cards as Christians by religion, regardless of their sentiments, loyalty, devotion and Israeli military service.

An Israeli identity card (*teudat-zehut*) states the ethnic and religious identity of the bearer. The official term for this category in Hebrew is *le'om*, and *qawmīya* in Arabic, translated as "nation," but understood in the sense of ethnic affiliation rather than citizenship. The objectionable feature of the I.D. card is instant "profiling" as to the ethnic/religious identity of the bearer. Jewish I.D. cards state date of birth using the Hebrew calendar, while Arab I.D. cards include the grandfather's and father's name.

Due to the objections, "ethnicity" has not been indicated since 2005, but this is a mere fig leaf. The category of religion (*dat*) remains. The religious parties have objected to the category of ethnicity altogether, believing that it may designate people as Jews who are not Jewish or did not undergo an Orthodox conversion. It should be in Israel's vital interest to cultivate a nondenominational sense of national identity in which the country's Arab citizens can share—a Hebrew Republic in which neither religion nor "nationality" (i.e., not in the sense of citizenship and passports, but rather a term used to denote "ethnic origin") will be listed in Israeli I.D. cards.

Several thousands of would-be converts to Judaism have often spent years and considerable resources to win acceptance as Israeli citizens, although their loyalty and sympathies have never been in doubt. Religious conversion is nevertheless the accepted way of winning entry into the country.

Opposition to the Concept of a Secular Hebrew Republic

There are more than a few Jews in Israel who are reluctant to visualize the concept of a secular Hebrew Republic. For many of them, the idea provokes feelings of betrayal or abandonment of the heritage of countless generations, regardless of the fact that they personally are not observant. The disastrous 1973 Yom Kippur War led many secular Israeli Jews to contemplate whether their own arrogance, overconfidence and fervent nationalist sentiments had in part contributed to the debacle of unpreparedness. The high losses sustained brought back painful memories of the 1948 War of Independence and much soul searching, including a return to religion for some. Dr. Steven Plaut of the University of Haifa, a frequent blogger and staunch defender of Israel in international forums, gave vent to many of these feelings in his article "The Collapse of Israeliness?"[8] Plaut accuses secular Zionism of a host of sins, first and foremost that it absorbed much of the anti–Semitism of the Gentiles in order to create its new secular culture, modern nationalist identity and language:

> One of the greatest ironies of Jewish history is that secular Zionism of the nineteenth century was formulated precisely for the purpose of offering an alternative to the assimilationism and "self-hatred" of the Diaspora.... Here we had the leaders of Israel from the Labor Party, the Israeli Left and the Likud insisting that peaceful relations with the Arabs could be achieved through a long process of Jewish self-deprecation, self-denial and self-humiliation. They claimed that peace could be achieved through Israel agreeing to turn over its heartland to terrorists, that security could be achieved by the abandonment of security and Israel distancing itself from its own Jewish roots.... The failure of Secular Zionism is one and the same with the crisis of "Israeliness." Oslo has shown how shallow and empty is the whole enterprise known as Israeliness.

Plaut looks at the equation and finds that in times of crisis, the secular Zionist ideology was wanting. He insists that most traditional Jews both inside and outside Israel will never accept the idea that Jews and Arabs can share "Israeliness" (the idea of a Hebrew Republic or the nativist anti-religious "Canaanism thesis" that denies the spiritual character of "the Jewish people"). His accusations give the impression that the gulf separating the Zionist ideology and ultra-orthodoxy only began in an independent State of Israel in 1948. He also blames the "secular Left" and the political right for the Oslo accords and what he terms an "abandonment of security." He believes that this self-delusion rests on the fundamental error that the "Israeli People" are "a normal nation" that could negotiate and reach compromises with the Arab states and Arab-Palestinian national movement.

His words, written a decade ago, put the cart before the horse and confuse cause and effect. Since then, much has changed. Secular Israelis (of both right and left) are confident in a stronger and much more powerful and secure Israel, one that is primarily secular and can avoid the mistakes of the past, one that need not fear a non–Jewish minority of 20 percent. In 2003, most of the left was still engaged in wishful thinking about granting far-reaching "autonomy" to Israel's "Arab" population.

Prospects for a Future Palestinian-Jordanian Entity Alongside the Hebrew Republic

The concept that speakers of Arabic today constitute one nation has never matched reality and has been repeatedly demolished by sporadic but numerous civil wars in Jordan, Lebanon, Syria, Libya, Yemen, Morocco, Algeria and among various Palestinian factions. Among the Palestinian Arab population in Jordan, which constitutes a majority, there is growing speculation that the king may not endure and that his personal rule over them will follow that of the other rulers deposed by the "Arab Spring."

This may happen sooner rather than later and pave the way for a realistic agreement between a true Palestinian Jordan and Israel to reach an accommodation over the territory presently administered by the PA (Palestinian Authority). There are already open calls from Jordanian citizens (in exile) for accommodation with Israel and assertions that the people must seize the initiative from the inept and corrupt PA in the "territories."[9]

The well-known Palestinian academic, Sari Nusseibeh, president of al-Quds University in East Jerusalem, once a strong proponent of the two-state solution and now in favor of some kind of three-way federation of Israel-Jordan-Palestine, has supported recognition of Israel as "a civil, democratic, and pluralistic state whose official religion is Judaism, and whose majority is Jewish," much as Greece is a largely secular state but one with close links to the Orthodox Church. Immediate pressure from Arab nationalists subsequently caused him to tone down his statements; yet his vision is close to that of Uri Avnery.

The Emergent Goal of a Hebrew Republic

A Hebrew republic is an idea based on the efforts of five generations of Zionist pioneers who created an authentic national community and for whom "a Jewish state is not a Judaic state." For secular Israelis who support the idea of a Hebrew Republic, Jewish identity has been decided in a national sense once and for all, and in only one place—in Israel, not Uganda, Argentina, Birobidzhan, affluent American suburbs or ultra–Orthodox Jewish Diaspora neighborhoods.

A "republic" has long been associated with full equality as in Switzerland, the ideal model for incorporating peoples of diverse cultures, languages and religions but sharing in common civic ideals and loyalty.

Keep the Flag—but Change the Anthem

One modest change that could and should accommodate all Israel's non-Jewish population would be a change in the national anthem, with its outdated lyrics of the two-thousand-year-old Jewish longing for Zion. It grates on the ears of many secular Jews, and even some religious ones as well, particularly those who were born in the country, so it is not only the Arabs who feel uncomfortable singing the lyrics. The anthem is clearly now obsolete.

DENMARK'S AND FINLAND'S DUAL ANTHEMS

Many states have dual anthems. Denmark has one sung on occasions of historical significance, in which a naval victory over the Swedes is recalled (*Kong Christian stod ved højen mast* [King Christian stood by the high mast]), and another civic one of a quite different tone (*Der er et yndigt land* [There is a beautiful country]), whose words describe the natural beauty of the landscape.

The Finnish national anthem has words in both Finnish and Swedish. The latter is sung by Finnish citizens of Swedish origin in the autonomous Åland islands, who enjoy special rights of local autonomy, control of migration and service in Swedish-speaking units of the Finnish armed forces. Such a model of distinct majority-minority relations would best serve a future Hebrew Republic.

Sponsoring a competition for Arabic words to a common anthem and replacing *ha-Tikvah* (or permitting creation of an alternative anthem that sings of love for a common homeland) would offend no one except the obtuse and obdurate. Israel must, of course, also strive to eliminate some of the major disparities in employment opportunities and municipal services to Arab towns and villages. Even high-ranking Israeli Arab officials such as judges and members of the Knesset often remain embarrassed and silent when the anthem is sung.

Example of Other "Ethnic States" That Ensure Equality Before the Law

For the liberal mindset, Israel is way out of line because the link between the religious establishment and state authority is so strong. The proclamation of a Hebrew Republic could follow the example of Slovakia, which states in its constitution:

> We the Slovak nation, mindful of the political and cultural heritage of our forebears, and of the centuries of experience from the struggle for national existence and our own statehood, in the sense of the spiritual heritage of Cyril and Methodius and the historical legacy of the great Moravian Empire, proceeding from the natural rights of nations to self-determination, together with members of national minorities and ethnic groups living on the territory of the Slovak Republic, in the interest of lasting peaceful cooperation with other democratic states, seeking the application of the democratic form of government and the guarantees of a free life and the development of spiritual culture and economic prosperity, that is, we the citizens of the Slovak republic, adopt through our representatives the following constitution.[10]

There is an initial mention of "We," clearly referencing the Slovak nationality, and a second "We," meaning all those who share in Slovak citizenship and live in the territory of the Slovak republic, including individuals who are members of national minorities and ethnic groups. Such individuals do not have to be labeled in an internal passport-type document. If these individuals of Hungarian, German, Croat, Gypsy or Jewish descent do not feel secure and equal, and cannot accept the terms of such a constitution and citizenship (like a considerable number of Israeli Arabs), they must choose to live somewhere else.

In comparison with Estonia, where the Russian-language minority has been subject to special regulations demanding near fluency of the local languages in order to enjoy full political rights, Israel appears more "liberal," but this overlooks several important considerations in which it falls short of being a true republic. Israel's Law of Return affords Jews (including immediate family members) from abroad automatic citizenship, not because they are in danger, and not because they have acquired the rudiments of Hebrew and knowledge of Israeli laws, but simply because of their shared religion.

Critics

Critics will immediately cry out, "But Israel is in the Middle East and not Europe," or "Arab-Jewish relations are burdened with more than a hundred years of intense religious and ethnic conflict and can hardly be compared with peaceful Scandinavia or Switzerland [whose national anthem may also be sung in all the various official languages] or other small ethnic states of Europe like Hungary and Slovakia." The claim that Arabs and Jews cannot be "integrated" in Israel is made by many on both sides. Typical of such views are the results of a poll conducted by Haifa University and the Israel Democracy Institute, stating that 70 percent of Israeli Arabs do not accept Israel's right to have a Jewish majority; 55 percent prefer to live in Israel rather than anywhere else, but 68 percent claim they fear being transferred out of the country.[11] Nevertheless, such opinions expressed in public polls are often standard for the "Arab street" in avoiding any unwanted repercussions due to intimidation.

Jews in the Diaspora—No Longer a Firm Ally?

Several prominent Jews who have served as foreign minister or secretary of state of their countries, such as Henry Kissinger and Hector Timmerman of Argentina, have taken rigid hard-line positions against Israeli interests and provoked the intense criticism of their fellow Jewish citizens at home, despite the fact that Israel's Fundamental Law of Return and ideology as the "Jewish State" regards them as enjoying a legal "right" to automatically acquire Israeli citizenship. These individuals are undeniably "Jews," and yet loyal to the nation to which they owe allegiance as opposed to Israel. This was the normal situation in most of the past 2,000 years of history and has not changed. It is no less true that there are "Arabs" and non–Jews who are loyal Israeli citizens and patriotically serve their homeland and are ready to defend it with their lives, even if under considerable animosity from family, friends and neighbors.

Since 1948, there has been a continual debate over three alternative concepts that differ from the Zionist narrative that the State of Israel is the homeland of the entire Jewish people, pondering whether it should be one of the following:

1. A secular republic in the original spirit of Herzl and other early founding fathers of political Zionism, in which religion and national identity are separated and in which the state would be as "Jewish" as France, Poland, or Ireland are "Catholic" by heritage, historical memories and associations and traditions. This is the ultimate objective of a Hebrew Republic and not too distant from an "ethnic nation-state" such as the modern states of Latvia, Estonia, Hungary, Greece, the Czech Republic or Slovakia—the state is the political embodiment of a distinct historical nation, including those throughout the world who still emotionally identify with it.
2. A non-ethnic liberal republic deprived of any national-historical content with ethnicity or religion, in which all citizens enjoy equal status as citizens, whatever their religious origin or profession, as in the multicultural United States or Brazil.

3. A "bi-national state" along the lines of Canada, Belgium and Switzerland in a federal arrangement. This format was much debated in the 1930s and 1940s but has lost much appeal because it tends to only exacerbate rivalry between the several constituent regions based on ethnicity, language and or religion. The central government of Spain has also played with a similar arrangement of "autonomous provinces," granting considerable authority in the areas of education, culture and language to Catalonia, the Basque provinces and Galicia, but the results have been equivocal and both Catalan and Basque separatists refuse such "halfway measures."

A Dynamic Profile of Competing Narratives Among "Jews" and "Arabs"

The use of the terms "Arabs" or "Jews" in reporting about Israeli society combines distinct but also shifting population groups with diverse opinions of the State of Israel. Most journalists reporting on conflict within Israel assume diametrically opposed attitudes between two hostile populations. Within the population defined as "Jewish" on their I.D. cards, there is a clear but challenged majority who endorse the Zionist definition of a Jewish state yet they are internally diverse and span a wide range of opinions, including both religiously observant and decidedly secular in outlook. Opposing them all is a militant minority opposed to the Zionist view of the state as the "home" of the Jewish People. They also run the gamut in their dissent from the "Zionist narrative," divided along the following lines:

1. ultra-Orthodox for whom the definition of "Jewish" is one founded on the traditional rabbinical interpretation of identity based on maternal descent, and who insist that the State of Israel function as a "Jewish Vatican," ensuring the religious character of all national institutions;
2. those Jews who subscribe to what has been called a "Post-Zionist" or ultra-liberal democratic state, in which the country, in their view, should have no prescribed national or ethnic character, and the individual rather than the community is fully guaranteed personal rights and liberties; and
3. supporters of a secular Hebrew Republic based on territory and language.

The diversity of opinion among "Arab" citizens is not as apparent. A great many coercive factors limit the willingness of many individuals to express opinions that deviate from what is referred to as "the Arab street." The official government definition of their status is that of a national and religious minority "enjoying full cultural autonomy and official recognition of their language and full freedom of worship."

Regardless of what customs, traditions, ethnic origins or religious sentiments Israel's non-Jewish population groups continue to cherish, many would probably accept some formula for a unified national identity, common educational system, and fully equal rights and responsibilities, including conscription, if a full-scale peace agreement were achieved and a choice given to become citizens of a Hebrew state. Few are willing to admit this publicly, however.

In the past, and especially on the eve of partition, a small minority of both Arab and Jewish opinion identified with the far left of the Zionist movement, *ha-Šomer ha-TZair*, and the Palestinian Communist Party supported the idea of a fully bi-national state like Belgium, with everything divided along ethnic lines. The Belgian-Swiss model of a bi-national state was much debated as a potential solution in the 1930s, but was ultimately unworkable. In the Belgian case, the "neutral status" of the country and its borders were guaranteed by the great powers, and there was a near-universal loyalty to the royal house.

In Mandatory Palestine, there was no bi-national formula that could be made to work on the most crucial issues. The "post-Zionist" formula of a kind of United States, with no identity except civil rights for all its citizens, likewise has neither gravity nor glue to hold it together at all. Even in the United States and Brazil, fluent knowledge of English and Portuguese, respectively, are considered absolutely essential as part of any national dialogue.

"World Jewry," or the Jewish Diaspora of many diverse communities throughout the world, ranges from the ultra-Orthodox (including a minority who oppose Zionism just as do their counterparts who live in Israel and are Israeli citizens) to a larger group who are largely secular, non-observant and often active on the political left. The latter group is not immune from feelings of hostility toward the State of Israel, and they are unresponsive to the appeal of Zionism and or Jewish religious tradition. Many "traditional" and moderate Jews who tend to be older have often shared a sense of close identity with Israel and Zionism, represented by the slogan "We Are One People." They include many families who define themselves as secular, observant, modern Orthodox, Conservative, Reform, Reconstructionist, and "non-affiliated." Even among them, however, are those who often support candidates or political figures who advocate policies that are inimical to Israeli interests.

It is very likely that even in a future secular Hebrew Republic of Israel, traditional Jewish holidays would continue to be celebrated and cherished, as they currently are in the Diaspora. Such a state (like the United States) would probably delegate some of these festivals and holidays to the private sphere. It would allow those who so wish to manage their own personal affairs—marriage, divorce, adoption, and so on—without intervention from the rabbinical establishment. Religious Jews would be free to continue to abide by *Halacha*, as they do today. Whether these changes would make Israel more palatable or attractive to the non–Orthodox segment of World Jewry is an open question.

Jewish sympathy in the Diaspora and the United States toward the State of Israel has generated only a small trickle of immigrants to Israel. The statistics below speak for themselves:

> According to the CBS, in 2012, just 16,557 people from around the world made aliya, which is slightly more than one-tenth of one percent of world Jewry.... Consider the following: last year's figure was the lowest recorded since 2009 and the third-lowest in the past two decades. Indeed, in 2002, 33,567 Jews moved to the Jewish state, which means that the immigration rate has dropped more than 50 percent in the past 10 years. No less disturbing is the fact that aliya from the West, where the bulk of Diaspora Jewry resides, managed to contribute barely one-third of the 2012 total. Out of the five to six million American Jews, a paltry 2,290 members of the tribe made the journey home to Zion last year according to the CBS. I've been to New York Knicks basketball games at Madison Square Garden with more Jews in attendance than that.... Despite the 2008 economic crisis and uncertainty over the future of the EU and America, the Jews of the United States and much of the West are quite comfortably ensconced where they are and don't appear to be moving to Israel any time soon.[12]

Nevertheless, Israel will continue to be the natural and obvious destination for all Jews in the Diaspora who are concerned about their future and the possibility of finding a path to foster what they find valuable and worth preserving of their Jewish heritage.

The Arabs of Israel, the Territories, Jordan and the Arab World

A large part of the Palestinian Arab population currently living in the territories administered by the PA—Jordan, Gaza and Lebanon—claim refugee status dating from 1948. The conflicting authorities of these areas assert the right to speak for those "refugees" from previous conflicts. There is, however, an enormous hidden gulf between the official position of these "authorities" and many ordinary Palestinians.

The kaleidoscope of facts on the ground of shifting opinion in the current State of Israel and the territories should not diminish the fact that there is a clear Jewish majority and "non–Jewish" minority in the State of Israel. Much of the conventional wisdom and the appeals made by many Jewish community leaders in the Diaspora, foreign heads of state (including President Obama), and the many UN resolutions imploring Israel to choose between democracy and a "Jewish State" are more than a generation behind the times.

As of 2013, Jews constitute a majority within the State of Israel of approximately 60 percent of the total population west of the Jordan River; 6.3 million vs. 1.65 million "Arabs" in Israel, a million in Gaza and an exaggerated number of 2.1 million in the West Bank "territories."[13] The Palestinian Authority's own Central Bureau of Statistics includes the 300,000 residents in East Jerusalem and several hundred thousand additional Arabs without residency status in this 2.1 million figure. If Gaza is excluded, the Jewish population constitutes more than two-thirds of the total and is growing. The excess of Jewish over "Arab" births in Israel proper continues to grow, and what is even more significant is that, in terms of the age structure of both populations, Israeli Arabs are clearly an aging population, while the demographic profile of Israeli Jews grows "younger."[14] According to birth data, the number of children born within the Jewish population rose from 90,900 in 2000 to 125,492 in 2012, resulting in an increase in the share of babies born to Jews from 67.9 percent in 2000 to 73.6 percent in 2012.[15]

Moreover, a significant percentage of both Israeli Arab youths and those in the "West Bank" territory (Judea and Samaria) would prefer to emigrate rather than remain where they are. A 2006 poll published by the Palestinian An-Najah University in Nablus found that "one in three Palestinians wanted to emigrate. The 1,350 people surveyed in the West Bank and Gaza Strip cited dire economic conditions as the first reason, followed by lawlessness, political deadlock, and fears of civil war."[16] For Arabs who prefer a "Palestinian state," there is the alternative to the Palestinian majority state in the Kingdom of Jordan; for Israeli Hebrew-speaking Jews, there is nowhere else. This requires a leap of faith and "thinking outside the box," but a Hebrew Republic of the future is less radical than the idea of a "Jewish state" was in 1880, when Ben-Yehuda arrived in Jerusalem with the fantastic idea of creating a spoken Modern Hebrew vernacular and national language for the twentieth century.

Would a "Hebrew Republic" Seek to Re-create the "Canaanite" Ideology?

The concept of Israel as a "Hebrew Republic" differs from the ideology of the Canaanite movement, which sought to build a new nation merging Jewish and Muslim identities in a new nation-state linked to the remote historical past of the ancient Israelite kingdoms. A Republic implies that language and territory are the basis for national life, and that there is a clear majority in

Israel that functions on the basis of a national framework created by the Hebrew language and the territory of the state regardless of past history, race, religious observance, gender or "ethnic" origin. Its citizens are free, just as the Welsh and Scots in the United Kingdom are able to cultivate a regional and minority language, traditions and folklore as long as these do not impinge on the rights and obligations of citizenship. It applies as much, and in equal fashion, to the ultra–Orthodox sector as to the Arab sector of the population, and to all those groups that have tried to use political leverage on the basis of a separatist identity.

14. Slang and Profanity in Spoken Hebrew

Modern Hebrew, which began only a little more than a century ago, has changed more since then to reflect the needs of a community of speakers than it had in the preceding two thousand years. Those who have learned Biblical, or Talmudic, Hebrew are thus often at a loss to understand modern colloquial Israeli Hebrew unless they have lived in the country for some time. Likewise, a turn-of-the-century American or Englishman waking up from a long sleep like Rip Van Winkle would not be familiar with the new meanings acquired by such words as "gay," "far out," "blue," "hot," "cool," "wicked," "boss" or even "brother" and "mother" in the sense that they are used today.

In the early 1970s a witty bestseller on classic Hebrew slang, *Milon Olami Le'Ivrit Meduberet*,[1] by Dan Ben-Amotz delighted Israeli audiences. Slang relies on being able to appreciate the context of the subjects under discussion and an implied familiarity with the social and political realities of the society in which the language is used. It is for this reason that Americans and Britons, or Irishmen and Englishmen, do not necessarily laugh at the same jokes.

Ben-Amotz's book still has many fans due to the humor and accompanying illustrations in the form of photos, sketches, advertisements and cartoons. Its success was startling. The first edition was sold out in three days (January 27–29, 1972), and then went through six more editions within four months! Many of the terms were pure English, Yiddish and Arabic, such as bullshit, babysitter, big shot, upside, overhaul, ex (former), happy end, *bubbeleh*, *amachaya*, *putz*, *alteh-zakin*, *manyak*, *bulbul* (nightingale), *abu-beten* (father of a big stomach—a popular name for very fat men), and *anah-aaref* ("Do I know?" in Arabic). A great many expressions are simply verbatim translations of slang expressions from English or Yiddish, such as the Hebrew equivalents for "the night is still young," "move your ass," and "nose in the air," or else they are combinations of invented Hebrew terms with Yiddish endings, such as *colboynik* (for col-bo—"everything in it") and *cloomnik* (from the Hebrew word for nothing—"a good for nothing").

Dr. Nissan Netzer, of the Department of Hebrew and Semitic Languages at Bar-Ilan University, found that 630 of the approximately 2,600 slang terms in contemporary Hebrew were inspired by Yiddish.[2] Less frequent, but more interesting, are the expressions that arose as part of the environment in which the Yishuv (Zionist settlements) found themselves, such as *'al ḥeshbon ha-Baron* ("at the expense of someone else"—a reference to the Baron de Rothschild's subsidies to half a dozen early settlements).

After thirty years, Ben-Amotz's book obviously called for an updated sequel. Ruvik (Reuven) Rosental, journalist, author and editor, added and revised much Hebrew slang in Israel with his 2005 edition of *Milon HaSlang HaMekif* (The Comprehensive Dictionary of Slang),[3] and more recently Danny Ben-Israel provided a handy reference guide to more vulgar profanity titled *ZUBI! The Real Hebrew You Were Never Taught in School*.[4] This most current reference work is a slim, profusely illustrated paperback volume that covers just about any vulgar term but is also humorous.

The last time I visited Israel, in May 2012, I noted among the many changes a much greater use of American profanity of the most vulgar kind—pertaining to sex, genitalia, body parts and excretory functions, homosexuality, sado-masochism, and drug use. Additional favorite topics are exasperation with the bureaucracy and ultra–Orthodox establishment, the kibbutz way of life, snobbism, the very wealthy and very poor, the rock music scene, thuggish gangs, undesirable behavior in public places, smuggling, Jews of different geo-cultural origins, Russians, Ethiopians, Arabs, and the army. Many of these slang terms are still essentially English, Arabic and Yiddish, but there is more use of inventive Hebrew, a trend that will grow.

For readers who cannot avoid the subject, what is most amusing is the growth of real native Sabra slang to reflect even the behavior of typical residents in specific geographic localities beyond the three largest cities of Tel-Aviv, Haifa and Jerusalem, to include Beersheba and Giv'atayim, where special slang terms are used to designate "dudes" (i.e., the local "cool" inhabitants), *rabanim* (normally used as the plural form of "rabbi" in a literal sense but used exclusively in Beersheba for the figurative meaning), and *urdunim* in Giv'atayim. According to Ben-Israel, "Let's go to Haifa" is an invitation to have sex, so be careful in planning your itinerary![5]

Most of these slang terms have originated spontaneously without any planned intervention from the Academy of the Hebrew Language.

In any daily conversation on the street, in a bus, or even at the marketplace, one can hear Hebrew terms that have undergone a transformation, so that although the root meaning of the words may be recognizable, it is not immediately obvious how to interpret their usage or the implied connotations.

The following is intended as a "Guide to the Perplexed" for Hebraists abroad, non–Hebrew speakers and those who intend to visit Israel and keep their ears open for expressions of Israeli humor. One need not even have an acute ear, since these expressions are repeated dozens of times a day.

The etymology of three common idiomatic expressions illustrates how the social development of Jewish society in Mandatory Palestine and into the modern State of Israel has changed the Hebrew language to adapt to reality in a way that could not have been foreseen in the two thousand years of Diaspora existence.

Israel is a society beset with many tensions, and the terms *Davka*, *Mah Pitom?* and *Col HaCavod* are frequently resorted to as tension-releasing devices. They are interjections or philosophical expletives used to combat the daily frustrations for which no tourist guidebook or standard Hebrew-language textbook, let alone Zionist sympathies, can prepare prospective immigrants and tourists. Most short-term visitors are aware of the country's "macro problems"—the constant threat of war and terrorism, massive taxation, the high cost of living and religious extremism. The "micro problems" of everyday life (shoddy products, arrogant bureaucrats and the very low level of politeness and respect for public property and private space) are usually what unfortunately drive many immigrant-idealists from Western countries to return home after a few years.

The Terms

In order to appreciate the "Davka mentality," one must have lived in Israel for some time and have been exposed to the everyday frustrations and irksome situations that are common but do not make screaming headlines, such as endless frustrations in trying to wait in line (i.e., the trivia of life that too often provoke intense conflicts, anger and frustration).

The etymology of the word is uncertain. It does not appear in the Bible, but it is probably related to the root D-Y-K (to be exact or on time). It conveys the idea of precision and came into use during the time of the Talmud to indicate something appropriate to a particular time and situation. In the course of the development of modern Israeli society, it has, however, acquired an ironic and sarcastic flavor.

Old-time Hebraists may still encounter it or use it in its original sense and say something like "Davka, I fancy a cup of tea just now." Its sarcastic connotations arise, however, in two ostensibly opposite situations to mean "just when least expected" or "just for spite." In fact, this last meaning of davka has become so common that it is frequently used, especially by children, as a verb— "to davka someone," meaning "to spite someone."

The two situations that provoke usage are negative and positive: the negative—not being able to carry out what should be an everyday trivial task in spite of increasingly heroic but vain attempts to do so; the positive—actually being able to accomplish the task at hand against all the odds and the usually expected frustrations based on the overwhelming weight of precedence. If, contrary to all expectations, one does manage to accomplish the task at hand, this is cause for a "positive" davka—much rarer than the ordinary negative one. A positive davka is sure to evoke the admiration and hearty approval of bystanders. They will most likely recall their last positive davka experience and bask briefly in an atmosphere of self-congratulation.

But is this really a specifically Israeli phenomenon? Other cultures have their own colorful expressions for ironical and paradoxical situations—fate, kismet, karma, fado, destiny. These, however, generally deal with the great issues of human existence, divine retribution, life, death and honor, and they are often immortalized in great literature or opera. What makes the Israeli "Davka complex" special is its close linkage with the mundane, trivial commonplace experiences of the ordinary citizen.

The second cliché is *Mah Pitom*?, literally meaning "What, suddenly!?" In the Bible, *pitom* (meaning "suddenly") is used to indicate an unexpected event that occurs very quickly. It is used twenty-five times, but nowhere does it indicate a question. In contemporary Hebrew, however, the combination of the interrogative *Mah* (What?) with *pitom* is both a form of rhetorical question and an exclamation on the order of "How can any serious person ask such a stupid question or really mean what he/she is saying?" As such, it is favored by teenagers in reply to their parents' questions. It is inherently sarcastic and can be translated as "You've got to be kidding!" or "You can't really mean that!" It seeks no actual reply, since the issue raised is not worthy of being discussed any further.

Shortly before the assassination of Prime Minister Rabin, his wife Leah was asked in an on-the-spot interview by a journalist from the Israeli newspaper *HaAretz*, "Aren't you concerned that your husband isn't wearing a bulletproof vest?" Mrs. Rabin sarcastically answered, "Why all of a sudden [*Mah Pitom?*] a bulletproof vest? Is this Israel or Africa?"[6] The press later used her remarks to call upon the public to do some soul searching. Mrs. Rabin's blind overconfidence was similar to that which caused Golda Meir and the Israeli political leadership to discount the threat of an imminent Egyptian attack in the 1973 Yom Kippur War in spite of accurate intelligence regarding Egyptian intentions.

Col haCavod (All the Honor!) sounds more like Biblical Hebrew. *Cavod* means honor. The root C-V-D signifies "heavy" and the liver (the heaviest organ in the body). *Cavod* is often used in conjunction with God, His throne, and one's parents (the fifth commandment requires us to "honor your father and your mother, so that your days may be long upon the land which the Lord your God is giving you").

Cavod and its many cognates appear several hundred times in the Bible, especially in some of the most poetic verses in Psalms and in the Book of Isaiah. *Col HaCavod* means that you are entitled by right to all the honors and recognition for your achievements. This phrase is the highest form of a compliment in modern Hebrew. It is, however, used by a much wider range of persons for lesser achievements, in keeping with the leveling tendency of Labor Zionism, which sought to create an egalitarian society of Jewish toilers. In fact, the example given in Dan Ben-Amotz's dictionary is "My kid made kaka [had a bowel movement] today in the potty!" to which the appropriate reply from a bystander is "Col haCavod!"[7]

Israelis love to make fun of themselves. The source of this humor is that life is equated with goodness and God's just laws. Goodness and human life belong together, as do death and evil. Even non-Jews recognize the traditional Jewish toast *L'chaim* ("To Life," offered at any joyous and festive occasion). Deuteronomy 30, verses 15–19, expand on the meaning of life as the hallmark of Jewish ethics: "See, I have set before you today life and good, death and evil, in that I command you today to love the LORD your God, to walk in His ways and to keep His commandments, His statutes, and His judgments that you may live and multiply.... I call heaven and earth as witnesses today against you, that I have set before you life and death, blessing and cursing, therefore choose life that both you and your descendants may live."

It is this cherishing of life—understood as God's greatest gift to humanity, whom He has endowed with all the faculties that animals lack, not least of which are laughter and humor—that is so typically "Jewish." The musical *Fiddler on the Roof*, based on a story by the great Yiddish humorist writer Shalom Aleichem, spells out a creed that ALL Jews (from the most Orthodox to the least observant and atheist) agree on, as sung in one of the most popular songs "To Life."

Previous Reliance on Arabic, Yiddish, German and English for Profanity

A great many foreign words are in everyday use for profanity, which was lacking in the vernacular speech of the early Zionist pioneers, who would use the expressions known to them in Yiddish, Russian, Polish, and German or heard from their Arab neighbors and Turkish administrators (see Chapter 3). All of the Arabic expressions below are heard every day in Hebrew conversation. They are an undeniable sign of Israeli Arabs and Jews sharing language.

ahlan washalan, or just *ahlan*—greetings, welcome

asli—authentic, real

kus emak—your mother's vagina! (the Russian equivalent, *kibinimat*, is also widely used)

inshallah—God willing

abu—literally "father of," but used to denote the characteristics of someone, like *abu-arba* (father of four = someone who wears glasses) *abu-beten* (father of the belly = a fat guy), and so on

achbar—all powerful, terrific, wonderful

dechilak—please, have a heart

yallah—let's go!

wallah—I swear to God

ya'ani—in other words, that is

keyf—joy, pleasure, delightful

dir balak—careful!

majnun—crazy, possessed

mastul—a bucket (drunk)

mabsoot—satisfied, okay

sabbaba—beautiful, excellent, terrific, awesome

sachteyn—for your health, good appetite, good luck

arse—pimp, or "lucky bastard"

fashla—screw-up

By and large, this is still the situation today, with the exception that English has entered the picture, initially through service in the British armed forces and the Mandatory period, and then much more through American films and the continuing close relations with the United States.

Due to the absence of vowels in most books and the propensity of Israelis to make up acronyms, a spoken short-hand Hebrew is much more apparent than in European languages. *Ramatcal* רמטכ"ל is the short-hand acronym for Chief of the General Staff (*Rosh ha Meetah haClali*), and the Israeli Armed Forces are universally referred to as *Tzahal* צ"ה ל (for the *Tzva haHagana Le-Yisrael*); *Matnas* מתנ"ס indicates a community center (literally *mercaz tarbut, noar vesport*, Culture, Youth and Sports Center.)

There are hundreds of these in use; the most entertaining one I came across on my last visit was "That's your problem"—*zabashka* זבשכ"ה (for *zot ha baiya shelcha!* זאת הבעיה שלך).

15. The Current Assault on Hebrew at Home

Hebrew's historical success story is well documented. By 1913, most primary schools in the Zionist agricultural colonies utilized Hebrew as the language of instruction,[1] a monumental advance from the turn of the century, when many schools under the guidance and support of the Baron Edmund de Rothschild utilized French. Hebrew teachers and educators also successfully protested the initial proposal that a new technical university in Haifa for the study of engineering, known as the Technikum—later to become the Technion—would teach scientific subjects in German, acknowledged as the most important language for a technical education.

Just three generations ago, in 1925, Hebrew won a startling victory—recognition as the chief language of instruction for all subjects by the Hebrew University of Jerusalem. No other event in the twentieth century had such a successful effect on convincing the world that Hebrew indeed had been made fit for modern life. A further victory was the triumph over Yiddish, cemented in 1948 by the recognition of Hebrew as the official language of the State of Israel. These triumphs, however, have lapsed into the background due to the worldwide appeal of English in the age of the Internet and the powerful attraction of American technology, business and popular culture.

Some voices still demanded a proper role for Yiddish or warned of the necessity of avoiding a linguistic provincialism that would ignore the need for learning a world language for practical purposes of diplomacy and business. In 1925, the editor of the largest Yiddish newspaper in New York offered a significant sum of money to establish a chair in Yiddish at the University in Jerusalem, provoking students there to circulate fliers calling a Yiddish chair an "idol in the sanctuary."[2]

By 1933, recorded minutes of the Zionist congresses were required to be published in Hebrew instead of German. English, of course, was the language of British Mandatory government in Palestine, alongside both Hebrew and Arabic, and was taught in most schools as a required academic subject.

A major element within the Zionist leadership foresaw the emerging dominance of the United States and also sought to ensure the Western, European and "cosmopolitan" nature of an eventual independent Jewish state. Ben-Zion Dinaburg (Dinur), head of the Jewish Teachers' Training College in Jerusalem and professor of history at the Hebrew University, called English "the chief conduit of European influence in the Jewish community of Palestine." On the eve of World War II, he wrote that studying English would help Jews avoid what he referred to as "the degenerative effects of the East and establish a functioning European society."

In a 1941 report from the Jewish National Council in Palestine, recommendations were made that the secondary school curriculum focus on "English life" and promote a connection with "modern values" in order to "provoke useful discussion and help to correct provincial tendencies." This pleased the British Mandatory authorities, who regarded it as a step toward diminishing growing Hebrew nationalism among Jewish youth in the country.

In 1943, Leon Roth, professor of philosophy at the University in Jerusalem, argued that English learning was necessary for many practical reasons, such as understanding news reports (including the events of the war as broadcast worldwide by the BBC), textbooks, road signs, packaging, and advertisements and manuals in fields important to the Jewish population in Palestine.

A 1960 Israeli stamp honoring the Hebrew University.

The Current Assault and Retreat of the Hebrew University

In spite of many successes, there is a growing concern that the use of Hebrew as the primary language of instruction and as a research tool is under assault in both Israel and the Diaspora. On January 16, 2013, as a "sign of the times," the senate of the Hebrew University of Jerusalem voted to permit PhD students to submit their dissertations in English, provoking a protest and public outcry from many Israeli educators as well as the Hebrew Academy. The arguments used to justify the measure have been used in many other places—namely, that the new global economy has increased pressure to be literate in English, the most important language in international use. Professor Moshe

Bar-Asher, the director of the Academy of the Hebrew Language, reacted by reminding the senate that "the Hebrew University's founders—giants among men—who were keen promoters and defenders of the Hebrew language, and taught in it, and demanded that all papers be submitted in Hebrew."[3] Through the new decision, Bar-Asher and others believe the status of Hebrew has been symbolically devalued.

Prior to this decision, Haifa's Technion had decided to teach its prestigious business courses in English only, a move that has also been criticized by Bar-Asher as a "fresh blow to the Jewish lingua franca."

The Jewish daily *Forward* contacted all seven Israeli universities for a comprehensive report on the rivalry between English and Hebrew in response to their article on the subject, "Should Israeli Science Speak English?[4] All seven confirmed that they had many classes taught, and coursework assessed, in English.

Gabriel Birenbaum, a senior researcher at the Academy of the Hebrew Language, has requested that the Education Ministry require universities in Israel to use less English: "We would like to see a situation where teaching must be in Hebrew for all courses, with only very particular exceptions, such as those for foreign students." In response, Minister of Education Gideon Saar, who chairs the Council for Higher Education, has asked colleagues to present a position statement on language use in universities.

"Hebrew is the language of the Jewish People, but if you write your thesis in Hebrew, it is buried," is a typical response of many academicians, such as Yehuda Band, chairman of the chemistry department at Ben-Gurion University of the Negev. He added that allowing students to write in English helps them to get their theses read and published, and also benefits their career trajectory: "A student who can't write in English is severely limited—it's the language of science."

At the Hebrew University of Jerusalem, Sarah Strouma, the rector, supports the idea that students should complete at least one course taught and assessed in English. She told the *Forward* that she would like to see this recommendation changed to a requirement. There is thus an open conflict between the government, which has proposed to scale back programs in English, and academica.

"I'm unabashedly Zionist and believe in Israel as the nation state of the Jewish people and all that that entails with symbols and language," was the reaction of Likud party member Moshe Koppel, computer scientist at Bar-Ilan University in Tel-Aviv. "But since all the computer science publications are in English and we expect students to publish their theses, it would be double the work for them to write it in Hebrew and translate to English."

Hebrew Academy spokesman Birenbaum explained in the *Forward* article that "in those days [of the Technion Board in 1913], even many words were lacking, but they managed. But today, when Hebrew is much richer, we have this deterioration toward English." He is "not against English," but states that its use must be limited to "maintain respect for our own language."

Both decisions were defended as an effort to keep Israelis competitive in an English-dominated world. This recent trend has built-in dangers because it reinforces the growing influence of Anglo-American dominance in the worlds of entertainment, finance, diplomacy, science and culture through books and films. Within Israel, Hebrew monoglots, no matter how sophisticated, literate and educated, are becoming an "underclass," something unthinkable in France, Spain, Italy, Russia, Germany or Argentina, for example, where few university graduates are really conversant in English or able to use it effectively in their research or careers.

Defense of Hebrew: The Counterattack

Several institutions and agencies have attempted to shore up their support for the official language against the assault from English. The Haifa municipality banned its officials from using English words in official documents, and it is conducting a campaign to stop businesses from using English-only signs to market their services.[5]

In 2012, a Knesset bill for the preservation of the Hebrew language was proposed, which included the stipulation that all signage in Israel must first and foremost be in Hebrew, as with all speeches by Israeli officials abroad. The initiator of the bill, Akram Hasson, stated that his proposal was intended to prevent Hebrew from "losing its prestige" and stop children incorporating more and more English words into their vocabulary. It is all the more gratifying to lovers of Hebrew and the vision of a "Hebrew Republic" that Mr. Hasson from Daliyat al-Karmel is a Druze, not a Jew, as well as a former mayor of Carmel City and member of the Haifa Planning and Building Committee. He was subsequently awarded the Golden Inkwell prize by the Hebrew Writers Association for outstanding service to the national language. He is the first non–Jew to receive the prize. The association was founded in 1921 in Tel-Aviv. Such Zionist luminaries as Nahum Sokolow, Ahad Ha'am and Haim Nahman Bialik also served as honorary presidents. It represents 450 distinguished writers, poets, directors and playwrights.

In accepting the award, Mr. Hasson said:

> I see myself as an Israeli for all intents and purposes. Israeli society must be one family, free from racism or bigotry. We need everyone to be equal. This is our national language. How come representatives from other countries speak in Italian

and Spanish, with simultaneous translation, and we don't? We don't need to be embarrassed by our language. You hear kids today who are putting English words all the time into their speech. The language is losing its prestige.[6]

An English language preference by an Israeli university is more than a practical measure to enable students to "compete" in the world market. It tells the Russian immigrant community in Israel, which is deeply attached to its culture and language and outnumbers English-speaking immigrants by a ratio of roughly 15:1, that their language enjoys a low priority. A huge majority of the recent Russian immigrants to Israel who now strongly identify with the state and its Hebrew culture as the most visible sign of their Jewish distinctiveness are not religious.[7] Spanish-speaking Jews in Israel who immigrated from Latin America also number close to half a million, and, like the Russians, they regard the Technion's decision as "Anglo-favoritism" and a sign of downgrading Hebrew.

Authors of a prominent study of Russian immigrants in Israel who arrived during the past twenty-five years agree that the immigrants acquired Hebrew quickly and thus were able to improve their employment prospects and social lives, but they are still closely attached to their mother tongue and their cultural world is mediated primarily through Russian. Their preference for Russian, however, should not be regarded as an index of ghettoization. On the contrary, many appreciate Hebrew and are fluent, or near fluent, in English or other languages, and, like Zionist heroic figures of the past, Jabotinsky and Trumpeldor, they feel both intensely Jewish in a secular sense and a part of what they regard as "Grand Russian Culture."[8]

The great majority of Russian Jews in Israel support weekly newspapers and many periodicals, as well as several cable TV stations; follow Russian soccer clubs; are avid customers of hundreds of Russian bookstores; and patronize scores of Russian "delicatessens" that specialize in pork products. Some even have Christmas decorations in their homes in December—none of this creates a feeling of guilt or any contradiction to being loyal patriotic Israelis (although for many ultra–Orthodox, "Russian" has become synonymous with pork, prostitution, hooliganism, crime and filth).

The Snob Appeal of English

There is a legitimate fear in Israel that the national language is being transformed into a two-tier system (diglossia) of low-caste usage for the home and workplace, and that English is increasingly acquiring the status of a "high-caste" language for official use in an international setting at conferences, seminars, and major entertainment events such as the "Eurovision" song contest.

Most Israelis who study abroad do so in English-speaking countries, and the *Jerusalem Post* continues to be the most widely read and cited foreign language daily newspaper in Israel. In 1959, when Yael Dayan, daughter of famous Israeli military hero Moshe Dayan, brought out her first novel written in English (rather than in Hebrew to be followed by an English translation), she was roundly criticized, but since then, such behavior hardly raises an eyebrow. The claim is made by many Israelis and tourists that British- or American-accented Hebrew speakers are rated by native Hebrew-speaking Israelis as being at the pinnacle of wealth, education, power and success.[9]

The growing appeal of English has been reinforced by the Internet, although a report on "English Around the World" as far back as 1975 found that 80 percent of the books in Israel university libraries were in English and only 10 percent in Hebrew.[10]

When David Levy, then foreign minister, was assigned to attend the Madrid Peace Conference in 1991, there was concern in Israeli diplomatic circles that the minister would speak in Hebrew or French, and he was ultimately replaced by then–prime minister Yitzhak Shamir, whose heavy Yiddish-accented English was felt to be more adequate to bring Israel's view to the English-speaking Diaspora and world.

The Prospects for the Future

Due in part to the oft-repeated view by many observers and the mistaken impression of journalists that "everyone speaks English," the informational and social gap between Israel and the Diaspora continues to grow. This tendency is aggravated by the media, which often select fluent English-speaking Israelis to interview. No interpreter is necessary and Hebrew monoglots are ignored as if they did not exist. This frequently leads to a distortion of what the "average Israeli" thinks. This is more than unfortunate. The preference of Israeli political figures for speaking English at all international gatherings sends the wrong political message that elegant and correct Hebrew speech is unimportant.

The growing Anglicization of Hebrew is one linguistic aspect of a weakening of the language's historical connections with Judaism and Jewish folkways.[11] This is not necessarily directly connected with a decline in formal religious belief, but symptomatic of the traditional cosmopolitan Jewish preference for the "great cultural languages" and a place on the world stage.

16. Outlook for Hebrew Education in the United States and the United Kingdom

Hebrew-language charter schools were established to overcome the neglect of the language by many parents and their dislike of being lectured by their children's teachers, who tend to be mostly *yordim* (Israelis who have left the country). Most often, they are the women Hebrew teachers employed by synagogues and the Jewish community.

The appearance of Hebrew charter schools at the elementary and secondary levels is an innovation and carries the promise of a new secular-oriented, Hebrew-based education that would repeat the success of the interwar European and South American *Tarbut* schools. In the United States there is at present nothing comparable to the *Tarbut* educational movement centers.[1]

Most American Jews—either immigrants or their children and grandchildren—were busy establishing themselves and building a new life during the period of mass immigration from 1890 to 1940, which naturally included learning English; their major (and often only) contact with the Hebrew language was in preparation of boys for their bar mitzvah ceremonies and learning to recite prayers and take part in synagogue services.[2]

There is a new fear expressed by some that such schools, founded on an ethnic or even a language basis, are a Trojan horse for bringing religion into taxpayer-funded schools. These schools are struggling to gain a new level of acceptance. They are privately sponsored primary and secondary schools but are publicly funded and promise, in exchange for taxpayer support, to meet minimum standards set by state or local education boards. The school rules prohibit selecting students on a religious basis, although it is natural that the most interested candidates come from secular Jewish families who are unaffiliated with a particular synagogue.

Hebrew charter schools, unlike the *Tarbut* schools, do not teach most other subjects using Hebrew as the language of instruction. Like other charter schools, they operate on a lottery system. The New York–based Hebrew Charter School Center (HCSC)[3] is the national headquarters for this movement and has provided seed money and training for five Hebrew charters, including a new Washington, D.C., school, Sela, that opened in August 2013. HCSC works with planning teams and existing charter schools across the country to realize these objectives:

1. Increase the capacity for designing new, high-quality Hebrew-language charter schools.
2. Provide resources for the established schools.
3. Develop a field of educators prepared to lead such schools and the movement.
4. Promote and support a network of high-quality Hebrew-language schools.
5. Support local communities to develop these schools and provide maximum benefit for children and families.

HCSC's executive director until February 2014, Aaron Listhaus, denied charges that the schools were designed to bolster Israel's public image at a time when it is facing increasing international criticism. "Our kids, we believe, have an affinity for Israel through the curriculum," he said. The Brooklyn Hebrew Language Academy has been more explicit and declared that its objective is to foster a love for the country of Israel in all of its diversity: "Selected subjects, such as art, music, social studies and physical education are conducted in Hebrew and English through a co-teaching model with both an English-speaking instructor and a Hebrew-speaking instructor. All formal and informal communication between students and the Hebrew instructor are exclusively in Hebrew. For example, all meals at HLA (breakfast and lunch) are looked at as instructional opportunities and are conducted in Hebrew."[4]

Harlem Hebrew was granted a charter by the New York State Board of Regents and opened in the fall of 2013 in Community School District (CSD) 3 in Manhattan. It is a free public charter school serving 168 students in grades K–1 in its first school year, and hopes to reach 450 in five years' time. It is modeled after the Hebrew Language Academy (HLA), which opened in CSD 22 in Brooklyn in 2009. The schools all stress the advantages of bilingual education and of studying Hebrew as a key to doing business with Israel, a leader in engineering and information technology, science, medicine, and business in a global economy. The HCSC network hopes to open an additional 20 Hebrew charters in five years. Common to all the websites of the Hebrew Charter Schools is the statement answering the question "Why Hebrew?":

Hebrew is a language that has gone through a profound revitalization over the past century and a half from a classical to a living language. The modernization and secularization of the language and its transformation to a spoken, cultural medium has been central to the development of a secular Hebrew speaking society and culture in the land of Israel. This unique historical occurrence the renaissance of a language and its role in the creation of culture and society-is deeply instructive, offering meaningful opportunities for students to explore the evolution and purposes of language and its function in building and sustaining communities worldwide.

The United Kingdom

Jewish educators in the United Kingdom had been dismayed by the recent change in policy made by British Education Minister Elizabeth Truss, who announced plans that, starting in 2014, the Ministry of Education would formally recognize seven foreign languages as a compulsory "elective" for children aged 7 to 11. Schools must offer at least one of these languages, excluding Hebrew. This meant that Jewish elementary schools that have traditionally offered Hebrew as part of the program in "Jewish studies," along with the national curriculum, would have had to add one of the additional "recognized" languages, making it more expensive and putting their students under a new burden with regard to the time and effort needed to graduate.

The senior vice president of the Jewish Board of Deputies, Laura Marks, said the government's proposals could be "extremely damaging to our community's identity.... Hebrew is a vital ingredient for the understanding of our faith and culture." She urged the government to "reject the idea of stipulating only a narrow range of languages."[5]

In May 2014, after a long eight months campaign, the Government reversed itself. The Rt. Hon Michael Gove, Secretary of State for Education, gave in and announced that the Jewish schools' governors, teachers and parents would be free to teach the language that they consider right for their own school. For the vast majority this is Hebrew, including in some cases, both modern and Biblical.

The importance of the reversal is highlighted by the fact that in April 2012, the syllabus had recognized that "the study of languages *may* include major European or world languages, such as Arabic, French, German, Italian, Japanese, Mandarin, Russian, Spanish and Urdu." Hebrew was again omitted. Schools could choose which languages they would teach. It is hard to understand the rationale in this directive for German, Italian and Japanese—perhaps it is a modern sign of goodwill toward Britain's former Axis enemies in World War II—but the importance of these languages has been diminishing for some time.

Four years ago, in a UK report, the Jewish Leadership Council urged all Jewish schools to teach Hebrew and said that it was "disappointing" that some had preferred French as their foreign language.

In contrast to the Welsh, Scots and Irish, who have distinct "home territories" within the British Isles, all other so-called minority groups face the dilemma of promoting appreciation for an alternative culture other than the overwhelmingly dominant and universally imitated and admired English one.

The basic instinct of many in the non–Orthodox Jewish community is that schools run a risk of segregating pupils from mainstream society and fail to provide a balanced, realistic view of the world around them. Nevertheless, many parents, while paying lip service to universal ideals, send their children to a state-supported Jewish school that they believe is academically superior to the alternative state comprehensive school. The same explanation has been given by cynics for the apparent success of bilingual (Welsh and English) schools in Wales, and even schools in Ireland that offer instruction in Irish Gaelic (Erse). Such schools have enjoyed a greatly increased popularity since the 1970s.[6] A socio-economic profile of pupil enrollment revealed a definite middle-class preponderance, and Labour Party critics assailed the trend as an attempt to preserve an "elitist environment" rather than promote Welsh or Irish cultural identity.

Jewish beliefs and traditions stem from an enormous variety of Diaspora experiences, foreign languages, customs, and beliefs—a diverse heritage that in today's reality has largely been reduced to preferences for "mother's kitchen" (i.e., smoked salmon, gefilte fish and salt beef [corned beef]—old-time Jewish favorites). If one reads the community newsletters of other ethnic groups in Britain, there is a lively debate regarding not just political developments in the ancestral homeland but also cultural creativity—literature, popular music, dance, the arts, and sport. The common denominators for enjoying this creativity are language and a commitment to community involvement.

I lived and worked in London from 1991 to 1999 and had the opportunity to teach Hebrew at the Jews' Free School (JFS), the largest Jewish school in the country, where I observed some of the dilemmas facing the role of Hebrew in the curriculum. JFS was established in 1817, and by the end of the nineteenth century it had over 4,000 pupils on the rolls, both boys and girls. In the years since then, the school has migrated across London, from the East End to Camden Town to the outer suburbs of northwest London, just as the descendants of the immigrants themselves did.

The school, in all its advertisements, insists on carefully stating that it "welcomes non–Jewish teachers" (for all subjects except Jewish studies and Modern Hebrew), but in my case, the fact that I am primarily non-observant created problems, even though no part of the modern language instruction in Hebrew relies on any commitment to religious observance. In practice, the school was satisfied that I wore a *kippah* (the head covering worn by observant Jewish males). On this same issue, the school once had to cancel an event at which the celebrated secular Israeli author A. B. Yehoshua was scheduled to talk. He had refused to wear the *kippah* and thereby posed a challenge to the religious ethos of the school.

These experiences at the school in teaching Hebrew and at an American university convinced me that the greatest failure of Jewish schools in both the United Kingdom and the United States is the inability to provide more than just a veneer of traditional observance of ritual rather than cultural counterpoint (not a replacement) through Hebrew to Anglo-American society. A new subject, "Israeli studies," was recently introduced in the JFS curriculum, and hopefully it will provide a better understanding of the links between British Jews and Israeli society.

In today's Britain, Jews are not, as they were in the past, the only significant and highly visible minority. At the turn of the previous century, Jews were highly concentrated geographically in the East End of London, and the great majority enjoyed a vibrant cultural and religious life in Yiddish. Over the past three generations, many have chosen to give up much of this heritage and draw closer to the English majority in every way except for the formal religious identification.

In many ways, the same process has occurred over the past five centuries for the Scots, Welsh and those Irish who have remained within the political framework of the United Kingdom. These three peoples of the "Celtic fringe" of Britain have witnessed the loss of much of their heritage. This is also what has happened to significant numbers of European immigrants—the Greeks, Germans, Poles, Italians and Maltese—and it is likewise occurring among "New Commonwealth" immigrants, many of whom are different in race and religion from the majority.

Jews differ from the majority in a religion that is visible only among a small number of devoutly Orthodox practitioners. The non–Orthodox tend, however, to be attracted to affluent "golden ghettos" of suburbia and are often seen only as a pale imitation of the affluent classes of the "Anglo-Saxon (English) majority."

One can have more than a single identity. Some of the greatest writers in the English language were Scots, Welsh and Irish. James Joyce did not feel less Irish, or Dylan Thomas less Welsh, or Robert Louis Stevenson less Scottish because they chose to write in English. Their subjects are recognizably Irish, Welsh and Scottish characters set in the towns and countryside of Ireland, Wales and Scotland with which they were intimately familiar. They wrote in English but expressed the fortunes and misfortunes of their respective region's native sons and daughters. It is more than a little ironic that the main character in Joyce's *Ulysses*, representing "everyman," is Bloom—an Irish Jew! And some of the greatest writers in the English language today are Asians who have been resident in Britain for many years and whose work reflects a dual cultural heritage (Salman Rushdie and V.S. Naipul) enjoyed by Asian-Britons.

A Welshman who chooses to vote for Plaid Cymru (the Welsh Nationalist Party) will argue with his fellow countrymen, only one-fifth of whom speak Welsh fluently (if only one-fifth of the British Jewish community could even read an Israeli newspaper!), that without national independence, Welsh culture is doomed in the face of the majority English domination of the United Kingdom.[7] However, the popularity of the Eisteddfod cultural festivals, the continued success and appeal of massed male choirs, the growth of a parallel Welsh elementary school system, and the success of the Welsh-language TV station all bode well for the survival of what makes Wales distinctive, and they make even non–Welsh speakers aware that the Welsh cultural and historical heritage is alive, presenting the opportunity for an added dimension in their lives.[8]

Jewish or Muslim or Catholic or Welsh or Gaelic pupils should not be separated or segregated from their friends even if they go to a sectarian school. They must share the same national symbols and culture, as well as have the choice, if they so wish, to preserve those distinctive cultural features that would allow a shared feeling of kinship and cultural connection with their ethnic or religious counterparts abroad. This should apply to Israel as well, and it is a challenge that Israel must eventually cope with.

Epilogue

The prediction was made in Chapter 1 that by 2030, a majority of the world's Jews will probably be Hebrew speakers living in Israel, and that the divergence of interests and outlooks between many Jews in the Diaspora, particularly in the United States, and the people of Israel will be greater than today. The difference in language will contribute to this trend, just as a growing proximity with a shared homeland and language will draw the Israeli citizens who have been branded on their identity cards as "Arabs" or Muslims or Christians closer to their Jewish compatriots. This was not possible in 1948 or 1967, when a triumphant Israel faced a cowed internal "Arab minority," very few of whom were able to communicate across the language divide and appreciate the benefits of living in a state with guaranteed rights, or called upon to shoulder the burden of shared obligations.

In 1880, Hebrew was not the daily habitual vernacular of anybody. In 1900, it was the first language in habitual or primary use of no more than several hundred families in Palestine, and by 1930 it was used by several tens of thousands of Jews accounting for no more than 3 percent of the world's Jewish population. By 1950, it was the first language of the successful defenders of Israel from the invasion of six Arab armies when the country's Hebrew-speaking Jews constituted no more than 8 percent of the world Jewish population. Today, it is approximately 45 percent.[1]

Jews in Israel now confront a minority that has already been able to use the mirror of the Hebrew language to make them more aware of how legitimate grievances as "Israeli citizens" need to be negotiated. In 1949, the remnants of the "Arab" population who remained in the State of Israel barely constituted 12 percent of the overall population. They represent 20 percent today. For many of them, especially the Druze, the Circassians, the Christians and the Bedouin, the reality is that Arab nationalism and the promise of a "Palestinian state" are less attractive than ever before due to the acrimonious and nearly constant armed conflict between Hamas and the Palestinian Authority, and the instability of neighboring Syria, Lebanon, Jordan and Iraq, with their large numbers of Palestinian refugees.

Appreciation of Israel's growing strength; newly discovered immense resources of natural gas, oil and shale reserves[2]; and vastly increased attraction for trade, tourism, and investment, as well as closer strategic relations with India,[3] China[4] and Russia, will all serve to make the goal of equal citizenship a more attractive alternative for the country's minority population. The Hebrew language continues to exercise an immense appeal, charm and fascination in enabling Israelis to simultaneously identify with both the biblical past's well-known scriptures and the most modern achievements in modern science and technology.

The 2009 Israeli stamp, with biblical injunction proclaiming the country to be a land "flowing with milk and honey" alongside modern achievements in the science of bee-keeping (apiculture) and honey production. Permission secured from the Israeli Ministry of Finance (designed by Yigal Gabai, courtesy Israel Postal Service).

Nevertheless, a barrier remains. Muslim and Christian Arabs, like the Russians who are the children and grandchildren of "mixed marriages," are largely shut out of sharing in the sense of common nationhood. This ideal can never be mediated with the ultra–Orthodox, for whom the only reality of identifying as a Jew is found in the rulings of the *halachah*, and for whom Israel can only be a "Jewish state," not a "state of the Jews" as envisioned by Herzl.

Knowledge of Hebrew, literacy and greater opportunities as well as equal treatment before the law will not by themselves entice or convince many Arabs to become a loyal minority. The same language has not prevented civil war in dozens of other countries. It must be combined, as was the civil rights movement in the United States, with a commitment to nonviolence. Another intifada and threats of violence will only confirm the hard-line expectations of many Jewish Israelis that Israel must preserve its religious character, but this, in the long run, would be self-defeating.

Prime Minister Netanyahu and some of his predecessors, particularly David Ben-Gurion, frequently demanded that their Palestinian counterparts recognize Israel as a "Jewish state," the combination of a red herring and straw man tactic that does not equate loyalty and good citizenship with the behavior of the individual citizen, but rather links it to membership in a category strictly determined by birth.

A Hebrew republic would continue to be the political expression of three thousand years of Jewish history and, like the republic of Slovakia, an ethnic state—a democratic one, to be sure, but one that demands equality before the law, with equal rights and obligations for all citizens. Those Arabs and others who feel that this is a denial of their group identity should be helped to emigrate, as should those ultra-Orthodox who refuse to accept the same equality of shared citizenship.

Eliezer Ben-Yehuda, while still a student in Paris in 1880, undertook a brief sojourn in Algeria for his health (he would later die of tuberculosis in 1923). While there, he was outraged to read in what was the leading periodical in Jerusalem, *HaŠaḥar*, an editorial rejecting the possibility of making Hebrew into a living language capable of serving as the vehicle of a modern nation. He wrote, with incredible prescience, "Today we may be moribund, but tomorrow we will surely awaken to life; today we may be in a strange land but tomorrow we will dwell in the land of our fathers; today we may be speaking alien tongues, but tomorrow we shall speak Hebrew."[5]

Ben-Yehuda rejected categorically the notion that the Jews are a "spiritual people" (i.e., a religious community), a belief ascribed to by many in the Diaspora. He asserted that it was no wonder that many Jewish youths were abandoning both the faith and the Hebrew language of their ancestors. He despaired because their identity had no representation on the world political stage.

> Despite exile from its homeland, the Jewish people will survive, for its spirit and Torah remain with it; it will live as long as the spirit itself.... If this is so, then all our efforts to make them appreciate the importance of the language to us, will be of no avail.... Only a Hebrew with a Hebrew heart will understand this and such a man will understand even without our urging. Let us therefore make the language really live again. Let us teach our young people to speak it and then they will never betray it.... Let us increase the number of Jews in our desolate land; let the remnants of our people return to the land of their fathers, let us revive the nation and its tongue will be revived too! ... the land of our fathers is waiting for us; let us colonize it and by becoming its masters, we shall again become a people like all others.[6]

Had a Jewish state been proclaimed in 1937 or 1938, it might well have been a haven for the many trapped Jews of Europe, including several hundred thousand fluent and near-fluent Modern Hebrew speakers in the Zionist youth movements, *Tarbut* schools and training farms, as well as supporters of the militant New Zionist "Revisionist" organization supporting Jabotinsky, mostly young people. These were precisely those Jews most convinced of the futility of remaining in Europe and who most strongly believed in the objective and personal need for the near-total transformation of Jewish society in order to create a Hebrew state in Palestine. Their numbers would have easily doubled or tripled the total Jewish community there by the time of the outbreak of World War II in September 1939, not just numerically but also in the Zionist-Hebrew and largely secular character of the *Yishuv*.

Ben-Yehuda's amazingly accurate prediction was made in the face of derision and ridicule. His firm conviction that the Hebrew language would live again when the land was restored and a Jewish majority was its master was echoed by the testimony delivered by Ze'ev Jabotinsky to the Palestine Royal Commission in 1937,[7] when he, practically alone, warned of the coming Holocaust. He argued that a Jewish majority state was the key to survival of the Jews as a nation, and also one that could offer equality of rights and obligations to an eventual Arab minority. His logic was unassailable and all the more accurate in hindsight, given that there was ample room for all the inhabitants living in Palestine at that time and the expected 3,000,000–4,000,000 Jews in Europe clamoring to escape impending doom. Jabotinsky and his spiritual successor in the Revisionist movement, Menachem Begin, maintained the same position regarding the inherent right of every people to a state of their own, as well as their stance that the Arab peoples would in the future have multiple states through which to realize their national potential, while for the Jews there was only one possibility—just as envisioned by Ben-Yehuda.

The Consequences of Ignorance of Modern Hebrew

THE DILEMMAS

For some American Jews, Israel has become an embarrassment, one that threatens their self-image as profoundly liberal and understanding of others' grievances. For them, the Israelis, as fellow Jews, living amid the cauldron of a strident, militant, exclusivist Islam and the legacy of repeated Arab nation-state failures, should shoulder the burden and responsibility of giving up much of their sovereignty for the delusion and illusion of rescuing the "Palestinians," and thus helping to ensure what they believe will be a "peaceful world order," although their parents and grandparents most likely rejoiced at the rebirth of Israel in 1948 and regarded it mystically as partial compensation for the Holocaust. The language divide between the Diaspora and Israel simply did not exist three generations ago, when Yiddish served as a lingua franca uniting most Jews.

In 1998, the Israeli Supreme Court reached a unanimous decision (endorsed by the two modern Orthodox judges who were members at the time) that the wholesale exemptions from conscription granted to ultra–Orthodox males create "a deep rift in Israeli society and a growing sense of inequality. The current situation has created an entire population that is not integrated into the labor market and is increasingly dependent on state stipends."[8]

Efraim Halevy, 78, served as head of Israeli Mossad under three prime ministers and negotiated the peace treaty with late King Hussein of Jordan in 1994. Yet even this pillar of the Israeli defense establishment, and spokesman for the official Zionist ideology of the state proclaiming it as the "Homeland of the Jewish People," has publicly noted with dismay how Jewish Orthodoxy has moved to the extreme in Israel and speculates that, with the continued growth of non–Zionist Orthodox communities, Zionists could become a minority in Israel even without the Arabs.

Halevy has condemned religious extremism in the Israel Defense Forces, warning that Israel's actual existential danger comes from within and is more threatening than Iran's nuclear program. He has also recounted his own experience in England, growing up in a religious home and as a member of the religious Zionist movement *Bnei-Akiva*. When speaking at a military academy meeting commemorating fallen soldiers, he said, "We have today a situation in Israel in which 100s of 1000s of Israelis do not have a personal status in the country. They are not recognized technically as Jews.... When they want to marry, they have no way to marry and have to go outside the country. Their Jewish identity is not recognized by the state. These are very serious problems, because in the end this could be a major split inside Israeli society. Which I have said in the past ... I think this is a greater threat to Israel than the Iranian nuclear threat."[9]

These statements are a measure of how far apart and divided "Jews" are in Israel regarding the nature of a "Jewish state." For many *Hareidim,* Yiddish continues to be their habitual language, and "elders" in the community continually admonish their children not to use Ivrit, a really hopeless task when, even in ultra–Orthodox residential quarters such as Mea Shearim or Bnei-Brak, Hebrew is constantly heard on the street and is the medium exerting pressure toward cultural uniformity, whereas in America, Britain or France, the *Hareidim* can more easily shut out modernity by associating it with the *goyim* through their languages—English or French.

The Prospect

An overwhelming majority of Israel's Jewish population, both observant and secular, loves and honors the Hebrew language as an essential ingredient of their faith and the national language as well as their mother tongue. A future Hebrew Republic based on language and territory in addition to the heritage of Jewish longing for an independent existence as a nation, and a state with equal rights and obligations for all citizens, is the only credible future framework for a political solution in harmony with the accepted views of democratic states.

Those who doubted the ability of "the Jews" to defend their homeland in 1948 also doubted the ability of Israel to defeat more powerful and numerous enemies on the field of battle over the course of four more wars; absorb massive immigration from numerous cultural backgrounds and languages, increasing its population many times over; create a powerful, productive economy; and achieve outstanding successes in the fields of science, medicine, technology, and agriculture—all while integrating a diverse population through the medium of the Modern Hebrew language, a modern education, economy and culture in all the arts. It did so for the first forty years of its existence while embattled, blockaded and besieged, and through an intensive campaign to integrate the many new immigrants in spite of their different concepts of Jewish religious identity, ranging from ultra–Orthodoxy to totally secular and agnostic or atheist. Before being able to appreciate the new culture created by the Zionist pioneers via Modern Hebrew in all its many art forms—literature, journalism, music, dance, painting and sculpture—the immigrant population had to be assimilated and receive a message in a common language. No matter how much they were able to relate to the Hebrew they knew as a liturgical language familiar from prayers and synagogue services, they were reduced to the level of near-illiterates upon their arrival in Israel. (Many Jews in the Diaspora still have in their minds the picture of new destitute arrivals on the immi-

The Jewish immigrant ship *Exodus*, 1947 (Palmach Photograph Gallery).

grant ships and an austere Israel drawn from the popular film and novel *Exodus*.)

Israel and the Hebrew Language of the Future

The Modern Hebrew language has been a principal ingredient in the creation of a dynamic, technologically advanced, modern and successful society, a factor that has increased a sense of solidarity among Israelis, including non–Jews. It was the cement that created a nation forged by love for a homeland and tested by war and adversity, rather than justifications based on the Bible, the Holocaust or the ancient tribal kingdoms of the Israelites. Israel's "legitimacy" cannot be weighed in the balance, as many try to do, with regard to how much "injustice" was done to the Palestinian Arabs. The lack of such an independent political state is entirely of their own doing, as is the maintenance now of three separate entities—Gaza, the West Bank and the Hashemite Kingdom of Jordan. Like other struggles between the Germans and their neighbors—Poles, Czechs, French, Lithuanians and Danes—the final borders determined for all time the political framework of coexistence, and not appeals to the past and who suffered a greater injustice.

The prospect for the future is that the growing facility in Hebrew by both the Arab and the Orthodox sectors will contribute to a greater sense of a shared identity of common citizenship. Israel is younger than such veteran colonial states as Argentina, the United States, Australia, or Uruguay, where a sense of common nationhood was established through generations of effort in unifying immigrants of diverse ethnic backgrounds. However, Israel is more mature as a modern state than countries such as the Central African Republic, Angola, Belize and East Timor, which lack any clear historical continuity or sense of nationhood. They were created amid conflicts between native indigenous peoples and migrants, rival tribes, great power colonial interests and imposed languages.

The increasingly bitter disputes between Sunni and Shi'a Muslims have long-range repercussions for peace and an acknowledgment by many in the "Arab world" that ties with Israel are in their best interest.[10] Israel's growing strategic superiority, coupled with its much improved economic outlook and massive new natural energy resources, as well as the increasing acrimonious disputes between potential adversaries, portend an imminent collapse of any united Arab front. Israel is neutral in the current Syrian civil war, and the longer the war goes on, the less the Druze on the Golan Heights will opt for a return to a regime run by the Assad clique, which is hated throughout most of the Arab world. This was a government they supported with the hope of a

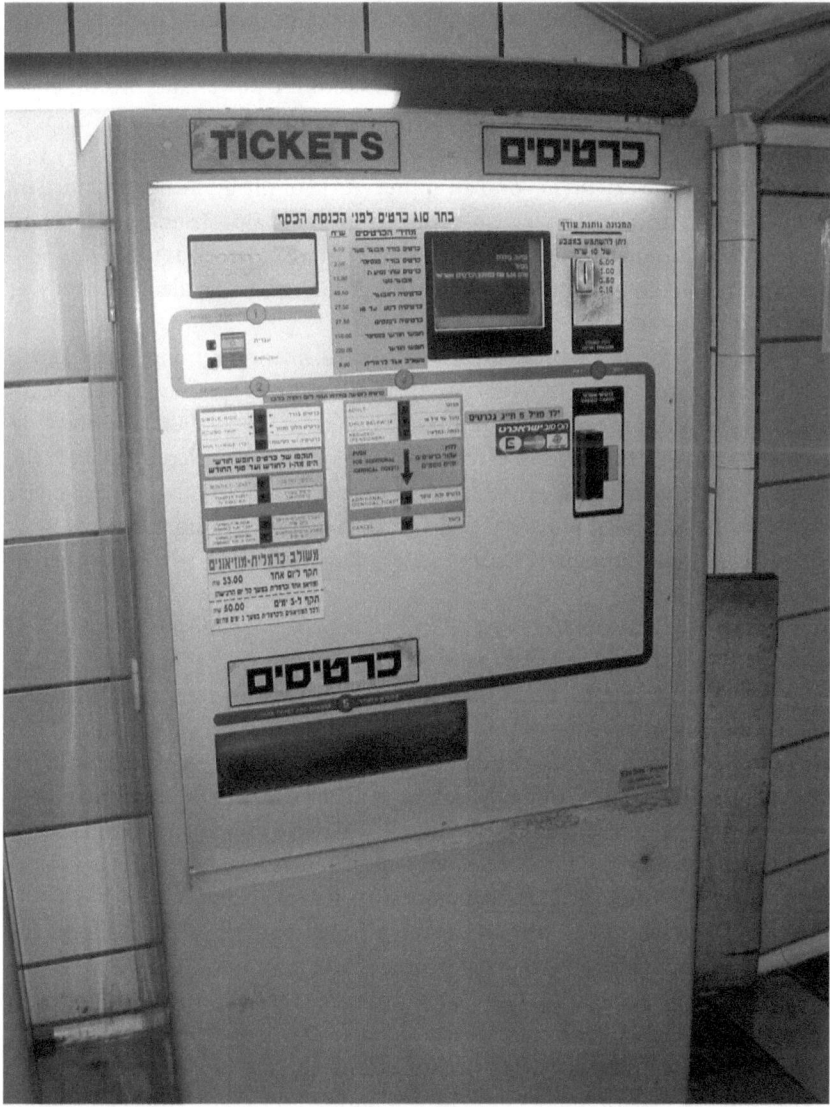

The Carmelit, a sophisticated ticket machine at the entrance to the Paris Square metro (Kikar Paris) station in Haifa (photograph by Deror Avi).

suitable reward, but the prospects are now that Israel will adamantly oppose any territorial concession there. Hamas has been seriously wounded and humiliated by the overthrow of the Morsi regime, and *Hezbollah* in Lebanon has become increasingly isolated by its support of the Assad regime. The Kurds in Iraq, enjoying a growing prosperity, have every reason to increase cooperation with Israel and forestall any future Arab attempt to reduce them to a position of weakness.

In light of Israel's growing influence, economic power and prominence, and the contributions made by all its citizens of diverse ethnic and religious origins, fluency in Modern Hebrew and a familiarity with contemporary secular Israeli culture extend beyond an appreciation of the biblical past, Judaism, or an ethical "universalist Jewish civilization." It is a profound asset for all those with an interest in and sympathy for the State of Israel, as well as its people, who created a vibrant and successful nation. It is a challenge worthy of the effort required.

The increase in Hebrew proficiency, even fluency, among many Israeli Arabs has created a new dynamic. Several generations ago, few Israeli Arabs had a higher education in Hebrew, read books (or even the daily press) in Hebrew, followed the news in Hebrew or had a computer to connect with the world outside their place of residence. These are commonplace occurrences today and have made it much more difficult to present the monolithic view of the world that monolingual Arabic speakers have had recourse to in the neighboring Arab states.

Further education and literacy and greater participation in the national workforce have all opened more than just greater career opportunities. Israeli Arabs are more and more aware that much of the picture presented in the Arabic media abroad is remote from the reality they experience at home. They are more sophisticated and adept at determining who, among their Jewish fellow citizens and the government, seeks and promotes their welfare and whose words can be accurately matched with their deeds. This is a prerequisite for active participation in politics, business, culture and social life, and it is a factor contributing to equality and acceptance on a national level.

Moreover, this new cultural existence is substantially different from the contact between the two groups of people in the past. For the Arabs of Israel, it has meant the acquisition of a new vocabulary that did not exist in Arabic and had to be learned not just as words but also as entirely new concepts, such as "compromise." The Egyptian author Nonie Darwish made this clear in a recent interview with Jamie Glazov,[11] explaining how many Arabs are handicapped not simply because of the prevalence of so many dialects that often frustrate mutual understanding among themselves but also by their need to assimilate concepts of political behavior they had not previously acknowledged. This point has been further elaborated by Tarek Heggy (born in Egypt in 1950), a petroleum expert and lecturer at several U.S., European and Moroccan universities, as well as the author of 13 books in Arabic. In a newspaper article published in the Cairo daily newspaper *Al Ahram* on September, 29, 2002, titled "Our Need for a Culture of Compromise," he wrote:

I went through all the old and new dictionaries and lexicons I could lay my hands on in a futile search for an Arabic word corresponding to this common English word ["compromise"], which exists, with minor variations in spelling, in all European languages, whether of the Latin, Germanic, Hellenic or Slavic families. The same is true of several other words, such as "integrity," which has come to be widely used in the discourse of Europe and North America in the last few decades and for which no single word exists in the Arabic language. As language is not merely a tool of communication but the depositary of a society's cultural heritage, reflecting its way of thinking and the spirit in which it deals with things and with others, as well as the cultural trends which have shaped it, I realized that we were here before a phenomenon with cultural (and, consequently, political, economic and social) implications.

How Acquisition of Modern Hebrew Was Instrumental in Creating the Sense of Nationality

Many Jews came to identify with Zionism and the sense of a Modern Hebrew nationhood not through any preexisting affinity for Biblical Hebrew, but rather from the painful realization that what they had regarded as a shared citizenship with fellow Germans, Poles, Hungarians, and Russians did not correspond with the largely fictitious model they had chosen as equal citizens of the "Mosaic faith." For many Israeli Hebrew-speaking Arabs in Israel, there is a growing suspicion that, as much they have been forced to pay lip service to the idea that they are "Arabs" (or even "Palestinians"), this does not correspond with the future they would wish for themselves upon facing a realistic (and not simply an ideological) choice of which side of the border they will end up on. Many for the first time can envision a place in a "Hebrew Republic" rather than a "Jewish" or "Palestinian" state.[12]

For some, the ideal of a Hebrew Republic will remain forever foreign and a matter of pure convenience. For most others, however, the appeal of such an idea is within the realm of possibility. This book is dedicated to those of whatever origin who sense a common obligation, historic or future loyalty, and the idea of a growing participation in the surrounding Israeli society, across sectarian boundaries.[13]

Even the world of fiction has begun to pay attention to the new and dynamic multicultural Hebrew society of Israel. A recent best-seller, *The Last Israelis* by Noah Beck, sets the action aboard an Israeli nuclear submarine with a "mixed" crew of 35 sailors, three of whom are a Christian Arab, a Druze and a Vietnamese-Israeli "gay," all of whom respond loyally to the call of a common patriotic sentiment to defend their homeland and give very plausible reasons for doing so. They portray a growing sense of Israeli civil society that is more powerful than differences of origin, ethnicity, religion, and sexual orientation.

More than 60 years ago, Mordechai Kaplan, one of the greatest Jewish thinkers of the twentieth century, and the founder of the Reconstructionist movement in the United States, argued,

> Once Hebrew becomes a foreign or ancient tongue to the Jew, he ceases to experience any intimacy with Jewish life.... The first practical step in any effort to live Judaism as a civilization should be to learn Hebrew. It should be included among the languages that Jewish children are taught in the high schools and colleges, and it should be given the same academic credit as Latin and Greek.[14]

For anyone who wishes to grasp the essence of Israel's rebirth as a modern nation and the spirit of the Hebrew language that animates it, listen to "The Convoy Song" (*Shir ha-Shayarah*)[15] as performed by the late icon of Hebrew song, Arik Einstein:

> The convoy keeps on coming since a century ago
> They are now far from us—the farmers and pioneers who worked so hard
> Without seeing the end of the road
> And now we are passing through and will not stay quiet or rest
> They won't continue without us—in this—our life's adventure
> [excerpts from stanza 1—translated from the Hebrew]

This is the great adventure of modern Israeli society's successful struggle against overwhelming odds—it is the spark that is ignited when two individuals meeting for the first time outside of Israel discover that their native or habitual language is Modern Hebrew, the tongue not of the Bible or the Mishnah, but of the songs of the Haganah, Palmach and Irgun, or the Hebrew of novelists, singers, and political figures such as Ze'ev Jabotinsky, Moshe Shamir, Amos Oz, Shoshana Damari, Rita, Nehama Hendl, and Arik Einstein.

In light of Israel's growing influence, economic power and prominence, and the contributions made by all Israeli citizens of diverse ethnic and religious origins, fluency in Modern Hebrew and a familiarity with contemporary secular Israeli culture extend beyond merely an appreciation for the biblical past, Judaism, or an ethical "Universalist Jewish civilization." It is a profound asset for all those with an interest in and sympathy for the State of Israel and its people, one that will continue to make progress in creating a common bridge through language with the country's non–Jewish Hebrew-speaking citizens.

Chapter Notes

Preface

1. Reuven Sivan, "Ben Yehuda and the Revival of Hebrew Speech," *Ariel: A Review of the Arts and Sciences in Israel*, no. 25 (1969): 35–39.

Chapter 1

1. See Yoram Ettinger, "Defying Demographic Projections," *Israel haYom* (Israeli daily newspaper online), April 5, 2013, and Jack Wertheimer, "The Jewish Birthrate," *Commentary* (October 2005).
2. "Baseball in Israel" website, Thursday, October 14, 2010. "The Yankles? New Team Takes New Swing at Bringing Professional Baseball to Israel!" http://israelibaseball.blogspot.com/2010/10/yankles-new-team-takes-new-swing-at.html.
3. See Daniel Rogov, "The Israeli Kitchen," *Ariel: A Review of the Arts and Sciences in Israel* (1985–1986): 40–51. In the late 1930s, the German Zionist organization produced an illustrated handbook, *How to Cook in Eretz Israel*, explaining to housewives from Europe how to adapt to the new climate and the preparation and selection of local fruit and vegetables.
4. Herman Hesse, *Beneath the Wheel*, translated by Michael Roloff (Bantam Books, 1968), 90–91.
5. Stewart Ain, "Poll: Romney Wins Among American Citizens," *Jewish Week*, November 12, 2012;
6. Adina M. Yoffie, in an article from August 23, 2012, in the *Jewish Ideas* daily website. See also Alan Mintz, "On the Question of Hebrew," *Forum*, nos. 46–47 (Fall/Winter 1982): 73–76.
7. Steven M. Cohen, "Beyond Distancing: Young Adult American Jews and Their Alienation from Israel," reprinted in *Camera on Campus* 18, no. 1 (Spring 2008): 12. (*Camera* is an abbreviation for Committee for Accuracy in the Middle East Reporting in America.)
8. Kenneth Hanson, *The Eagle and the Bible* (New English Review Press, 2012).
9. Eric Herschthal, "Israeli Authors Lost in Translation as Few Hebrew-Language Books Published in English," *Jewish Week*, May 25, 2010.
10. *The Forward*, April 9, 2012, and reposted on the *Jewish Ideas* daily website in the April 13, 2012, issue, titled simply "Memo to American Jews: Learn Hebrew—Gulf Between Israel and Diaspora Is Growing Fast." See http://forward.com/articles/154253/memo-to-american-jews-learn-hebrew/?p=all#ixzz2LwlvgzTA.

Chapter 2

1. Cecil Roth, *Jewish Contributions to Civilization*, 2nd ed. (Macmillan, 1938).
2. Cyrus Gordon, *The Common Background of Greek and Hebrew Civilizations* (W. W. Norton, 1962).
3. Michael Macrone, *Brush Up Your Bible!* (Harp Perennial—division of HarperCollins, 1993). The book explains the background to both the Old and the New Testaments' most frequently used and well-known verses.
4. Roger Williams Wescott, "Colonial American Belief in Hebrew as the Primal Language," *Geolinguistics* (1991)—paper presented at the conference on "Hebrew and the Bible in

Colonial America," Dartmouth College, May 22, 1990.

5. G. G. Coulton, *St. Francis to Dante* (David Nutt, 1906), 242–43. Salimbene was more honest in reporting the actual results than the innovator of the alleged first such experiment by Psammeticus, an Egyptian Pharoah during the seventh century BCE, who believed language was inborn and that children isolated from birth from any linguistic influence would develop the language they had been born with. He isolated two children, who were reported to have spoken a few words of Phrygian, an Indo-European language spoken in Turkey. Psammeticus concluded that this therefore must be the first, or original, language of all mankind.

6. According to the *Cambridge Encyclopedia of Language*, "Human language seems to have emerged within a relatively short span of time perhaps as recently as 30,000 years ago, but that still leaves a gap of over 20,000 years before the first unequivocal evidence of written language." Edited by David Crystal (Cambridge University Press, 1992), 291.

Chapter 3

1. "Ireland and the Irish," in *Languages in Competition*, Richard Wardhaugh, ed. (Basil Blackwell, 1987), 90–95; J. Macnamara, "Successes and Failures in the Movement for the Restoration of Irish," in *Can Language Be Planned? Sociolinguistic Theory and Practice for Developing Nations*, J. Rubin and B. H. Jernudd, eds. (University of Hawaii Press, 1971), 65–94; John Ardagh, *Ireland and the Irish—Portrait of a Changing Society* (Penguin Books, 1994).

2. Ardagh, *Ireland and the Irish*.

3. Geoffrey Hull, *The Malta Language Question* (Said International, 1993).

4. Brian Weinstein, ed., *Language Policy and Political Development* (Ablex, 1990). See also Jacob Landau, "Language Policy and Political Development in Israel and Turkey," in *Language Policy and Political Development*, 133–49; Eliezer Ben-Rafael, *Language, Identity and Social Division: The Case of Israel* (Oxford Studies in Language Conflict/Clarendon Press, 1994); Joshua A. Fishman, *Ideology, Society and Language* (Karoma, 1987) and *The Rise and Fall of the Ethnic Revival: Perspectives on Language and Ethnicity* (Mouton, 1985); Einar Haugen, *Language Conflict and Language Planning: The Case of Norwegian* (Harvard University Press, 1966); Mark Kurlansky, *The Basque History of the World* (Random House, 1999); Geoffrey Lewis, *The Turkish Language Reform: A Catastrophic Success* (Oxford University Press, 1999); W. Moleas, *The Development of the Greek Language* (Bristol Classical Press, 1989); Jonathan Eric Lewis, "Freedom of Speech—In Any Language," *Middle East Quarterly* (Summer 2004): 1–9; Itamar Even-Zohar, "Language Conflict and National Identity," in *Nationalism and Modernity: A Mediterranean Perspective*, Joseph Alter, ed. (Praeger, 1986), 126–35; Norman Berdichevsky, *Spanish Vignettes: An Offbeat Look into Spain's Culture, Society and History* (Santana Books, 2004).

5. Norman Berdichevsky, "Why Esperanto Is Different," *New English Review* (December 2007); Tamás Biró, "Weak Interactions: Yiddish Influences in Hungarian, Esperanto and Modern Hebrew," in *On the Boundaries of Phonology and Phonetics: A Festschrift Presented to Tjeerd de Graaf*, D. Gilbers et al., eds. (University of Groningen, 2004), 123–45.

6. Norman Berdichevsky, "Zamenhof and Esperanto," *Ariel: A Review of Arts and Sciences in Israel* 64 (1986): 58–71.

7. For an explanation of the different verb formats, or *binyanim* (constructions), corresponding to the passive, active, intensive and reflexive forms, see Edward Horowitz, *How the Hebrew Language Grew* (KTAV Publishing House, 1960), and William Chomsky, *Hebrew: The Eternal Language* (Jewish Publication Society, 1957), especially chapter 6, "How the Study of Hebrew Grammar Began and Developed," 117–54, which explains the different functions of the *binyanim*.

8. The most complete treatment of the persecution of the Esperanto movement and its advocates is Ulrich Lins, *La Dan̂ĝera Lingvo: Studo pri la persekutoj kontraŭ Esperanto* (Belicher Eldonejo, 1988). See chapter 2, "Lingvo de Judoj kaj Komunistoj," 91–145.

9. Ibid., 190–241.

10. Ibid., 383–96.

11. The only biography that gives full treatment to Zamenhof's Jewish background is *La Kaŝita Vivo de Zamenhof* (Zamenhof's Hidden Life) by N.Z. Maimon (Japanese Esperanto Institute, 1978).

Chapter 4

1. Bill Bryson, *Mother Tongue: The English Language* (Penguin Books, 1992), 62.
2. Ibid., 66.
3. For a more complete inventory of the languages that Hebrew borrowed from in the course of its three-thousand-year-long history, see E. Y. Kutscher, "Words and Their History," *Ariel: A Review of the Arts and Sciences in Israel*, no. 35 (1969): 65–74. Also in Hebrew, *Milim shehadru le-Ivrit* (Words that Penetrated Hebrew) on the website www.safa-ivrit.org/imported./php. Rabbi S. Farbush, *HaLashon HaIvrit beYisrael uveAmim* (The Hebrew Language in Israel and Among the Nations) (Israel, 1969); Ora (Rodrigue) Schwarzwald, "The Components of the Modern Hebrew Lexicon: The Influence of Hebrew Classical Sources, Jewish Languages and Other Foreign Languages on Modern Hebrew" (in Hebrew, with English abstract), *Hebrew Linguistics* 39 (1995): 79–90.
4. Milton Himmelfarb, "Hebraism and Hellenism Now," *Commentary* (July 1969): 50–57.
5. Joshua Blau, *The Renaissance of Modern Hebrew and Modern Standard Arabic*, Vol. 18, Near Eastern Studies (University of California, 1981).
6. The Templars were members of the Temple Society (German: *Tempelgesellschaft*), a German Protestant sect that evolved from the Pietist movement of the Lutheran Church. They were expelled from the church in 1858 because of their millennial beliefs holding that settlement of the Holy Land was a necessary condition for the second coming of Christ. In the latter half of the nineteenth century, they established six agricultural settlements in Palestine and generally had good relations with the Zionist settlers, who learned from them modern practices of agriculture, crafts, scientific research, business and building. At its height, the Templar community in Palestine numbered 2,200 just before the outbreak of World War I, when relations with the Jewish settlements were generally excellent and made particularly congenial by mutual use of the German language.
7. Hillel Halkin, "Hebrew as She Is Spoke," *Commentary* (December 1969): 55–60; David Gold, "An Introduction to English in Israel," *Language Problems and Language Planning* 5, no. 1 (Spring 1981): 11–54; Bernard Spolsky and Elana Shohamy, "Language in Israeli Society and Education," *International Journal of the Sociology of Language* (2002): 1–16.
8. Leo Rosten, *The Joys of Yiddish* (W. H. Allen, 1968), and *Leo Rosten's Treasury of Jewish Quotations* (Bantam Books, 1972).
9. John Geipel, *Mame Loshin: The Making of Yiddish* (Journeyman Press, 1982), 37. See chapter 4, "The Debt to the Holy Tongue," 37–42.

Chapter 5

1. For a biography of Eliezer Ben-Yehuda, see Robert St. John, *Tongue of the Prophets: The Fascinating Biography of Eliezer Ben-Yehuda, the Father of Modern Hebrew* [paperback] (Wilshire Book Company, 1979).
2. Judith Cooper-Weil, "Early Hebrew Schools in Eretz-Israel," *Ariel: A Review of the Arts and Sciences in Israel*, no. 104 (1997): 33–37.
3. Benjamin Harshav, *Language in a Time of Revolution* (University of California Press, 1993), 109.
4. For the source of estimates for the size of Biblical, Mishnaic and Modern Hebrew vocabulary, see Ghilad Zuckermann and Azzam Yadin, "'Blorit'—Pagans' Mohawk or Sabra's Forelock? Ideological Secularization of Hebrew Terms in Socialist-Zionist Israeli," in *The Sociology of Language and Religion*, Tope Omoniyi, ed. (Palgrave Macmillan, 2009).
5. Vardit Ringvald et al., *Brandeis Modern Hebrew—Ivrit biHeksher* (Hebrew in Context) (Brandeis University Press, 2005). See chapter 4, the unit on food, 161–99.
6. Dominican friar Giordano da Pisa told his parishioners in a sermon delivered on February 23, 1306, "It is not yet twenty years since the founding of the art of making eyeglasses, which make for good vision." Cited in Elong Gilad, *Mishkafayim* ("Word of the Day"), *HaAretz* online, June 12, 2013.
7. Gilad, *Mishkafayim*.
8. Rami Tal, "The Israeli Press," *Ariel: A Review of the Arts and Sciences in Israel* (1995): 99–100.
9. Meir Medan, "The Academy of the Hebrew Language," *Ariel: A Review of the Arts and Sciences in Israel*, no. 25 (1969): 40–47.
10. Moshe Atar, "Title not available."

Leshonenu La'Am [Our Language for the People], issue 457, page 21.

11. Ahad ha-Am, in his article "Ĥevlei Lashon," in *ha-Shiloaĥ* 18 (1908): 9–19, cited in Shelomo Morag, "The Emergence of Modern Hebrew," in *Hebrew in Ashkenaz: A Language in Exile*, Lewis Glinert, ed. (Oxford University Press, 1993).

12. C. Rabin, "Hebrew," in *Current Trends in Linguistics, 6: Linguistics in South West Asia and North Africa*, T. A. Sebeok et al., eds. (Mouton, 1970).

13. Dr. Reuven Sivan, *Leksikon leshipur ha-Lashon* (Karni Publishers, 1969), 173–83.

14. Chaim Rabin, "The Revival of the Hebrew Language," *Ariel: A Review of the Arts and Sciences in Israel*, no. 25 (1969): 25–34; David Tene, "Israeli Hebrew," *Ariel: A Review of the Arts and Sciences in Israel*, no. 25 (1969): 49–63.

Chapter 6

1. Ghil'ad Zuckermann, *Yisraelit, Safah Yafah* (Israeli—A Beautiful Language) (Am Oved, 2008).

2. Zuckermann's controversial theory attracted responses from numerous linguists, Israelis and the entire Jewish world. Yiddish linguist Dovid Katz refers to Zuckermann as a "fresh thinking Israeli scholar," while a highly respected authority who writes widely for the *Forward* under the pseudonym "Philologus" accuses Zuckermann of a political agenda. Zuckermann's reply appeared on December 28 in *The Mendele Review: Yiddish Literature and Language*. See also Paul Wexler, *The Schizoid Nature of Modern Hebrew: Slavic Language in Search of a Semitic Past* (O. Harrassowitz, 1990).

3. Many teachers of Ivrit (Modern Hebrew) in high schools and universities often find it convenient and less troublesome to avoid many of the peculiarities of formal grammar, even though they are still prescribed by the Academy and in almost all textbooks. Most notable among the difficulties are the two sets of numbers when they apply to denoting the quantity of objects according to the "gender" of the noun (masculine and feminine) and that, contrary to expectations, the so-called masculine numbers end in the vowel sound "ah," as in *shlosha ĥayalim* (three soldiers) שלושה חיילים, whereas "three dresses" is *shalosh simalot* שלוש שמלות. Another major problematic concept is that of *smichoot*.

4. See Shmuel Yelvin, "The Hebreo-Phoenician Writing Signary," *Ariel: A Review of the Arts and Sciences in Israel*, no. 25 (1969): 7–18.

5. *Milon Megiddo Hadish* (New Megiddo Dictionary) (Megiddo Publishing Company, 1990).

6. Werner Weinberg, *Tikun HaKtiv haIvr vehanisyonoy liftorah* (The Orthographic Reform of Hebrew: The Problem and the Attempts to Solve It) תיקון הכתיב העברי (Hebrew University, 1971).

7. Ibid. See also On Ben Pela, *Ktav Oz, HaKtav HaLatino-Ivri* (The Latin-Hebrew Script), *HaTnua limaan Ktav Ivri ĥad-Mashma'i* (The Movement for a Decisive Hebrew Script) (Jerusalem, 1990), for a very recent proposal for a reformed alphabet using Latin letters; see also "The Karmeli Alphabet" online (illustrating an alternative way to write Modern and Classical Hebrew based on the Latin alphabet and developed by Michael Avinor of Haifa, Israel). The Karmeli alphabet can likewise be used to write English and German (www.omniglot.com/writing/karmeli.com).

8. Hillel Halkin, "A Movable Feast," *Jerusalem Report*, April 22, 1993.

9. Hillel Halkin (Philologos), "Revamping the Aleph-Bet," *Forward*, March 23, 1993.

10. Alberg is the author of a brochure titled "Efficient Reading in Hebrew—The Hillel Writing System and Spelling" (Telegraph Press, 1991). It is a detailed account of the insufficiencies of continued use of the traditional "square" Hebrew alphabet.

11. Dan Almagor, "How 'The Rain in Spain' Fell in Eretz-Israel," *Ariel: A Review of the Arts and Sciences in Israel*, no. 104 (1997): 38–46.

12. Lewis Glinert, *Modern Hebrew: An Essential Grammar*, 2nd ed. (Routledge, 1994).

13. Ibid., xiii.

Chapter 7

1. On the eve of World War II, there were between 11 and 12 million Yiddish speakers in the world. In the 1897 official czarist census of the population of the Russian Empire, including large parts of what today are Poland and the Baltic States, 97 percent reported Yiddish as their first language. See *Carta's Atlas of the*

Jewish People in the Middle Ages (Carta, 1991), maps 30–31; Neil G. Jacobs, *Yiddish: A Linguistic Introduction* (Cambridge University Press, 2005).

2. Bernard K. Johnpoll, *The Politics of Futility: The General Jewish Workers Bund of Poland, 1917–1943* (Cornell University Press, 1967); Jack Lester Jacobs, *Bundist Counterculture in Interwar Poland* (Syracuse University Press, 2009).

3. Leo Rosten, *The Joys of Yiddish* (W. H. Allen, 1968), and *Leo Rosten's Treasury of Jewish Quotations* (Bantam Books, 1972).

4. Theodore Herzl, *Altneuland* (Old-New Land) (Create Space Independent Publishing Platform, 2011).

5. See Uri Avnery, *Israel Without Zionism* (Macmillan, 1973), a partial autobiography of the noted journalist and editor of *HaOlam HaZeh* as well as his program for Israel-Arab peace negotiations.

6. Ze'ev Jabotinsky, *Hebrew Pronunciation* (HaSefer Publishing, 1940), 37–38.

7. Benjamin Harshav, *Language in a Time of Revolution* (University of California Press, 1993), "Social Desert."

8. Judith Cooper-Weil, "Early Hebrew Schools in Eretz Israel," *Ariel: A Review of the Arts and Sciences in Israel*, no. 104 (1997): 33–37.

9. In 1996, the Knesset passed laws to establish a National Authority for the Preservation and Cultivation of both Yiddish and Ladino in a special "Heritage Law." Similar proposals have since been proposed for other heritages of regional-local Jewish ethnic groups and their languages from Bukhara, Ethiopia, Iraq, Libya and Morocco.

10. Eliezer Ben-Rafael, *Language, Identity and Social Division: The Case of Israel* (Clarendon Press, 1994), 208.

11. Hillel Halkin, *Letters to an American Jewish Friend: A Zionist Polemic* (Jewish Publication Society, 1977).

12. *Commentary* (June 1967)—criticism of Hillel Halkin's view of Yiddish revivalism by an American Jewish feminist.

13. Hillel Halkin, *Commentary* (June 1997)—reply to feminist defense of "Yiddishkeit" (Jewish culture in Yiddish)" and characterization of Israelis and secular Zionists as "Hebrew-speaking goyim."

14. See the lively exchange of views in the Letters to the Editor column, "*Lingua Franca Iudaica*," in the March 2003 issue of *Commentary*.

15. Steven J. Gold, *The Israeli Diaspora* (University of Washington Press, 2002).

16. Lawrence Epstein, *At the Edge of a Dream: The Story of Jewish Immigrants on New York's Lower East Side*, An Arhur Kurzweil Book (Jossey-Bass, 2007), chapter 14, "Jewish Journalism," 221–237; Ehud Manor, *Forward: The Jewish Daily Forward (Forverts) Newspaper: Immigrants, Socialism and Jewish Politics in New York, 1890–1917* (Sussex Academic Press, 2009).

17. Hillel Halkin, "Hebrew as She Is Spoke," *Commentary* (December 1969): 60.

Chapter 8

1. Itamar Even-Zohar, "The Emergence of a Native Hebrew Culture in Palestine 1882–1948," *Poetics Today* 11 (Spring 1990): 175–191; Itamar Even-Zohar, "Who Is Afraid of the Hebrew Culture?" *Papers in Culture Research* (2005).

2. Jonah 1:9.

3. Bernard Spolsky and Robert Cooper, *The Languages of Jerusalem* (Clarendon Press, 1991), chapter 5, "The Revitalization and Spread of Hebrew," 57–73; William Chomsky, *Hebrew: The Eternal Language* (Jewish Publication Society, 1957), 184–244; David Gold, "Sketch of the Linguistic Situation in Israel Today," *Language in Society* 18 (1989): 373–87.

4. Dan Miron, "Between Rabbi Shach and Modern Hebrew Literature," *Israel Affairs* 4, nos. 3–4 (Spring/Summer 1998): 86–100.

5. Nurit Gertz, "From Jew to Hebrew in the Israeli Cinema of the 1940s and 1950s," *Israel Affairs* 4, nos. 3–4 (Spring/Summer 1998): 175–99.

6. See Boaz Evron, *Jewish State or Israeli Nation?* (Indiana University Press, 1995); Yaakov Shavit, *The New Hebrew Nation: A Study in Israeli Heresy and Fantasy* (Frank Cass, 1987).

7. Benjamin Harshav, *Language in a Time of Revolution* (University of California Press, 1993), 167.

8. Benzion Kaganoff, *A Dictionary of Jewish Names and Their History* (Routledge and Kegan Paul, 1978).

9. Martin Gershom, "Some Preliminary Notes on Israeli Family Names," http://theo

chem.weizmann.ac.il/~comartin/israelinames.txt; Wikipedia, "Hebraization of Surnames."

10. Yitzhak Ben Tzvi, *Collected Writings*, vol. 4, (in Hebrew), Jerusalem, 1925. Zionist Labor Movement; reissued 1944. pp. 11–14[3].

11. Even-Zohar, "The Emergence of a Native Hebrew Culture in Palestine."

12. Amos Oz, *A Tale of Love and Darkness*, translated by Nocholas de Lange (Vintage Books, 2005), 186.

13. "Tarbut Schools"; see Miriam Eisenstein, *Jewish Schools in Poland, 1919–1939* (King's Crown Press, 1950).

14. Norman Berdichevsky, "Zohar Argov and the Hebrew Language Gap," *New English Review* (May 2013).

15. Norman Berdichevsky, "The Impact of Urbanization on the Social Geography of Rehovot: An Israeli Case Study of Residential Differentiation, 1890–1874," PhD thesis, excerpt published in *Studies in Israeli Society*, vol. 1, edited by Ernest Krausz (Transaction Books, 1980), 73–96.

16. "Post-Zionism," the term used during the past two decades to describe the view of some Israelis, notably in academia, that Zionism fulfilled its mission with the independence of Israel and that the state should no longer be the bearer of a distinct ethnic or religious identity but rather become the state of "all its citizens," modeled on the United States; see also Rachel Feldhay Brenner, *Inextricably Bonded: Israeli Arab and Jewish Writers Re-visioning Culture* (University of Wisconsin Press, 2003), 19–26.

17. See Shavit, *The New Hebrew Nation*, and Evron, *Jewish State or Israeli Nation?*.

18. Cited in Shavit, *The New Hebrew Nation*, 116

19. *Yediot Ahronot*, June 18, 1982.

20. A. G. Horon, *Eretz haKedem—Madrich histori uMidini le-Mizrah ha-Karov* (Hermon Publishers, 1970) (in Hebrew).

21. Moshe Pelli, *HaTarbut HaIvrit beAmerika: 80 Shana HaTnu'ah HaIvrit beArtzot HaBrit 1916–1985* (The Hebrew Culture in America: 80 Years of the Hebrew Movement in the United States) (Reshafim Publishers, 1998), summary in English, p. XVII. See also Alan Mintz, ed., *Hebrew in America* (Wayne State University Press, 1993).

22. David Passow, *The Prime of Yiddish* (Gefen Publishing, 1996), and Wikipedia, "The Yiddish Press."

23. S. Farbush, *HaLashon HaIvrit beYisrael uveAmim* (The Hebrew Language in Israel and Among the Nations) (Israel, 1969), chapter 30, "The Impression of Hebrew's Rebirth on the Nations of the World," 365–68.

Chapter 9

1. Dov Levin, "They Fought Back: Lithuanian Jewry's Armed Resistance to the Nazis 1941–45," *Yad vaShem: Martyrs' and Heroes' Remembrance Authority*, Institute of Contemporary Jewry—Hebrew University, Jerusalem, 1974 (in Hebrew). Soloveichik repeated this phrase on numerous occasions.

2. Chaim Bialik on a visit to Kaunas in 1931. Several years later, Revisionist Zionist leader Ze'ev Jabotinsky also visited the city. Both visits drew huge crowds.

3. An academic high school with emphasis on the mechanical arts, sciences and mathematics.

4. Georg Von Rauch and Gerald Onn, *The Baltic States: The Years of Independence: Estonia, Latvia, Lithuania, 1917–1940* (University of California Press, 1974); T. G. Chase, *The Story of Lithuania* (Stratford House, 1946).

5. Moshe Pelli, *Haskalah and Beyond* (University Press of America, 2012); Marcin Wodzinski, *Haskalah and Hasidism in the Kingdom of Poland: A History of Conflict* [paperback] (Littman Library of Jewish Civilization, 2007); Olga Litvak, *Haskalah: The Romantic Movement in Judaism* [paperback] (Rutgers University Press, 2012); Jacob S. Raisin, *The Haskalah Movement in Russia* [paperback] (Echo Library, 2007).

6. Lucy Dawidowicz, *The War Against the Jews* (Bantam, 1986), English edition, 422.

7. *Doar Ha-Yom*, October 11, 1930.

8. Yitzhak Kissin, ed., *Antologia shel Ha Sifrut HaLitait* (Kaunas, 1932).

9. Binyamin Eliav, "HaMedinot HaBaltiot," in *HaTfutza: Mizrach Europa*, Yaakov Tzur, ed. (Keter Publishers, 1967), 106.

10. Norman Berdichevsky, "A Tale of Two Cities: Lithuania's See-Saw Struggle to Gain Control of Vilnius and Klaipeda (Memel)," *Boundary Bulletin*, University of Durham (July 1991): 5–9; John A. Gade, "The Memel Controversy," *Foreign Affairs* 2, issue 3 (1924): 410.

11. Shmuel Katz, *Lone Wolf: A Biography*

of Vladimir (Ze'ev) Jabotinsky, 2 vols. (Barricade Books, 1996); Ya'akov Shavit, *Jabotinsky and the Revisionist Movement, 1925–1948* (Frank Cass, 1988).
   12. Levin, "They Fought Back." On the formation of the 16th Lithuanian Division and the role of Jewish volunteers in its ranks, see 37–110.
   13. Wolf Vilensky, *Tahufuchot Goral: Sipur-Hayyim shel Gibor Brit HaMoatzot* (Vicissitudes of Fate: The Story of a Hero of the Soviet Union).
   14. *Antologia shel HaSifrut HaLitait*.
   15. Suniti Kumar Chatterji, *Balts and Aryans in Their Indo-European Background* (Indian Institute of Advanced Study, 1968).
   16. Von Rauch and Onn, *The Baltic States*.
   17. Samuel Gringauz, "Jewish National Autonomy in Lithuania (1918–1925)," *Jewish Social Studies* (July 1952).

Chapter 10

   1. See, for example, a textbook in Brazilian Portuguese—*Brasil: Lingua e Cultura*, by Thomas A. Lathrop and Eduardo M. Dias (Lingua-Text, 1992). Each chapter follows a storyline set in Brazil and introduces specifically Brazilian colloquialisms and social, cultural and political issues, as well as real restaurants, cafes, beaches and food specialties, not found in the Portuguese of Portugal. See also Norman Berdichevsky's review of the book in *Port Vitoria*, issue 5 (2012).
   2. Persky was a leading American Hebraist who coined the phrase "I am an eternal slave of the Hebrew language," which he put on his visiting card. He was born in Minsk and settled in the United States in 1906. He devoted the remainder of his life to strengthening the Hebraist movement.
   3. Cited in Dwight MacDonald, "Profiles: The Slave of Hebrew," *New Yorker*, November 28, 1959, p. 57.
   4. Chaim Rabin, *Everyday Hebrew: Twenty-Nine Simple Conversations with English Translation and Full Grammatical Introduction* (J.M. Dent & Sons, 1943).
   5. Ibid., 55.
   6. Benjamin Harshav, *Language in a Time of Revolution* (University of California Press, 1993).
   7. Rabin, *Everyday Hebrew*, 65.

   8. Ibid., 67.
   9. Ibid., 69.
  10. Ibid., 71.
  11. Ibid.
  12. Ibid., 73.
  13. Ibid., 75.
  14. Ibid., 85.
  15. Ibid., 99.
  16. Ibid., 121.

Chapter 11

   1. Yehoshua A. Gilboa, *Hebrew Silenced: The Suppression of Hebrew Literature and Culture in the Soviet Union* (translation of *Ha-Lashon Omedet al Nafsha*) (Herzl Press, 1982), 1–42; *Yivo Encyclopedia of Jews in Russia* (online).
   2. The Yiddish-speaking population in the Soviet Union according to the 1897 czarist Russian census.
   3. "The Hebrew Communist," a pamphlet by Eliezer Steinman, appeared in Odessa in 1919. It appealed to the authorities to permit dedicated Jewish communists loyal to the Soviet regime to contribute works of literature in the Hebrew language, as a legitimate national expression of creativity by Jewish writers.
   4. Editorial by K. Nelson in the first issue of the Yiddish newspaper *Emes* (Truth), August 7, 1918, cited in Gilboa, *Hebrew Silenced*, 63
   5. Gilboa, *Hebrew Silenced*, chapter 5, "The Pain of Yearning," 99–123.
   6. *HaAm* (Hebrew journal), June 16, 1917, p. 12.
   7. Norman Yitzhak, ed., *Bireshit HaBimah* (At the Beginning of Habimah) (Jerusalem, 1967), 309–10.
   8. David Ben-Gurion, "Bishlichut HaBimah" (On a Mission for HaBimah), in *Bireshit HaBimah*, Norman Yitzhak, ed. (Jerusalem, 1967), 111–12.
   9. R. Ben-Ari, *Habimah* (in Yiddish) (L.M. Shtayn, 1937), 61.
  10. "Refuseniks" was the unofficial term for individuals, typically mostly Soviet Jews, who were denied permission to emigrate by the authorities in the former Soviet Union and other countries of the Eastern Bloc. See Deborah Lipson, "Hebrew in the Soviet Union," *Ariel: A Review of the Arts and Sciences in Israel*, no. 85–86 (1991): 140–54. Many of them started their re-association with Jewish identity and

culture as a result of Israel's victory over the Arab states in the Six-Day War of 1967 and sought to learn Hebrew and/or cultivate Jewish religious festivals and traditions.

11. Nathan Sharansky, a leading "refusenik," human rights activist and author, who spent years in a Soviet prison. Sharansky was denied an exit visa to Israel in 1973. The reason given for denial of the visa was that he had been given access, at some point in his career, to information vital to Soviet national security and could not be allowed to leave. In February 1986, he was released and immediately immigrated to Israel, adopting the Hebrew name "Natan." In 1988, he wrote *Fear No Evil*, his memoirs of his time as a prisoner, and founded an organization of Soviet emigrant Jewish activists dedicated to helping new Israelis and educating the public about absorption issues In 1986, Congress granted him the Congressional Gold Medal.

12. Moissaye Ossigin, long-time editor of the Yiddish-language communist newspaper in the United States, *Freiheit* (Freedom). See Alexander Bittelman, *Program for Survival: The Communist Party Position on "The Jewish Question"* (New Century, 1947), 16 and 52–53.

13. *Political Affairs* (American communist periodical), February 1948, 146–55, and August 1948, 720–30.

14. Uri Waller, *Israel Between East and West: Israel's Foreign Policy Orientation, 1948–56* (Cambridge University Press, 1990); Zdroje Lederer, *The Soviet Union and the Middle East: The Post–WWII Era* (Stanford University Press, 1974); M. Confino and Sh. Shamir, *The USSR and the Middle East* (Israel Universities Press, 1973); Susan Hattis, *Political Dictionary of the State of Israel* (Jerusalem Publishing House, 1987).

15. "In Putin's Russia, Jews Adopt Silence as Best Protection," *Times of Israel*, October 28, 2012.

Chapter 12

1. M. Amara and Abd Al-Rahman Mar'i, *Language Education Policy: The Arab Minority in Israel* (Kluwer Academic Publishers, 2002).

2. Avraham Zuroff, "Some Arab Citizens of Israel Prefer Hebrew," Arutz 7 website, June 13, 2009. This article, citing Cairo's Al Azhar Al Sharit Islamic Research Academy, noted that in some Israeli towns, "Up to 30 percent of Arabs prefer speaking Hebrew over Arabic. About 60 percent prefer Arabic, while 10 percent speak English. In other towns, it is the other way around and Hebrew is dominant." The author faults the Israeli educational system for the Arabic language's loss of popularity among Israeli Arabs. See also Raphael Patai, *The Arab Mind* (Charles Scribners' Sons, 1983), especially chapter 4, "Under the Spell of Language," 41–72; Rachel Feldhay Brenner, *Inextricably Bonded: Israeli Arab and Jewish Writers Re-visioning Culture* (University of Wisconsin Press, 2003).

3. Habeeb Shehade, University of Helsinki, Third Nordic Conference on Middle Eastern Studies: Ethnic Encounter and Culture Change, "The Hebrew of the Arabs of Israel," June 19–22, 1995.

4. List of languages by number of native speakers, from Wikipedia, the free encyclopedia. All similar lists note that the Arabic language consists of many diverse regional dialects, some of which are mutually unintelligible. See also "Most Widely Spoken Languages in the World: What Are the Most Spoken Languages in the World?" http://www.nationsonline.org/oneworld/most_spoken_languages.htm.

5. United Nations Educational, Scientific and Cultural Organization—Index Translationum statistics. See http://portal.unesco.org/culture/en/ev.php-URL_ID=7810&URL_DO=DO_TOPIC&URL_SECTION=201.html.

6. Eliezer Ben-Rafael, *Language, Identity and Social Division: The Case of Israel* (Clarendon Press, 1994), especially chapter 13, "The Case of a National Minority," 166–79.

7. Protocols of the Elders of Zion—a czarist forgery intended to implicate Jews both in czarist Russia and throughout the world as fomenting unrest and strife—first published in Russia in 1903, translated into multiple languages, and disseminated internationally in the early part of the twentieth century. Henry Ford funded printing of 500,000 copies that were distributed throughout the United States in the 1920s.

8. Fouad Ajami, "Five Myths about the Arab Spring," *Washington Post*, February 12, 2012.

9. The Druze are a minority Muslim sect considered heretical by most traditional Sun-

nis. They constitute just under 2 percent of Israel's total population and are concentrated in Galilee. See Donna Rosenthal, *The Israelis: Ordinary People in an Extraordinary Land* (Free Press, 2003), chapter 14, "The Druze," 303–15. They have volunteered for military service and more than half serve in combat units. Several have acted as Israeli ambassadors and ministers. See also Hillel Cohen, *Army of Shadows: Palestinian Cooperation with Zionism, 1917–1948* (University of California Press, 2008) (translated from Hebrew), 237–49; Peter Beaumont et al., *The Middle East: A Geographical Study* (John Wiley & Sons, 1976), 370–82.

10. Circassians are an ethnic Turkic–Sunni Muslim minority in Israel, numbering 5,000 in two Galilean villages, who are the descendants of migrants from the Caucasus Mountains. They maintain a separate ethnic identity and have loyally served in the Israel Defense Forces. See Hillel Cohen, *Good Arabs: The Israeli Security Agencies and the Israeli Arabs, 1948–1967* (University of California Press, 2010), 174–79; Chen Bram, "Muslim Revivalism and the Emergence of Civil Society: A Case Study of an Israeli Circassian Community," *Central Asian Survey* 22, no. 1 (March 2003): 5–21.

11. Daniel Pipes, "Happy Israel," *Washington Post*, June 5, 2013.

12. Arab men in Israel prefer brides who, if they are from the West Bank, know or will learn Hebrew. Many expect an Israeli Arab woman to be engaged in the workforce and speak Hebrew well. See Rosenthal, *The Israelis*, chapter 4, "Schizophrenia: Non-Jews in a Jewish State," 257–335.

13. Dianna Attalah, "West Bank Hebrew Language Study Is Growing," *Jerusalem Post*, March 27, 2013.

14. Ibid.

15. Ibid.

16. *The algemeiner*, July 5, 2013.

17. Interview by video of Heba Abu Seif, on YouTube, from Israeli television, Channel 10, Tuesday, July 2, 2013, http://www.algemeiner.com/2013/07/05/hebrew-speaking-egyptians-come-front-and-center-during-revolution-2-0-video/. See *algemeiner*, July 5, 2013.

18. For a detailed account of the life and work of Israel's major Arab writers in Hebrew, see Brenner, *Inextricably Bonded*, and Michael M. Caspi and Jerome D. Weltsch, *From Slumber to Awakening, Culture and Identity of Arab Israeli Literati* (University Press of America, 1998).

19. Translated into English by Salma Khadra Jayyusi and Trevor LeGassick (Zed Books, 1985).

20. A region adjacent to the 1949 cease-fire line between Israel and Jordan in the Sharon plain among the Samarian foothills and heavily populated by Muslim Arabs. It is a stronghold of the Islamic movement. The largest village is Umm-al-Fahm. It was originally agreed that the region would be annexed by Jordan, but the Israelis insisted in having it fall under Israeli jurisdiction. This was achieved in the armistice agreement as part of a territorial swap.

21. Sayed Kashua and Miriam Schlesinger (English translation), *Dancing Arabs* (Grove Press, 2004).

22. Shoshana London Sapir, "Letter from Haifa: An Official Language Gets More Respect," *Hadassah Magazine* (January 2010).

23. Roberta Kraemer, "A Test of Gardner's Socio-educational Model," in *Social Psychological Factors Related to the Study of Arabic Among Israeli High School Students*, Studies in Second Language Acquisition, Vol. 15 (Cambridge University Press, 1993).

24. Dan Almagor, "How 'The Rain in Spain' Fell in Eretz-Israel," *Ariel: A Review of the Arts and Sciences in Israel*, no. 104 (1997).

25. Published by Simon and Schuster in 2007; translated into English by Yael Lotan in 2002. It was also made into a popular film, and the Wadi Nisnas area of lower Haifa with a largely Arab population, where the story is set, is frequently the site of guided tours attended by those who have read and enjoyed the book and its message.

26. Yoram Ettinger, "Defying Demographic Projections," *Israel haYom*, April 5, 2013.

27. *HaAretz*, July, 29, 2012.

28. "The Palestinians of Jerusalem: What Do They Really Want? Round Table Discussion," Pechter Middle East Polls, American Task Force on Palestine, December 20, 2010.

29. *HaAretz*, "A Surprising Process of 'Israelization' Is Taking Place Among Palestinians in East Jerusalem," December 29, 2012.

30. Tal Law (July 23, 2002). The law authorizes a continuation of the exemption of yeshiva students from military service subject to the conditions within the law. At the age of 22, yeshiva students have a "decision year" and can choose between one year of civilian national

service alongside a paying job or a shortened 16-month military service and future service in the reserves as an alternative to continuing to study. In 2005, the state admitted that the Tal Law had failed to change enlistment arrangements, as only a few dozen ultra-Orthodox students had enlisted in the army as a result. The law was then extended in 2007 for another five years. On February 21, 2012, the High Court ruled that the law is unconstitutional. The final disposition of the law is still in abeyance and subject to a heated political debate.

31. Cohen, *Army of Shadows*, and *Good Arabs*.

32. Isabel Kershner, "Noted Arab Citizens Call on Israel to Shed Jewish Identity," *New York Times*, February 14, 2009.

33. Khaled Abu Toameh, *Islam Today*, May 18, 2009.

34. Khaled Abu Toameh, "The Palestinian Authority's Inconvenient Truth," Gatestown Institute, International Policy Council, January 13, 2013.

35. See an interview with her on YouTube at www.youtube.com/watch?v=pvhJAZlY030.

36. Qassem Ziyad, cited in Middle East Research Institute, "Israeli Arabs Object to Ideas of Israeli-Palestinian Territorial Exchanges," Special Dispatch No. 374, May 2, 2002.

37. Oren Kessler, "An Arab Maverick," *Tablet*, October 12, 2012. For a thorough documentation of sporadic but significant Arab cooperation with Zionism and the State of Israel, see Efraim Karsh, *Palestine Betrayed* (Yale University Press, 2010); Cohen, *Good Arabs*; Zeidan Atashi, *Druze & Jews in Israel: A Shared Destiny* (Sussex Academic Press, 1997); Raphael Israeli, *Green Crescent Over Nazareth: The Displacement of Christians by Muslims in the Holy Land* (Routledge, 2002).

38. Phillip Assouline, "Telling Israel Like It Is—in Arabic," *Time of Israel*, October 17, 2012.

39. Phillip Assouline, "Israeli Arab Urges Full Integration with Israel," *Times of Israel*, October 30, 2012.

40. James Bennet,"Israeli Arab Hero Is Praised but Not Embraced," *New York Times*, September 26, 2002.

41. Ibid.

42. *The algemeiner*, February 4, 2013.

43. *The algemeiner*, "Israeli Priest Hounded for His Support of Israel," January 4, 2013.

44. Lazar Berman and Elhanan Miller, "New Christian Arab Party Calls for IDF Enlistment," *Times of Israel*, July 10, 2013.

45. www.pbs.org/independentlens/shadya/film.html.

46. Atara Beck, "First Bedouin IDF Tank Commander," *Jewish Press*, October 30, 2013. Read more at http://www.jewishpress.com/blogs/united-with-israel/first-bedouin-idf-tank-commander/2013/10/30/.

47. Dana Kessler, "Upscale Arab Restaurants Gain a Wider Audience," *Tablet*, July 10, 2013.

48. Cited in Brenner, *Inextricably Bonded*, 106.

49. Bernard Horn, *Facing the Fires: Conversations with A.B. Yehoshua* (Syracuse University Press, 1997), 74–75.

50. Anton Shammas, "Kitsch 22: On the Problems of the Relations Between Majority and Minority Cultures in Israel," *Tikkun* 2, no. 4 (September–October 1987): 22, 26.

Chapter 13

1. Haganah (Defense)—underground military forces of the majority Socialist and Labour Zionist parties. See Yigal Lossin, *Pillar of Fire: The Rebirth of Israel—A Visual History* (Shikmona, 1983), and Dan Kurzman, *Genesis 1949: The First Arab-Israeli War* (New American Library, 1970), for background on the underground groups.

2. Irgun—the National Military Organization, *Irgun Tzvai Leumi* (*Etzel*), dissident underground group led by Menahem Begin, who went on to become the leader of the main opposition party *Herut* (Freedom) in the first decade of Israel's independence. Yaakov Shavit, *Jabotinsky and the Revisionist Movement, 1925–1948* (Frank Cass, 1988).

3. Stern Gang (Fighters for the Freedom of Israel; known by the Hebrew acronym Lehi)—most "radical" of the underground groups fighting against the British to achieve Israel's independence. See Joseph Heller, *The Stern Gang: Ideology, Politics and Terror 1940–1949* (Frank Cass, 1995).

4. Ernest Renan (1823–1892) was an important French theorist who wrote about a variety of social and political topics. His famous essay "What Is a Nation?" (*Qu'est-ce qu'une nation?*) was first delivered as a lecture at the Sor-

bonne in 1882. It continues to be cited in much of the literature on nationalism.

5. Uri Avnery, an Israeli author, political figure and journalist, was for many years the gadfly of the Zionist establishment, with his "heretical" views calling for Israel to be part of proposed union of the neighboring countries in a "Semitic region" and a rejection of maintaining close identity with the West and Jewish Diaspora. His early political thought was influenced by the nativist ideology known as Canaanism. Avnery edited the weekly magazine *HaOlam HaZeh* (This World), which was regarded as the primary popular opposition journal and featured many sensational scoops. Its use of "pornography" (by Israeli standards of the 1960–1970 era) also helped make it into the leading alternative media organ.

6. Zeidan Atashi, "The Druze in Israel and Compulsory Military Service," Jerusalem Center for Public Affairs, no. 464 (October 2001).

7. Several Israeli Jews, citizens of Israel, have been convicted of treason, espionage and murder for political purposes. They include Yigal Amir, convicted assassin of Prime Minister Yitzhak Rabin; General Yisrael Baer, a close associate of David Ben-Gurion and a member of the General Staff during the War of Independence; Aharon Cohen, ultra-leftist from kibbutz Mishmar HaEmeq, who spied for Syria; wealthy businessman Nahum Manbar, who illegally sold chemical and biological information to Iran; Sammy Baruch, a textile merchant who sold military secrets to several Arab states; Mordechai Vanunu, who revealed Israel's nuclear capacity; and others. Many Israeli Arabs have also been arrested for spying for Israel.

8. Steven Plaut, "The Collapse of Israeliness?" *Jewish Magazine*, "Zion Without Judaism" issue (March 2, 2003).

9. Mudar Zahran, "Jordan Is Palestinian," *Middle East Quarterly* 19, no. 1 (Winter 2012): 3–12, http://www.meforum.org/3121/jordan-is-palestinian.

10. English translation of Slovak Constitution in Moshe Berent, *A Nation Like All Nations: Towards the Establishment of an Israeli Republic* (in Hebrew) (Carmel, 2009), 262.

11. Poll conducted over ten-year period by University of Haifa and Israel Democracy Institute. By contrast, 75 percent of Jewish respondents believe that Arabs deserve equal rights as a minority in the country, 69 percent blame the Arabs for prolonging the conflict between the two peoples, and a large majority (78 percent) believes that the country must maintain a Jewish majority. See *algemeiner*, June 12, 2012.

12. Israel's Central Bureau of Statistics—see Michael Freund, "Orthodox Jews and the Aliyah Crisis," *Jerusalem Post*, March 8, 2013.

13. Yoram Ettinger, "Defying Demographic Projections," *Israel haYom*, April 5, 2013; Wikipedia, "West Bank," en.wikipedia.org/wiki/West Bank.

14. Yakov Faitelson, "A Jewish Majority in the Land of Israel: The Resilient Jewish State," *Middle East Forum* (Fall 2013): 15–27.

15. Ettinger, "Defying Demographic Projections."

16. An-Najah University report, cited in Reuters, November 22, 2006.

Chapter 14

1. Dan Ben-Amotz, *Milon Olami Le'lvrit Meduberet* (The World Dictionary of Spoken Hebrew) (Levin-Epstein, 1972).

2. Heidi Gleit, *Eretz Magazine* (March 2013).

3. Tamara Traubman, "Wallah, Long Time No See," *HaAretz*, February 1, 2006 (review of Rosenthal's dictionary).

4. Danny Ben-Israel, *ZUBI! The Real Hebrew You Were Never Taught in School* (Plume, 2011).

5. Ibid., 93.

6. Short radio interview before leaving the stage at the rally, in which she told listeners, "People have their personal security but they do not have doubts that the path of peace should be pursued."

7. Ben-Amotz, *Milon Olami Le'lvrit Meduberet*, 118.

Chapter 15

1. Judith Cooper-Weil, "Early Hebrew Schools in Eretz-Israel," *Ariel: A Review of the Arts and Sciences in Israel*, no. 104 (1997): 33–37.

2. JTA, December 4, 1927. A proposed gift in the amount of $100,000 offered by the editor of the Yiddish-language New York daily *Der Tag* (The Day), although accepted on behalf of the university by Chancellor Judah L.

Magnes, provoked demonstrations by students organized in the *Gdud Migenei HaSafah* (Batallion for the Defense of the Language (Hebrew) and notable luminaries such as Norman Bentwich, M. M. Ussishkin, and Dr. David Yellin as well as professors Klausner and Epstein.

3. *HaAretz*, June 28, 2013.

4. Nathan Jeffay, "Should Israeli Science Speak English?" *Forward*, April 13, 2012.

5. *HaYom*, June 28, 2012. Haifa mayor Yona Yahav publicly expressed his frustration over the growing use of English in the streets of Haifa. Under his direction, the Haifa government launched a campaign forbidding the use of English words such as "global," "order," "auditions," "fine-tuning," "scouting," "project" and many others in all official municipal documents. The mayor initially began the campaign when he objected to the use of a large sign in English for a barbershop where he had always had his hair cut. When asked to change the sign so that it would be include the Hebrew word *misparah* (at least with larger letters than the English "barbershop"), the barber refused, and Lahav stopped getting his hair cut there.

6. Deborah Danan, "Druze MK Wins Prize for Helping Hebrew," *Jerusalem Post*, June 18, 2012. Hasson represents the Kadima Party in the Knesset. His bill further stipulates that all speeches that take place overseas by senior officials representing Israel be conducted in Hebrew.

7. See Larissa Remick, *Russian Jews on Three Continents: Identity, Integration and Conflict* (Transaction Publishers, 2012), especially chapter 6, "Social Issues in Israel," and Donna Rosenthal, *The Israelis: Ordinary People in an Extraordinary Land* (Free Press, 2008).

8. Moshe Lissak and Eli Leshem, "The Russian Intelligentsia in Israel: Between Ghettoization and Integration," *Israel Affairs* 2, no. 2 (Winter 1995).

9. David Gold, "An Introduction to English in Israel," *Language Problems and Language Planning* 5, no. 1 (Spring 1981): 24.

10. Ibid., 14.

11. Bernard Spolsky and Elana Shohamy, "The Penetration of English as Language of Science and Technology into the Israeli Linguistic Repertoire: A Preliminary Inquiry," in *The Dominance of English as Language of Science: Effects on Other Languages and Language Communities*, Ulrich Ammon, ed. (Mouton de Gruyter, 2001); Nina G. Kheimets and Alek D. Epstein, "The Role of English as a Central Component of Success in the Professional and Social Integration of Scientists from the Former Soviet Union in Israel," in *Language in Society*, no. 30 (2001): 187–215; Eliezer Ben-Rafael, *Language, Identity and Social Division: The Case of Israel* (Clarendon Press, 1994); Gold, "An Introduction to English in Israel," 11–55.

Chapter 16

1. Steven J. Gold, *The Israeli Diaspora* (University of Washington Press, 2002), chapter 4, "Family and Gender Relations," 105–43.

2. Irving Howe, *World of Our Fathers: The Journey of East European Jews to America and the Life They Found and Made* (Simon & Schuster, 1976). See chapter 13, "The Yiddish Word," and chapter 16, "The Yiddish Press."

3. A nonprofit organization created by the Areivim Philanthropic Group in 2009 to help advance the Hebrew-language charter school movement. Its goal is to foster the development and sustainability of the Hebrew charter school movement by supporting a network of excellent schools that serve diverse populations of students, encourage strong interpersonal relationships, advance overall academic and social/emotional well-being, and promote high levels of Hebrew language proficiency and understanding of the culture and history of Israel and its immigrant communities (CHIIC).

4. "Hebrew Instruction," on the school's website.

5. Laura Marks, senior vice president of the Jewish Board of Deputies. See Lori Lowenthal Marcus, "Jewish Schools Endangered by New U.K. Curriculum," *Jewish Press*, December 16, 2012.

6. Holly Williams, "Mind Your (Minority) Language: Welsh, Gaelic, Irish and Cornish Are Staging a Comeback," *The Independent*, January 19, 2013.

7. See Philip Jenkins, *A History of Modern Wales, 1536–1990* (Longman, 1993), especially chapter 19, "A Nation One Again," 385–406, for the role of the Welsh language in the preservation of Welsh ethnic identity and the national movement.

8. Public opinion among non-Welsh speakers has remained strongly in favor of non-

coercive tax-supported programs in support of the language. A 1995 opinion poll recorded a massive 88 percent claiming pride in the Welsh language, 83 percent in favor of bilingual public bodies and 68 percent agreeing that the government's goal should be "to enable the language to become self-sustaining and secure as a medium of communications in Wales." See François Grin and François Vaillancourt, *The Cost-Effectiveness Evaluation of Minority Language Policies: Case Studies on Wales, Ireland and the Basque Country*, monograph no. 2 (European Center for Minority Issues, 1999), 17.

Epilogue

1. Mordechai Kaplan, 'Judaism as a Civilization'; Toward a Reconstruction of American-Jewish Life,' Schocken Books, 1972. 452.
2. Crispian Balmer, "Gas Discoveries Give Israel New Regional Clout," Reuters, May 22, 2013. Once totally dependent on fuel imports, Israel has made the largest gas discoveries in the world over the past decade off its Mediterranean coastline, and it is expected to become an exporter by the end of the decade.
3. Anshel Pfeffer, "Israel-India Relations: Strong, But Low-Key," *HaAretz*, December 1, 2008. The two countries currently enjoy extensive economic, military and strategic relationship. India is the largest customer of Israeli military equipment, and Israel is the second largest military partner of India. Military and strategic ties between the two nations include joint military training and space technology. In August 2012, they signed an academic research agreement, and there are considerable joint ventures in the areas of information technology, biotechnology and agriculture. India is Israel's eighth largest trading partner.
4. Sam Chester, in "As Chinese-Israeli Relations Enjoy a Second Honeymoon, America Frets," *Tablet*, June 28, 2013, reported the growing trade and cultural contacts between China and Israel. Arms sales to China, especially Israeli drones, were particularly significant over the past decade, and there are ambitious future plans, including eventual financing and construction of a rail line to run from Ashdod to Eilat and bypass the Suez Canal, exports of natural gas from its major new finds off the Israeli Mediterranean coast, and growing cultural ties. More than 800 Israeli students are currently undertaking advanced study of Chinese. Beijing has opened a Confucius Cultural Center in Tel-Aviv and it is no accident that the Chinese embassy on Ben-Yehuda Street in Tel-Aviv is marked by the largest flag flying from a public building in the city (or at least it was in May 2012, when I visited a café across the street). China is Israel's largest Asian trading partner and has sought Israel's expertise in solar energy, manufacturing robotics, irrigation, construction, agricultural and water management, and desalination technologies to combat water shortages.

5. Eliezer Ben-Yehuda, letter written to the editor of the Hebrew newspaper, *HaŠaḥar*, in Jerusalem from Igazier, Algeria, in 1880. See English translation in Arthur Hertzberg, *The Zionist Idea: A Historical Analysis and Reader* (Jewish Publication Society, 2011), 160–65.
6. Ibid.
7. Ze'ev Jabotinsky, "An Answer to Ernest Bevin: Evidence Submitted to the Palestine Royal Commission" (House of Lords, London, February 11, 1937) (Bernard Ackerman/Beechhurst, 1946). A booklet comprising Vladimir Ze'ev Jabotinsky's testimony before the Peel Commission (Palestine Royal Commission) in 1937. This speech, highlighting the possibility and inevitability of Palestine housing the majority of the world's Jewish population, was printed in this 1946 publication as a reply to Ernest Bevin, the foreign secretary, in his support of limiting Jewish immigration.
8. The 1998 Israeli Supreme Court decision in *The Ministry of Defense vs. Rubenstein* had to determine the potential conflict between the right to freedom of religion (via the pursuit of religious studies) and the obligations of citizenship (via an equitable public sharing of the burden of military service). The controversy led to continued bitterness, as the issue was not resolved, pitting those who serve for three or more mandatory years of military service from ages 18 to 21, followed by decades of reserve duty, against those who perform no military service at all. This ruling found that the military draft deferments lacked any specific legal authorization. Subsequently, the "Deferment of Military Draft for Yeshiva Students Whose Occupation is the Study of Torah Law" (the Tal Law) was enacted in 2002, authorizing the defense minister to defer the military service of any Israeli national who requests it, provided he studies in a yeshiva on a regular basis for at

least forty-five hours a week and does not engage in any other occupation.

9. Efraim Halevy, *Jerusalem Post*, November 4, 2011.

10. See statements by Kuwaiti officials on arms deals with Israel to provide aid to the Syrian rebels fighting the Assad regime. *The algemeiner*, 2013.

11. See the video at http://hasbara-videos.blogspot.com/2011/02/jamie-glazov-interviews-nonie-darwish.html.

12. See Norman Berdichevsky, *Nations, Language and Citizenship* (McFarland, 2004).

13. *The algemenier*, "Must a Jewish State Be Zionist?" June 28, 2013.

14. Mordechai Kaplan, *Judaism as a Civilization: Toward a Reconstruction of American-Jewish Life* (Schocken Books, 1972), 452.

15. Music by Stavros Xarhakis, and lyrics by Eli Mohar.

Bibliography

Abu Toameh, Khaled. "The Palestinian Authority's Inconvenient Truth." Gatestown, International Institute Policy Council, January 13, 2013.
Ain, Stewart. "Poll: Romney Wins Among American Citizens." *Jewish Week*, November 12, 2012.
Ajami, Fouad. "Five Myths About the Arab Spring." *Washington Post*, February 12, 2012.
Alberg, Robert. "Efficient Reading in Hebrew—The Hillel Writing System and Spelling" (*Kriyah Yeilah bi'Ivrit*). *Telegraph Press* (Bnei-Brak, 1991).
Almagor, Dan. "How 'The Rain in Spain' Fell in Eretz-Israel." *Ariel: A Review of the Arts and Sciences in Israel*, no. 104 (1997).
Amara, M., and Abd Al-Rahman Mar'i. *Language Education Policy: The Arab Minority in Israel*. Kluwer Academic Publishers, 2002.
American Task Force on Palestine. "The Palestinians of Jerusalem: What Do They Really Want? Round Table Discussion." Pechter Middle East Polls, December 20, 2010.
Ardagh, John. *Ireland and the Irish: Portrait of a Changing Society*. Penguin Books, 1994.
Assouline, Phillip. "Israeli Arab Urges Full Integration with Israel." *Times of Israel*, October 30, 2012.
———. "Telling Israel Like It Is—in Arabic." *Times of Israel*, October 17, 2012.
Attalah, Dianna. "West Bank Hebrew Language Study Is Growing." *Jerusalem Post*, March 27, 2013.
Atar, Moshe. *Ivrit Safah ḥaya*. S. Friedman Publishers, 1989.
———. *Leshonenu La'Am* (Our Language for the People) (issue 457).
Atashi, Zeidan. "The Druze in Israel and Compulsory Military Service." Jerusalem Center for Public Affairs, no. 464 (October 2001).
———. *Druze & Jews in Israel: A Shared Destiny*. Sussex Academic Press, 1997.
Avinor, Michael. "The Karmeli Alphabet." www.omniglot.com/writing/karmeli.com.
Avneiri, Uri. "Benjamin's Inn: A Tribute to Artist, Writer and Editor Benjamin Tammuz, The 'Canaanite,' on the Occasion of the Publication of a New Edition of His Writings in Hebrew." *HaAretz*, Dec. 27, 2007.
Avnery, Uri. *Israel Without Zionism*. Macmillan, 1973.
Balmer, Crispian. "Gas Discoveries Give Israel New Regional Clout." Reuters, May 22, 2013.
Bartal, Israel. "From Traditional Bilinguals, to National Monolinguals." In *Hebrew in Ashkenaz: A Language in Exile*, Lewis Glinert, ed., 141–50. Oxford University Press, 1993.
Beaumont, Peter, et al. *The Middle East: A Geographical Study*. John Wiley & Sons, 1976.
Beck, Atara. "First Bedouin IDF Tank Commander." *Jewish Press*, October 30, 2013.
Beck, Noah. *The Last Israelis*. Create Space Independent Publishing, 2013.
Ben-Amotz, Dan. *Milon Olami Le'Ivrit Meduberet* (The World Dictionary of Spoken Hebrew). Levin-Epstein, 1972.
Ben-Israel, Danny. *ZUBI! The Real Hebrew You Were Never Taught in School*. Plume, 2011.
Bennet, James. "Israeli Arab Hero Is Praised but Not Embraced." *New York Times*, September 26, 2002.
Ben On, Pela. *Ktav Oz, HaKtav HaLatino-Ivri* (The Latin-Hebrew Script). *HaTnua limaan Ktav Ivri had-Mashma'i* (The Movement for a Decisive Hebrew Script). Jerusalem, 1990.

Ben-Rafael, Eliezer. *Language, Identity and Social Division: The Case of Israel*. Clarendon Press, 1994.
Berdichevsky, Norman. "The Impact of Urbanization on the Social Geography of Rehovot: An Israeli Case Study of Residential Differentiation, 1890–1874." Ph.D. thesis. Excerpt published in *Studies in Israeli Society*, vol. 1, Ernest Krausz, ed., 73–96. Transaction Books, 1980.
_____. *Nations, Language and Citizenship*. McFarland, 2004.
_____. "A Tale of Two Cities: Lithuania's See-Saw Struggle to Gain Control of Vilnius and Klaipeda (Memel)." *Boundary Bulletin*, University of Durham (July 1991).
_____. "Why Esperanto Is Different." *New English Review* (December 2007).
_____. "Zamenhof and Esperanto." *Ariel: A Review of Arts and Letters in Israel* 64 (1986): 58–71.
_____. "Zohar Argov and the Hebrew Language Gap." *New English Review* (May 2013).
Berent, Moshe. *A Nation Like All Nations: Towards the Establishment of an Israeli Republic*. Carmel, 2009.
Berman, Lazar, and Elhanan Miller. "New Christian Arab Party Calls for IDF Enlistment." *Times of Israel*, July 10, 2013.
Biró, Tamás. "Weak Interactions: Yiddish Influences in Hungarian, Esperanto and Modern Hebrew." In *On the Boundaries of Phonology and Phonetics: A Festschrift Presented to Tjeerd de Graaf*, D. Gilbers et al., eds., 123–45. University of Groningen, 2004.
Bittelman, Alexander. *Program for Survival: The Communist Party Position on "The Jewish Question."* New Century, 1947.
Blau, Joshua. *The Renaissance of Modern Hebrew and Modern Standard Arabic*. Vol. 18, Near Eastern Studies. University of California, 1981.
Bram, Chen. "Muslim Revivalism and the Emergence of Civil Society: A Case Study of an Israeli Circassian Community." *Central Asian Survey* 22, no. 1 (March 2003): 5–21.
Brenner, Rachel Feldhay. *Inextricably Bonded: Israeli Arab and Jewish Writers Re-visioning Culture*. University of Wisconsin Press, 2003.
Bryson, Bill. *Mother Tongue: The English Language*. Penguin Books, 1992.
Cambridge Encyclopedia of Language. Edited by David Crystal. Cambridge University Press, 1992.
Carta's Atlas of the Jewish People in the Middle Ages. Carta, 1991.
Caspi, Michael M., and Jerome D. Weltsch. *From Slumber to Awakening: Culture and Identity of Arab Israeli Literati*. University Press of America, 1998.
Chase, T. G. *The Story of Lithuania*. Stratford House, 1946.
Chatterji, Suniti Kumari. *Balts and Aryans in Their Indo-European Background*. Indian Institute of Advanced Study, 1968.
Chester, Sam. "As Chinese-Israeli Relations Enjoy a Second Honeymoon, America Frets." *Tablet*, June 28, 2013.
Chomsky, William. *Hebrew: The Eternal Language*. Jewish Publication Society, 1957.
_____. *How the Hebrew Language Grew*. Jewish Publication Society, 1957.
Cohen, Hillel. *Army of Shadows: Palestinian Cooperation with Zionism, 1917–1948*. University of California Press, 2008.
_____. *Good Arabs: The Israeli Security Agencies and the Israeli Arabs, 1948–1967*. University of California Press, 2010.
Cohen, Steven M. "Beyond Distancing: Young Adult American Jews and Their Alienation from Israel." Reprinted in *Camera on Campus* 18, no. 1 (Spring 2008).
Confino, M., and Sh. Shamir. *The USSR and the Middle East*. Israel Universities Press, 1973.
Cooper-Weil, Judith. "Early Hebrew Schools in Eretz-Israel." *Ariel: A Review of the Arts and Sciences in Israel*, no. 104 (1997).
Coulton, G. G. *St. Francis to Dante*. David Nutt, 1906.
Danan, Deborah. "Druze MK Wins Prize for Helping Hebrew." *Jerusalem Post*, June 18, 2012.
Dawidowicz, Lucy. *The War Against the Jews*. Bantam, 1986.
Domb, Risa. "'Hebrew, Speak Hebrew': The Place of Hebrew in Modern Hebrew Literature." In *Hebrew Study from Ezra to Ben-Yehuda*, William Horbury, ed. T & T Clark, 1999.
Eisenstein, Miriam. *Jewish Schools in Poland, 1919–1939*. King's Crown Press, 1950.
Eliav, Benyamin. "HaMedinot HaBaltiot" (The Baltic States). In *HaTfutza: Mizrach Europa*, Yaakov Tzur, ed. Keter Publishers, 1967.

Epstein, Lawrence. *At the Edge of a Dream: The Story of Jewish Immigrants on New York's Lower East Side*. An Arthur Kurzweil Book. Jossey-Bass, 2007.
Ettinger, Yoram. "Defying Demographic Projections." *Israel haYom*, April 5, 2013.
Even-Zohar, Itamar. "The Emergence of a Native Hebrew Culture in Palestine 1882–1948." *Poetics Today* 11 (Spring 1990).
_____. "Language Conflict and National Identity." In *Nationalism and Modernity: A Mediterranean Perspective*, Joseph Alter, ed. Praeger, 1986.
_____. "Who Is Afraid of the Hebrew Culture?" *Papers in Culture Research*, 2005.
Evron, Boaz. *Jewish State or Israeli Nation?* Indiana University Press, 1995.
Faitelson, Yakov. "A Jewish Majority in the Land of Israel: The Resilient Jewish State." *Middle East Forum* (Fall 2013): 15–27.
Farbush, Rabbi S. *HaLashon HaIvrit beYisrael uveAmim* (The Hebrew Language in Israel and Among the Nations). Israel, 1969.
Fishman, Joshua A. *Ideology, Society and Language*. Karoma Publishers, 1987.
_____. *The Rise and Fall of the Ethnic Revival: Perspectives on Language and Ethnicity*. Mouton, 1985.
Freund, Michael. "Orthodox Jews and the Aliyah Crisis." *Jerusalem Post*, March 8, 2013.
Gade, John A. "The Memel Controversy." *Foreign Affairs* 2, issue 3 (1924).
Geipel, John. *Mame Loshin: The Making of Yiddish*. Journeyman Press, 1982.
Gertz, Nurit. "From Jew to Hebrew in the Israeli Cinema of the 1940s and 1950s." *Israel Affairs* 4, nos. 3–4 (Spring/Summer 1998).
Gilad, Elong. *Mishkafayim* (Word of the Day). *HaAretz* online, June 12, 2013.
Gilboa, Yehoshua A. *Hebrew Silenced: The Suppression of Hebrew Literature and Culture in the Soviet Union*. Translation of *HaLashon Omedet al Nafsha*. Herzl Press, 1982.
Glick, Caroline. *The Israeli Solution: A One-State Plain for Peace in the Middle East*. Crown Forum, Random House, 2014.
Glinert, Lewis, ed. *Hebrew in Ashkenaz: A Language in Exile*. Oxford University Press, 1993.
_____. *Modern Hebrew: An Essential Grammar*. 2nd ed. Routledge, 1994.
Gold, David. "An Introduction to English in Israel." *Language Problems and Language Planning* 5, no. 1 (Spring 1981): 11–55.
_____. "Sketch of the Linguistic Situation in Israel Today." *Language in Society* 18 (1989).
Gold, Steven J. *The Israeli Diaspora*. University of Washington Press, 2002.
Gordon, Cyrus. *The Common Background of Greek and Hebrew Civilizations*. W. W. Norton, 1965.
Greenbaum, Avraham. "The Status of Hebrew in Soviet Russia from the Revolution to the Gorbachov Thaw." In *Hebrew in Ashkenaz: A Language in Exile*, Lewis Glinert, ed., 242–48. Oxford University Press, 1993.
Grin, François, and François Vaillancourt. *The Cost-Effectiveness Evaluation of Minority Language Policies: Case Studies on Wales, Ireland and the Basque Country*. Monograph no. 2. European Center for Minority Issues, 1999.
Gringauz, Samuel. "Jewish National Autonomy in Lithuania (1918–1925)." *Jewish Social Studies* (July 1952).
Habibi, Emile. *The Secret Life of Saeed, the Pessoptimist*. Translated by Salma Khadra Jayyusi and Trevor LeGassick. Zed Books, 1985.
Halkin, Hillel. "Hebrew as She Is Spoke." *Commentary* (December 1969).
Halkin, Hillel. *Letters to an American Jewish Friend: A Zionist Polemic*. Jewish Publication Society, 1977.
_____. "A Movable Feast." *Jerusalem Report*, April 22, 1993.
_____ (Philologos). "Revamping the Aleph-Bet." *Forward*, March 23, 1993.
Halperin, Liora. "Modern Hebrew, Esperanto and the Quest for a Universal Language. " *Jewish Social Studies, History, Culture Society* 19, No. 1 (Fall, 2012) pp. 1–33.
Hanson, Kenneth. *The Eagle and the Bible*. New English Review Press, 2012.
Harshav, Benjamin. *Language in a Time of Revolution*. University of California Press, 1993.
Hattis, Susan. *Political Dictionary of the State of Israel*. Jerusalem Publishing House, 1987.
Haugen, Einer. *Language Conflict and Language Planning: The Case of Norwegian*. Harvard University Press, 1966.

Hazony, David. "Memo to American Jews: Learn Hebrew—Gulf Between Israel and Diaspora Is Growing Fast." *Jewish Ideas Daily*, April 13, 2012. http://forward.com/articles/154253/memo-to-american-jews-learn-hebrew/?p=all#ixzz2LwlvgzTA.
Heggy, Tarek. "Our Need for a Culture of Compromise." MidEastWeb Opinion Forum, October 27, 2002.
Heller, Joseph. *The Stern Gang: Ideology, Politics and Terror 1940–1949*. Frank Cass, 1995.
Herschthal, Eric. "Israeli Authors Lost In Translation as Few Hebrew-Language Books Published in English." *Jewish Week*, May 25, 2010.
Hertzberg, Arthur. *The Zionist Idea: A Historical Analysis and Reader*. Jewish Publication Society, 2011.
Herzl, Theodore. *Altneuland* (Old-New Land). Create Space Independent Publishing Platform, 2011.
Hesse, Herman. *Beneath the Wheel*. Translated by Michael Roloff. Bantam Books, 1968.
Himmelfarb, Milton. "Hebraism and Hellenism Now." *Commentary* (July 1969).
Hoffman, Joel. *In the Beginning: A Short History of the Hebrew Language*. New York University Press, 2006.
Horn, Bernard. *Facing the Fires: Conversations with A.B. Yehoshua*. Syracuse University Press, 1997.
Horon, A. G. *Eretz haKedem—Madrich histori uMidini le-Mizrah ha-Karov*. Hermon Publishers, 1970.
Horowitz, Edward. *How the Hebrew Language Grew*. KTAV Publishing House, 1960.
Howe, Irving. *World of Our Fathers: The Journey of East European Jews to America and the Life They Found and Made*. Simon & Schuster, 1976.
Hull, Geoffrey. *The Malta Language Question*. Said International, 1993.
Israeli, Raphael. *Green Crescent Over Nazareth: The Displacement of Christians by Muslims in the Holy Land*. Routledge, 2002.
Jabotinsky, Ze'ev. "An Answer to Ernest Bevin: Evidence Submitted to the Palestine Royal Commission." House of Lords, London, February 11, 1937. Bernard Ackerman/Beechhurst, 1946.
———. *Hebrew Pronunciation*. HaSefer Publishing, 1940.
Jacobs, Jack Lester. *Bundist Counterculture in Interwar Poland*. Syracuse University Press, 2009.
Jacobs, Neil G. *Yiddish: A Linguistic Introduction*. Cambridge University Press, 2005.
Jenkins, Philip. *A History of Modern Wales, 1536–1990*. Longman, 1993.
Johnpoll, Bernard K. *The Politics of Futility: The General Jewish Workers Bund of Poland, 1917–1943*. Cornell University Press, 1967.
Kaganoff, Benzion. *A Dictionary of Jewish Names and Their History*. Routledge and Kegan Paul, 1978.
Kaplan, Mordechai. *Judaism as a Civilization: Toward a Reconstruction of American-Jewish Life*. Schocken Books, 1972.
Karsh, Efraim. *Palestine Betrayed*. Yale University Press, 2010.
Kashua, Sayed, and M. Schlesinger. *Dancing Arabs* (English translation). Grove Press, 2004.
Katz, Shmuel. *Lone Wolf: A Biography of Vladimir (Ze'ev) Jabotinsky*. 2 vols. Barricade Books, 1996.
Kershner, Isabel. "Noted Arab Citizens Call on Israel to Shed Jewish Identity." *New York Times*, February 14, 2009.
Kessler, Dana. "Upscale Arab Restaurants Gain a Wider Audience." *Tablet*, July 10, 2013.
Kessler, Oren. "An Arab Maverick." *Tablet*, October 12, 2012.
Kheimets, Nina G., and Alek D. Epstein. "The Role of English as a Central Component of Success in the Professional and Social Integration of Scientists from the Former Soviet Union in Israel." *Language in Society*, no. 30 (2001): 187–215.
Kissin, Yitzhak, ed. *Antologia shel Ha Sifrut HaLitait* (Hebrew). Kaunas, 1932.
Kraemer, Roberta. "A Test of Gardner's Socio-educational Model." In *Social Psychological Factors Related to the Study of Arabic Among Israeli High School Students*. Studies in Second Language Acquisition, Vol. 15. Cambridge University Press, 1993.
Kurlansky, Mark. *The Basque History of the World*. Random House, 1999.
Kurzman, Dan. *Genesis 1949: The First Arab-Israeli War*. New American Library, 1970.
Kutscher, E. Y. "Words and Their History." *Ariel: A Review of the Arts and Sciences in Israel*, no. 35 (1969).

Landau, Jacob. "Language Policy and Political Development in Israel and Turkey." In *Language Policy and Political Development,* Brian Weinstein, ed. Ablex, 1990.

Lapide, Pinchas E. *Hebrew in the Church: The Foundations of Jewish-Christian Dialogue.* William B. Eerdmans, 1984.

Lederer, Zdroje. *The Soviet Union and the Middle East: The Post–WWII Era.* Stanford University Press, 1974.

Levin, Dov. "They Fought Back: Lithuanian Jewry's Armed Resistance to the Nazis, 1941–45." *Yad vaShem: Martyrs' and Heroes' Remembrance Authority.* The Institute of Contemporary Jewry—Hebrew University, Jerusalem, 1974.

Lewis, Geoffrey. *The Turkish Language Reform: A Catastrophic Success.* Oxford University Press, 1999.

Lewis, Jonathan Eric. "Freedom of Speech—In Any Language." *Middle East Quarterly* (Summer 2004).

Lins, Ulrich. *La Dangera Lingvo: Studo pri la persekutoj kontraŭ Esperanto.* Belicher Eldonejo, 1988.

Lipson, Deborah. "Hebrew in the Soviet Union." *Ariel: A Review of the Arts and Sciences in Israel,* no. 85–86 (1991).

Lissak, Moshe, and Eli Leshem. "The Russian Intelligentsia in Israel: Between Ghettoization and Integration." *Israel Affairs* 2, no. 2 (Winter 1995).

Litvak, Olga. *Haskalah: The Romantic Movement in Judaism* [paperback]. Rutgers University Press, 2012.

Lossin, Yigal. *Pillar of Fire: The Rebirth of Israel—A Visual History.* Shikmona, 1983.

MacDonald, Dwight. "Profiles: THE SLAVE OF HEBREW." *New Yorker,* November 28, 1959.

Macnamara, J. "Successes and Failures in the Movement for the Restoration of Irish." In *Can Language Be Planned? Sociolinguistic Theory and Practice for Developing Nations,* J. Rubin and B. H. Jernudd, eds. University of Hawaii Press, 1971.

Macrone, Michael. *Brush Up Your Bible!* Harp Perennial (division of HarperCollins), 1993.

Maimon, N. Z. *La Kaŝita Vivo de Zamenhof* (Zamenhof's Hidden Life). Japanese Esperanto Institute, 1978.

Mandel, George. "Why Did Ben-Yehuda Suggest the Revival of Spoken Hebrew?" In *Hebrew in Ashkenaz: A Language in Exile,* Lewis Glinert, ed., 193–207. Oxford University Press, 1993.

Manor, Ehud. *Forward: The Jewish Daily Forward (Forverts) Newspaper: Immigrants, Socialism and Jewish Politics in New York, 1890–1917.* Sussex Academic Press, 2009.

Marcus, Lori Lowenthal. "Jewish Schools Endangered by New U.K. Curriculum." *Jewish Press,* December 16, 2012.

Medan, Meir. "The Academy of the Hebrew Language." *Ariel: A Review of the Arts and Sciences in Israel,* no. 25 (1969): 40–47.

Meir, Orna. *How to Cook in Eretz-Yisrael.* World's Women's Zionist Organization, 1936.

Mendes-Flohr, Paul. "Hebrew as a Holy Tongue: Franz Rosenzweig and the Renewal of Hebrew." In *Hebrew in Ashkenaz: A Language in Exile,* Lewis Glinert, ed., 222–41. Oxford University Press, 1993.

Michael, Sami. *Trumpet in the Wadi.* Translated by Yael Lotan (2002). Simon & Schuster, 2007.

Middle East Research Institute. "Israeli Arabs Object to Ideas of Israeli-Palestinian Territorial Exchanges." Special Dispatch no. 374, May 2, 2002.

Milon Megiddo Hadish (New Megiddo Dictionary). Megiddo Publishing Company, 1990.

Mintz, Alan, ed. *Hebrew in America.* Wayne State University Press, 1993.

———. "On the Question of Hebrew." *Forum,* nos. 46–47 (Fall/Winter 1982).

Miron, Dan. "Between Rabbi Shach and Modern Hebrew Literature." *Israel Affairs* 4, nos. 3–4 (Spring/Summer 1998).

Modern Language Association of America. *Enrollments in Languages Other than English in United States Institutions of Higher Education.* Fall 2009.

Moleas, W. *The Development of the Greek Language.* Bristol Classical Press, 1989.

Morag, Shelomo. "The Emergence of Modern Hebrew: Some Sociolinguistic Perspectives." In *Hebrew in Ashkenaz: A Language in Exile,* Lewis Glinert, ed., 208–21. Oxford University Press, 1993.

Mozeson, Isaac E. *The Word: The Dictionary that Reveals the Hebrew Sources of English.* Jason Aronson, 1995.
Oz, Amos. *A Tale of Love and Darkness.* Translated by Nocholas de Lange. Vintage Books, 2005.
Passow, David. *The Prime of Yiddish.* Gefen Publishing, 1996.
Patai, Raphael. *The Arab Mind.* Charles Scribner's Sons, 1983.
Patai, Raphael. *The Jewish Mind.* Charles Scribner's Sons, 1977.
Pelli, Moshe. *Haskalah and Beyond.* University Press of America, 2012.
_____. *HaTarbut HaIvrit beAmerika: 80 Shana HaTnu'ah HaIvrit beArtzot HaBrit 1916–1985* (The Hebrew Culture in America: 80 Years of the Hebrew Movement in the United States). Reshafim Publishers, 1998.
Pfeffer, Anshel. "Israel-India Relations: Strong, But Low-Key." *HaAretz*, December 1, 2008.
Pipes, Daniel. "Happy Israel." *Washington Post*, June 5, 2013.
Plaut, Steven. "The Collapse of Israeliness." *Jewish Magazine*, "Zion Without Judaism" issue (March 2, 2003).
Rabin, Chaim. *Everyday Hebrew: Twenty-Nine Simple Conversations with English Translation and Full Grammatical Introduction.* J.M. Dent & Sons, 1943.
_____. "Hebrew." In *Current Trends in Linguistics, 6: Linguistics in South West Asia and North Africa*, T. A. Sebeok et al., eds. Mouton, 1970.
_____. "The Revival of the Hebrew Language." *Ariel: A Review of the Arts and Sciences in Israel*, no. 25 (1969).
Raisin, Jacob. *The Haskalah Movement in Russia* [paperback]. Echo Library, 2007.
Remick, Larissa. *Russian Jews on Three Continents: Identity, Integration and Conflict.* Transaction Publishers, 2012.
Ringvald, Vardit, et al. *Brandeis Modern Hebrew—Ivrit biHeksher* (Hebrew in Context). Brandeis University Press, 2005.
Rogov, Daniel. "The Israeli Kitchen." *Ariel: A Review of the Arts and Sciences in Israel* (1985–1986).
Rosenthal, Donna. *The Israelis: Ordinary People in an Extraordinary Land.* Free Press, 2003.
Rosten, Leo. *The Joys of Yiddish.* W. H. Allen, 1968.
_____. *Leo Rosten's Treasury of Jewish Quotations.* Bantam Books, 1972.
Roth, Cecil. *Jewish Contributions to Civilization.* 2nd ed. Macmillan, 1938.
Saenz Badillos, Angel. *A History of the Hebrew Language* (English edition). Cambridge University Press, 1993.
Sapir, Shoshana London. "Letter from Haifa: An Official Language Gets More Respect." *Hadassah Magazine* (January 2010).
Schniedewind, William M. *A Social History of Hebrew: Its Origins Through the Rabbinic Period.* Yale University Press, 2013.
Schwarzwald, Ora (Rodrigue). "The Components of the Modern Hebrew Lexicon: The Influence of Hebrew Classical Sources, Jewish Languages and Other Foreign Languages on Modern Hebrew." *Hebrew Linguistics* 39 (1995): 79–90.
Shammas, Anton. *Arabesques.* Harper & Row, 1986.
_____. "Kitsch 22: On the Problems of the Relations Between Majority and Minority cultures in Israel." *Tikkun* 2, no. 4 (September–October 1987).
Shavit, Ya'akov. *Jabotinsky and the Revisionist Movement, 1925–1948.* Frank Cass, 1988.
_____. *The New Hebrew Nation: A Study in Israeli Heresy and Fantasy.* Frank Cass, 1987.
Shehade, Habeeb. University of Helsinki, Third Nordic Conference on Middle Eastern Studies: Ethnic Encounter and Culture Change. "The Hebrew of the Arabs of Israel." June 19–22, 1995.
Sivan, Reuven. "Ben Yehuda and the Revival of Hebrew Speech." *Ariel: A Review of the Arts and Sciences in Israel*, no. 25 (1969): 35–39.
_____. *Leksikon le-Sipur ha-LaSon.* Karni Publishers, 1969.
Sneir, Reuven. "Hebrew as the Language of Grace: Arab-Palestinian Writers in Hebrew." Translated by M. 'Awda and R. Sneir. *Prooftexts* 15, no. 2 (1995): 163–83.
Spolsky, Bernard, and Robert Cooper. *The Languages of Jerusalem.* Clarendon Press, 1991.
Spolsky, Bernard, and Elana Shohamy. "Language in Israeli Society and Education." *International Journal of the Sociology of Language* (2002).

_____. "The Penetration of English as Language of Science and Technology into the Israeli Linguistic Repertoire: A Preliminary Inquiry." In *The Dominance of English as Language of Science: Effects on Other Languages and Language Communities*, Ulrich Ammon, ed. Mouton de Gruyter, 2001.

St. John, Robert. *Tongue of the Prophets: The Fascinating Biography of Eliezer Ben-Yehuda, the Father of Modern Hebrew* [paperback]. Wilshire Book Company, 1979.

Stampfer, Shaul. "What Did 'Knowing Hebrew' Mean in Eastern Europe?" In *Hebrew in Ashkenaz: A Language in Exile*, Lewis Glinert, ed., 129–40. Oxford University Press, 1993.

Tal, Rami. "The Israeli Press." *Ariel: A Review of the Arts and Sciences in Israel* (1995).

Tene, David. "Israeli Hebrew." *Ariel: A Review of the Arts and Sciences in Israel*, no. 25 (1969).

Times of Israel. "In Putin's Russia, Jews Adopt Silence as Best Protection." October 28, 2012.

Torstrick, Rebecca L. *Culture and Customs in Israel*. Greenwood Press, 2004.

Traubman, Tamara. "Wallah, Long Time No See." *HaAretz*, February 1, 2006.

Ullendorff, Richard. "Hebrew in Mandatory Palestine." In *Hebrew Study from Ezra to Ben-Yehuda*, William Horbury, ed., 300–306. T & T Clark, 1999.

Von Rauch, George, and Gerald Onn. *The Baltic States: The Years of Independence: Estonia, Latvia, Lithuania, 1917–1940*. University of California Press, 1974.

Waller, Uri. *Israel Between East and West: Israel's Foreign Policy Orientation, 1948–56*. Cambridge University Press, 1990.

Wardhaugh, Richard, ed. *Languages in Competition*. Basil Blackwell, 1987.

Weinberg, Werner. *Tikun HaKtiv haIvr vehanisyonoy liftorah* (The Orthographic Reform of Hebrew: The Problem and the Attempts to Solve It). Hebrew University, 1971.

Weingrad, Michael. *American Hebrew Literature: Writing Jewish National Identity in the United States*. Syracuse University Press, 2011.

Weltsch, Jerome D. *From Slumber to Awakening: Culture and Identity of Arab Israeli Literati*. University Press of America, 1998.

Wertheimer, Jack. "The Jewish Birthrate." *Commentary* (October 2005).

Wescott, Roger Williams. "Colonial American Belief in Hebrew as the Primal Language." *Geolinguistics* (1991).

Wexler, Paul. *The Schizoid Nature of Modern Hebrew: Slavic Language in Search of a Semitic Past*. O. Harrassowitz, 1990.

Williams, Holly. "Mind Your (Minority) Language: Welsh, Gaelic, Irish and Cornish Are Staging a Comeback." *The Independent*, January 19, 2013.

Wodzinski, Marcin. *Haskalah and Hasidism in the Kingdom of Poland: A History of Conflict* [paperback]. Littman Library of Jewish Civilization, 2007.

Yelvin, Shmeul. "The Hebreo-Phoenician Writing Signary." *Ariel: A Review of the Arts and Sciences in Israel*, no. 25 (1969).

Yitzhak, Norman, ed. *Bireshit HaBimah* (At the Beginning of Habimah). Jerusalem, 1967.

Yoffie, Adina M. "Jewish Studies, Once and Future." *Jewish Press*, August 23, 2012.

Zahran, Mudar. "Jordan Is Palestinian." *Middle East Quarterly* 19, no. 1 (Winter 2012): 3–12.

Zakim, Eric. *To Build and Be Built: Landscape, Literature and the Construction of Zionist Identity*. University of Pennsylvania Press, 2006.

Zuckermann, Ghil'ad. *Yisraelit, Safah Yafah* (Israeli—A Beautiful Language). Am Oved, 2008.

_____, and Azzam Yadin. "'Blorit'—Pagans' Mohawk or Sabra's Forelock? Ideological Secularization of Hebrew Terms in Socialist-Zionist Israeli." In *The Sociology of Language and Religion*, Tope Omoniyi, ed. Palgrave Macmillan, 2009.

Zurofit, Avraham. "Some Arab Citizens of Israel Prefer Hebrew." Arutz 7 website, June 13, 2009.

Index

Page numbers in ***bold italics*** indicate pages with illustrations.

Abbas, Husam, and Nashat 155
Abraham 16
Abramovitsch, Shalom Jakob *see* Mendel Mokher Seforim
Abu Seif, Heba 141
Abu-Toameh, Khaled 149
Academy of the Arabic Language (Haifa, Israel) 142
Academy of the Hebrew Language 47, 56, 67, 73, 144, 173, 180
Africa 4
Afulah 21
Agriculture ***90***
Ahab, King 16
Aḥei Natzeret FC 139
Akkadia and Akkadian 18, 28, 44
Akko (Acre) 155
al-Ahram 198
Al Amal Lat'gir Arab Political Party 152
Alamiya, Father André 153
Åland islands 64
Al-Assad, Bashar 196–197
al-Azhar Islamic University, Cairo 141
Albania 42
Alberg, Robert 73
Aleichem, Shalom (Shalom Rabinowitz) 142, 176, 180
Aleph 103
Algeria 163
Al ha–Mishmar 57
Aligheri, Dante 27
Allen, Ethan 17
Allen, Woody 94
Almah 23
al-Quds University 163
Altneuland 77
American Community Service Report on Language Use at Home 86
Amihai, Yehuda 144
Amman 150

Anglo-Saxon 43
Angola 196
Antwerp 110
"Arab Spring" 140, 163
Arabesques 142
Arabia 43–44
Arabic Academy, Israeli 142
Arabic and Arabic dialects 1, 10–11, 27, 45–46, 48, 54, 63, 65, 71–73, 78, 136–139, 142, 164, 172–174, 176–178, 186, 198–199
Aramaic 16, 26, 28, 31
Argentina 100, 138, 140, 163, 166, 180, 196
Argov, Zohar 100
Armageddon 21
Armenian 4, 158
Arnold, Benedict 141
Assady, Dr. Suheir 150
Assyria 18, 44
Atzmon, Shmuel 82
Auguries of Innocence 20
Australia 108, 132, 136, 159, 166
Avnery, Uri (Helmut Ostermann) 159

Babel, Tower of 27
Babylonia 18, 44
Babylonian square letters 110
Baghdad 29
Balfour Declaration 104
Band, Yehuda 180
Baqa-al-Gharbiye 150, 155
Bar Ilan University 47, 173, 180
Bar-Kochba Revolt 158
Baseball 8
Bashevis Singer, Isaac 77
Basque and the Basques 30, 33, 43
Beck, Noah 199
Bedouin volunteers and casualties in the IDF 151, 154, 161, 190
Beersheba 173

223

Index

Begin, Menachem 89, 92, 193
Behemoth 21
Belgium 100, 110, 136, 158–159, 168
Belize 196
Ben-Amotz, Dan 173, 176
Ben-Ari, S. 130
Ben-Asher, Prof. Moshe 180
Ben-Avi, Itamar 42
Beneath the Wheel 9
Ben-Gurion, David 59, 60, 69, 81, 89, 91, 130, 147, 160, 191
Ben-Gurion University of the Negev 180
Ben-Israel, Danny 173
Benny, Jack 94
Ben-Rafael, Eliezer 139
Ben-Shaul, Haim, of Saragosa 56
Ben-Yehuda, Eliezer (Eliezer Perlman) *2*–*3*, 34, 37–44, 46, 49–51, 53–60, 65, 69, 77, 82–83, 88, 98, 109–110, 117, 143–144, 170, 180, 192–193
Ben-Zvi, Yitzhak 89, 91
Ber, Shlomo 100
Berbers 103, 158
Berger, Victor 105–106
Berle, Milton 94
Berlin, Irving 119
Beta Israel 29
Betar 113
Bethlehem 16
Bethulah 23
Bialik, Chaim Nachman 96–*97*, 107, 126, 129, 181
Bible, Biblical Hebrew, Biblical verses and place names 1, 9–10, 17, 20–29, 48, 60–61, 64–67, 70, 136, 176
Bilingualism (Hebrew and Arabic) in Israel 143–144
Birenboam, Gabriel 180
Birnbaum, Nathan 78
Birobidzhan 130–133
Blake, William 15
Blumberg, Harry 119
Bnei-Akiva 194
Bnei-Sachnin FC 139
Brazil 137, 166, 168
Brenner, B.M. 150
British English 137, 173
The Bronx 5
Brooklyn 185
Brooks, Mel 94
Brown University 16
Buenos Aires *5*
Bukhara, Uzbekistan 97
Bulgarian 38, 138
The Bund 76
A Burning Question 53

Byalistock 38
Byron, Lord 20

Cabal 21
Cairo 150, 198
Canaanites and "Canaanism" 26, 31, 44, 65, 101–103, 162, 170
Canada 117, 132, 136, 158
Carmelit *197*
Carthage 18, 31
Catalan and Catalonia 30, 33, 42, 167
Ceausescu, Nicolai 42
Census, U.S., Report on Language Use at Home 85
Central African Republic 196
Chabon, Michael 132
Chaldo-Assyrians 158
Charter schools 184–189
Chase, Edward Azriel 108
Cherubim and Seraphim 20
Chile 100
China and Chinese 4, 11–13, 28, 42–43, 132, 191
Chomsky, William 3
Christian IV, King of Denmark 24
Christianity 5, 9, 18, 21–24
Circassians 157, 161, 190
City College of New York (CCNY) 5
Clinton, Bill 16
Cohen, Rachel 149
Cohen, Steve 12
Col HaCavod 175–176
Coleridge, Samuel 20
Common Background of Greek and Hebrew Civilizations 18
"The Convoy Song" 200
Copenhagen 24
Copenhagen Round Tower *25*
Coptic Christians 158
Crete 18
Cromwell, Oliver 16
Cronin, Sean 31
Cyprus 18
Czechoslovakia 98, 133, 158, 196

Dabberu Ivrit 117
Daliyat-al-Carmel 181
Damari, Shoshanna 100, 200
Dancing Arabs 142
Dartmouth University 16
Darwish, Mahmoud 145
Darwish, Nonie 198
Davar 105–106
David, King 21
davka 174–175
Dayan, Moshe 183

Index

Dayan, Yael 183
Deir Hanna 151
Democrat Party, American 10
Denmark and Danish 38, 43, 100, 116, 138, 165
De Reynold, Gonzague 37
Deror 69
de Rothschild, Baron Edmund 173, 178
Dhomnaill, Nuala Ni 136
Diaspora, Jewish 1–2, 8–9, 30, 64, 72–73, 75–83, 91–94, 100–105, 118, 129–130, 162–163, 166–167, 169, 183, 190–200
Diglossia 182
Dinur, Ben-Zion 179
Doar ha-Yom 42
"Doctors' Plot" 134
Dreyfus trial 40
Druze 157–158, 196, 199
Druze volunteers and casualties in the IDF 146, 151, 161
Durban, South Africa 154
Duryanov, Alter 95
Dutch 38, 43
The Dybbuk 129
Dylan, Thomas 188

East Jerusalem 145–146
Egypt 103, 139–140
Eilat 134
Einstein, Albert 38, 199
Einstein, Aric 200
Eisteddfod 189
"Elem hen" 23
Emes 127
English 3, 12–13, 17, 28, 31, 35, 38, 40, 41, 46–48, 50–51, 53, 56, 60, 63, 65, 70, 73, 77–78, 89, 91, 117, 119, 121–123, 125, 137–138, 144, 150, 188, 172, 173, 176, 178–179, 184
Envy Tyre 103
Eretz Israel Museum 149
Eshkol, Levi 91
Esperanto 34–42
Estonia and Estonian 42, 108
Ethiopia 19, 29
Everyday Hebrew 118
Exodus (ship) **195**

Farsi (Persian) 28, 45, 48, 63, 127
Feast of Balshazzar 15
Fiddler on the Roof 142, 176
Fidling Arabs 142
Finland and Finnish 38, 72, 136, 164
Fishing **90**
Flemish 110
Fort Ticonderoga 17

Forward (Forvaerts –Yiddish daily newspaper) 105, 180
France 100, 181; French 11–13, 38, 43, 48, 54–55, 70, 85, 89, 116, 136, 140, 183, 196
Frederick II, Holy Roman Emperor 27
Fribourg, University of 37
Friedman-Yellin, Nathan 160
Frumkin, Dov 48

Gabai, Yigal 191
Gaelic 189
Ga'on, Yehoram 100
Gaza 21, 150, 169–171, 196
Gemara 54
Germany 16, 39, 76, 78, 84, 105, 108, 111–114, 118, 122, 132, 181, 188–189; German 11–13, 15, 38–39, 43, 46–48, 54–55, 60, 63, 65, 68, 70, 76–78, 81, 85, 89, 91, 99, 109, 116, 140, 176, 178–179, 186, 186, 199
Gilgamesh Epic 4
Givatayim 173
Glazov, Jamie 198
Glinert, Lewis 74
Golan Heights 196–197
Golden Inkwell Prize 181
Golem 21
Goliath 21
Gordon, Cyrus 18
Gorky, Maxim 128–129
Gourevitch, Adolphe *see* Horon, A. G.
Gove, Michael 186
Greece 17–18, 21, 44, 48, 163; Greek and Greeks 1, 5, 7, 11–14, 16, 27–28, 30, 33–34, 39, 43–45, 67, 136, 186–189, 200
Greek Catholics 158
Greek Orthodox Church 153
Green Mountain Boys 17
Greenberg, Uri Zvi 101
Grossman, David 144, 155
Gymnasia Herzliyah **83**

Ha-'Am 57
Ha-Aretz 57, 146
Habibi, Emile 141, 145
HaBimah National Theater 83, 119, 121, 124, 129–130
Habimah Theater 83, 122, 129–130
Ha-Boker 57
Hadar 112–113
Hadera 122
Ha-Doar 117, 177
Ha-Ezra 46
Haganah 91, 158, 199–200
ha-Havatzelet 48
ha-Histadrut ha'Ivrit 104
Haifa 46, 144, 173, 179, 181, 197

Haifa University 151, 162, 166
Haile Selassie, Emperor 19
Haiti 43, 137
Hakim, Dr. Azmi 153
Halacha 169
Ha-Lbanon 49
HaLevy Efraiim 193
Halkin, Hillel 72, 83–86
Halkin, Prof. Simon 5
Halleleujah 21
Hamas 139–140, 148, 197
Ha-Modia 57
Ha-Olam Ha-Zeh 159
Ha-Or 48
Hareidim 146, 194–196
Harshav, Benjamin 82
Harvard University 16
Ha-Šahar 53
Ha-Šomer ha-TZair 168
Haskalah 38, 40, 77, 109
Hassidism 99, 109
Hasson, Akram 181
"*Ha-Tikvah*" 41, 157
Hazan, Haim Leiv 56
Hazony, David 14
Hebraization Campaign 87–97
Hebrew Charter School Center (HCSC) 185
Hebrew Charter School Movement 184–187
Hebrew Literature 2, 72, 104, 127, 129
"Hebrew Republic," concept of a 147–171
Hebrew: The Eternal Language 3
Hebrew University 47, 63, 82, 146, 150, *179*, 180
Heggy, Tarek 198
Hendl, Nehama 200
Ĥerut 57
Herziliya Hebrew Teachers' College 117
Herziliyah Gymnasium *83*
Herzl, Theodore 77, 99–100
Herzog, Haim 143
Hezbollah 197
Hindi 28–29
Hiram of Tyre, King 102
Histadrut Labor Federation 150
Holocaust 81, 102–103, 108–112, 115–116, 131, 157, 196
Honey *191*
Horn, Bernard 156
Horon, A. G. 102–103
Horowitz, Edward 3
Hosanna 21
How the Hebrew Language Grew 3
Hoxha, Enhver 32
Hungarian 38–39, 81, 116

IDF *see*{en}Israel Defense Forces
The Iliad 18
India 191
Indo-European languages 28
Indonesia 4
Industry *90*
International Academy of Sciences, San Marino 41
Intifadas 157
Iraq 4, 139
Ireland 148; Irish 30–31, 187–189
Irgun 133, 158, 200
The Irish Times 31
Ishtar 44
Islam 18
Israel (Land of [Palestine] and State of Israel) 1–3, 18–19, 45, 48, 61, 76–86, 118–119, 130–133, 137, 141–148, 164, 178–181, 186–190, 193–200
Israel Communist Party 153
Israel Defense Forces (IDF) 89, 146, 151–154, 161, 176
Israel Democracy Institute 166
Israeli—A Beautiful Language 64
Israeli Arabs, Druze, Circassians and Bedouins 136–171
Israeli banknotes *90*
Israeli I.D. cards (teudot-zehoot) 161
Italy and Italian 11–13, 31, 45, 85, 182, 186, 193, 200
Ivory Coast 136
Ivri Anokhi 117

Jabotinsky, Ze'ev 80, *97*, 100–101, 110–115, 192–193, 200
Jaffa 103, 155
James IV, King of Scotland 28
Japan and Japanese 11–13, 42, 186
Jehovah and Yahweh *see* YHWH
Jehovah's Witnesses 24
Jericho 16
Jerusalem 38, 54, 57–58, 63, 73, 88, 103, 107, 111, 120–121, 130, 136, 143, 145–146, 150, 173, 178–180, 183, 192
Jerusalem Post 140, 183
Jesus 31
Jewish Leadership Council in the UK 187
Jewish National Council 179–180
Jews' Free School (JFS) 187–188
Job, Book of 18
Johns Hopkins University 167
Jokes and Witticisms 95
Jordan 4, 162–163, 196
Joyce, James 188
The Joys of Yiddish 76
Judaic (or Jewish) Studies 10

Judaism and Jewish religious communities 18, 21–24, 26–29
Juhja, Yousef 151

Kabbalah 19, 99
Karinaoui, Aatef 151–152
Kashua, Sayed 141–142
Katsav, Moshe 151
Kaunus 108, 114
Keaton, Dianne 7
Kenan, Amos 103, 144
Kerensky, Alexander 127
Khalaila, Boshra 151
Kharkov 127
Khrushchev, Nikita 133
Kibbutz 30–*31,* 47, 80, 122, 150–151, 173
The Kidney 150
Kiev 102
"Kippah agreement" at JFS 188
Kissinger, Henry 166
Klauszner, Joseph 89
Klingon 42
Knesset 2, 19, 30, 73, 83, 141, 143, 145–148, 150–152, 160, 164, 181
Kol ha-Am 57, 131, 133
Kol Yisrael 80
Koppel, Moshe 180
Koran (Quran) 137
Korean 11–12
Kovno 61, 110
Kurds 158, 197

La-Merħav 57
Ladino (Judeo-Spanish) 29, 30, 48, 65, 75, 83
"A Land Flowing with Milk and Honey" *191*
The Land of Kedem—A Historical and Political Guide to the Near East{en} 103
The Last Israelis 198
Latin 1, 11–13, 16, 27, 34, 37, 110, 200
Latvia and Latvian 108–110, 116
Law of Return 165
Lazar, Rabbi Berel 135
Lebanon 103, 162
Leħi (FFI Fighters for the Freedom of Israel, the "Stern Gang") 102, 133, 158
Letters to an American Jewish Friend 84
Letzte Nayes 82
Levine, S. 33
Levy, David 183
Lewis, Jerry 94
Lewittes, Mordechai 119
Libya 4, 152, 157, 162
Lilienblum, Moshe Leib 61
Linna, Väin 72

Listhaus, Aaron 185
Lithuania, Lithuanian and "Litvaks" 38–39, 61, 96, 107–116, 138
Lithuanian 16th Rifle Division 114
Lod *see* Lydda
London 97, 186–188
Lutzky, Brigadier General Dov 153
Luzhki 38
Lydda 122

Ma'ariv 140
Madrid Peace Conference 183
Mah Pitom? 175–176
Mahamid, Rami 153
Mahmoud, Mounir 140
Majadla, Ghaleb 150
Major, Sir John 20
Makkabi Games **88**
Malta and Maltese 30–33, 103, 188
Mandarin 186
Manhattan 185
Mansour, Atallah 141
Marks, Laura 186
Marsh Arabs 158
Marx Brothers 94
Masada 158
Maskilim 53
Mazzini, Giuseppe 112
Meir, Golda 89, 107, 174–175
Memel (Klaipeda), Lithuania 112
Mesopotamia 18, 103
Messiah 22
Mexico 136
Michael, Sammi 144
Michaux, A. 41
Midler, Bette 7
Milon HaSlang HaMekif 173
Milon Megiddo Ħadish 68
Milon Olami le'Ivrit Meduberet 172
Milton, John 15, 20
Milwaukee 105
Minsk 117
Misezhnikov, Stas 92
Mishna and Mishnaic Hebrew 44, 53–54, 61, 65–66, 70–71, 136
Mizrahi identity 144
Modern Hebrew: An Essential Grammar 74
Mongolia 132
Morgen Freiheit 105, 132
Morocco 29, 163, 198
Moscow 125, 127, 129–132
Moshe, Haim 100
Mossad 193
Mozeson, Isaac 28
Muhammad 139
Mussolini, Benito 42

My Big Fat Greek Wedding 7
My Fair Lady (in Hebrew) 144
My Michael 144

Nablus 170
Nadaf, Father Gabriel 153–154
Naipul, V.S. 189
Najar, Atallah 155
Nasser, Azmi, and Ruthy 148
Navon, Yitzhak 143
Nazareth 149–150, 153, 155
Neologisms 48, 61–63
Netanyahu, Benjamin 135, 191
The Netherlands 13
Netzer, Nissan 47, 173
New Norwegian 30
New Zealand 136, 158
Nikud 50, 67–69
Nimer, Samer 140
Nixon, Richard 16
Northern Ireland 20
Norway 148
Nusseiba, Sari 163

Obama, Barack 9–10
Odessa 127
The Odyssey 18
Olami 97
Olgin, Moissaye 132
Organization of the Islamic Conference (OIC) 139
Orpaz, Yitzhak 91
ORT 114–115, 135
Orthodox Jews in Israel 29, 46, 57, 60, 69, 77–78, 82–84, 94, 98, 100, 103, 106, 109, 125–126, 146, 161, 163, 167–169, 171, 173, 176
Orthodox Jews in the UK 186–189
The Orthographic Reform of Hebrew 69
Oslo Agreement 162
Oxford University 119
Oz, Amos 96, 98–99, 144, 155, 200

Pakistan 4, 158
Palestine Royal Commission of 1937 193
Palestinian Authority (PA) 140, 148, 151, 163, 190
Palestinian Communist Party 131, 148
Paradise Lost 20
Pechter Middle East Polls 146
Pelli, Dr. Moshe 104
Pennsylvania, University of 16
Persia 44
Perski, Daniel 117–118
Philippines 43
Philistines and Philistinism 21

Philologus 73
Phoenicia 18, 19, 32, 67, 102–103
Piers Plowman 20
Pines, Rabbi Yechiel Michel 60
Plaid Cymru 189
Plaut, Steven 162
Plene spelling 67
Poalei-Zion 12–26
Poalei-Zion Smol *125*–126
Poland 46, 57, 77, 97–98, 108, 111–114, 125, 166; Polish 38, 60, 65–66, 81, 94, 176
Portugal and Portuguese 11–12, 76, 116, 148, 168
Preca, Annibale 33
Princeton University 16
Profanity 172–177
"Protocols of the Elders of Zion" 139
Puritans 16, 19
Putin, Vladimir 135
Putnam, General Israel 17

Ra'a'nanah 122
Rabin, Chaim 118–122
Rabin, Leah 175
Rabin, Yitzhak 175
Rahat 151
Ramallah 150
Ramat-Gan 149
Rambam Healthcare, Haifa 150
Ratosh, Yonatan 102
Reconstructionism 200
"*Refuesenik*" movement 124–135
Rembrandt 15
Renan, Ernest 158
Republican Party, American 9
Reuchlin, Johann 15
Revisionism 192–193
Rhadanites 77
Rhyme of the Ancient Mariner 20
Riga 110, 113, 130
Rita 200
The Road to Ein Harod 144
Romania and Romanian 42, 47, 96
Rome 17, 44
Romney, Mitt 9–10
Rosenteil, Ruvik 173
Rosenzweig, Franz 98
Rosten, Leo 76
Roth, Cecil 17
Rovno 96, 98
Rushdie, Salman 189
Russia (Soviet Union and Russian language) 1, 15, 38, 39, 43, 47–48, 61, 63, 65–66, 70, 82, 85, 91, 95, 107, 108, 11, 113–117, 124–135, 138–40, 144, 157, 161, 165, 173, 176–177, 181–182, 185, 191, 199

Saar, Gideon 180
Salem 16
Salimbene di Adam 27
Samarkand 127
Sardinia 18
Satan 1, 19, 22
Scots in the UK 187–189
Secret Life of Saeed, the Pessoptimist 141
Seforim, Mendele Mokher (Shalom Jacob Abramovitsch) 41
Sela 185
Selden, John 16
Sephardim and Sephardi pronunciation 29, 47, 53–54, 69–70, 73, 76–78, 80, 100, 128, 130, 148
The Septuagint 67
Serbo-Crotian 39
Shamir, Moshe 200
Shamir, Yitzhak 183
Shammas, Anton 141, 154–155
Shar'abi, Boaz 100
Sharansky, Natan 131
Shaviv Strategy and Campaign Service 9
Shazar, Zalman 89, 105–107
Sheba, Queen of 19
Shelach, Uriel *see* Yonatan Ratosh
Shem Revue d'Action 102
Sheol 22
Shibboleth 19, 20
Shibolim 97
Shiloh 16
Shlayan, Bishara 153
Sholem, Gershom 98
Sicily 18
Sidon 18
Slang 172–177
Slovakia 165–166
Smart, Christopher 20
Sokolow, Nahum 31, 97, 181
Solomon, King 16, 18–19, 102
Somekh, Sasson 142
A Song to David 20
Spain 11, 12, 18, 29, 42, 76, 119, 136, 148; Spanish 5, 11–13, 38, 43, 85, 65, 85, 137–138, 182, 186
Stalin, Josef 39, 132–133
Stern Gang 158; *see also* Lehi
Stevenson, Robert Louis 188
Strouma, Sarah 180
Sudan 158
Swedes and Swedish 137, 164
Switzerland 164–165, 168
Syria 4, 139, 162

Tabash, Mustafa 154
Der Tag (Yiddish daily newspaper) 105

Tagalog 43
Tal Committee and Law 146
A Tale of Love and Darkness 98
Tallin (Reval) 110
Talmud 16, 19, 40, 50–51, 54, 56, 69, 99, 118, 122, 174
Tamra 154
Tarbut schools 94–98, 100, 113, 127, 184, 192
Tat 29
Technion (Technikum) 46, 178–182
Tel Aviv 9, 38, 95, 98, 132–143
Tel Aviv, University of 142
Thirteen Principles of the Faith 101
Timmerman, Hector 166
Tin Pan Ally 119
Tira 142
Treasury of Jewish Quotations{en}76
Trumpet in the Wadi 144–145
Truss, Elizabeth 186
Tschernikhowski, Shaul 96
Tulkarem 149
Tunisia 139
Turcomans 158
Turkish 30, 33–34, 45, 48, 127
Turniansky, Chava 82
Tyre 18

Ulpan 30–**32**, 63
Ultra-Orthodox Jews in Israel *see* Hareidim
Ulysses 189
Umm-al-Fahm 153, 155
UNESCO 137–139
United Kingdom 10, 171, 184–190
United Nations' Partition Plan for Palestine 132
United States 13–15, 117, 136, 130, 158, 168, 196, 198; 2012 presidential campaign 10
University of Fribourg 37
University of Pennsylvania 16
University of Tel Aviv 142
The Unknown Soldier 72
Ur 44
Urdu 186
Urdunim 173
Uruguay 196
U.S. Communist Party 132–133

Vardi, Herzl 91
Vatican 42
Vermont 17
Vilensky, General Wolf 114
Vilna 110–111, 114
Vilnius *see* Vilna
Virgin *see* Almah; Bethulah
Vowels *see* Nikud

Wadi 'Ara 151
Wales and Welsh 30, 33–34, 42, 138, 171, 186–189
Wallace, Henry 133
Walloons 158
Warsaw 56, 96–98
Warsaw Ghetto Uprising 158
Washington, D.C. 185
Webb, Arthur 31
Weinberg, Werner 69
Weizmann, Chaim 89
West Bank 149–150, 170, 196
Wilde, Oscar 21
The Word: The Dictionary That Reveals the Hebrew Source of English 28
World War I 111
World War II 63, 114–115, 179, 186

Yadin, Yigal 91
Yarkoni, Yaffa 100
Yavne religious schools 113
Yediot Ahronot 57, 103
"Yehoash" 51
Yehoshua, A. B. 155–156
Yellin, Dr. David 60
The Yellow Wind 144
Yemen 78, 100, 139, 162
Yevanic 29
Yevin, Yechiel Heschel 101
Yevsektsia 124–135

YHWH 9, 17, 19, 24–25
Yiddish 3–4, 8, 9, 11–14, 29, 34, 39, 45, 47–49, 51, 56, 60, 63–66, 75–85, 89–96, 104–110, 113, 115, 124–128, 130–133, 146, 172–173, 176, 183, 188, 193–194
The Yiddish Policeman's Union 132
Yokneam 155
Yom Kippur War 162, 175
Yordim 3, 14, 85, 184
Yugoslavia 148, 158

Zamenhof, Dr. Ludwig Lazar 34–42
Zichron Ya'akov 72
Zionism 2, 4, 8–9, 13–14, 29, 34, 39, 41, 45, 47, 49, 51, 56, 63–66, 75–85, 87–97, 105–107, 113–115, 118–119, 124–133, 146, 172–173, 183, 188, 193–94
Zionist Organization of America (ZOA) 103–104
Ziyad, Qassim 151
Zlatopolsky, Hillel 127
Zoabi, Mazen 154
Zoabi, Shadya 154
Zohar 99
Zohar, Guy 141
ZUBI! The Real Hebrew You Were Never Taught at School 173
Zuckermann, Ghil'ad 64–67, 74
Zvi, Raphael 129

www.ingramcontent.com/pod-product-compliance
Lightning Source LLC
Chambersburg PA
CBHW032049300426
44116CB00007B/665